THE SOCIOLOGY OF LAW AND ORDER

by the same author

SOCIAL CLASS AND DELINQUENCY

THE SOCIOLOGY OF LAW AND ORDER

Lynn McDonald

BOOK CENTER · MONTREAL · QUEBEC

WESTVIEW PRESS · BOULDER · COLORADO

364
McD

Copyright © 1976 by Lynn McDonald

Published in 1976 in London, England, by
Faber & Faber Ltd.

Published in 1976 in Canada by
Book Center, Inc.
1140 Beaulac Street
Montreal, Quebec H4R 1R8 Canada

Published in 1976 in the United States of America by
Westview Press, Inc.
1898 Flatiron Court
Boulder, Colorado 80301
Frederick A. Praeger, Publisher and Editorial Director

Printed and Bound in Great Britain

Library of Congress Cataloging in Publication Data

McDonald, Lynn.
  The sociology of law and order.

  Bibliography: p.
  Includes index.
  1. Crime and criminals. 2. Law enforcement.
3. Criminal justice, Administration of. I. Title.
HV6025.M28   1976   364   76-9753
ISBN 0–89158–614–8 (United States)
ISBN 0–920094–00–7 (Canada)

Contents

Preface

The material reported in this book represents a number of years' work, with a variety of research approaches, so that many people are owed thanks for assistance at various stages. The research strategy required a great deal of computer analysis of statistical data, most of which work was done by my research assistant, Margaret Latchford. Officials at Interpol provided data and information. A survey was part of the strategy, and again Mrs Latchford's contribution must be acknowledged. Officials of the organizations involved in the study provided lists of members and some sort of introduction to them. Without the respondents, of course, the study could not have been done, and I am grateful that many of them were exceedingly generous with their time. The Canada Council provided the funds for all this work.

The pursuit of ideas on law and order, notably the historical development of sociological theories thereon, required work of quite a different order. It early became clear that scholarship was not nearly so international as I had been led to believe, so that if I was to attain any remotely adequate knowledge I would have to travel to it. Practically speaking, knowledge resides in the major libraries of the countries whose scholars have worked on the problems at issue. My quest involved a year's stay in Paris, where I worked mainly at the Bibliothèque Nationale. In France I was a guest of the ministry of Foreign Affairs, in a programme jointly sponsored by the Canada Council. I also spent some time in London, at the British Library and the British Library of Political and Economic Science. A couple of short trips, to the Académie Royale in Brussels, and the library of the University of Basel rounded out the search. I am grateful to the librarians and officials of all these institutions for their help. The European stage of my research got off to a good start in Sweden, where I spent a term as a visitor at the University of Gothenburg. Colleagues there whose help I would like to acknowledge particularly are Bengt Rundblad, Helena Streiffjert, Kerstin Lindskoug, Edmund Dahlström and Rita Lilljeström.

9

A number of people read and criticized portions of the manuscript: David Downes, John O'Neill, Lorne Tepperman, Ernest Oksanen, Susanne Mowat, Frank Jones, Judith Blackwell, Richard Quinney and Roy Carr-Hill. Jeff Cody and Linda Armani did most of the typing. The book is dedicated to my mother, Mary Alice McDonald.

Paris
July 1975   L. M.

PART I

General Theories of Crime, Law and Sanctions

Chapter 1

LAW, ORDER AND SOCIOLOGY

This book began with a concern over the law and order issue, and the role social scientists have played in legitimating it as a problem of grave social consequences. I was concerned, firstly, with the widespread belief in the 'rising crime rate', a part of the official ideologies of the western world and, to a lesser extent, Soviet bloc countries and the Third World, excluding China. It is a view which has broad public acceptance and is taken seriously to signify real and growing threats to life, property and important social values. The response to the threat has seemed to enjoy almost as much consensus as the belief itself—a 'strengthening' of the law, an increase in the forces of order, and a search for ever more effective means of crime prevention and repression. In the United States this was dignified into a 'war on crime', while in other societies more modest schemes have sufficed, such as expanding the police force, building more prisons and hiring more social workers.

The beneficial effects of these policies remain to be clearly demonstrated, but certain inconveniences are immediately obvious. From the point of view of the customers of these social services, there are such consequences as deprivation of liberty, loss of job, and damage to reputation and self-respect. The public as a whole suffers, for punishment and rehabilitation are often more expensive than crime. Certain individuals resent the increased intrusion in their personal lives.

More important, perhaps, the law and order issue serves to deflect public attention from more pressing issues, like death, destruction, war, torture and starvation. These are hardly the lot of the average European or North American, to be sure, but even in the prosperous countries of the west there are large numbers of people who suffer.

Minorities, like Canadian and American Indians, live in genuine and growing squalor, and inflation means an insecure and ignoble old age for substantial numbers of people. The more fortunate miss that round of misery, but cannot be sure that they will do so well in the next, and are less sure about the problems passed on to their children and grandchildren. The rapid extinction of non-renewable resources, pollution and the deterioration of city life increasingly affect even the most comfortable members of the richest, safest countries.

Yet, all the while, ministers of the crown give speeches about juvenile delinquency and newspapers report them. Nor, given the grimness of the alternatives do we blame them. The subject of crime seems important enough to deserve some attention, but does not really hurt. For people who can no longer distract themselves with the problems of 'what the servants are up to', the crime problem is an admirable substitute. Nothing more controversial than probation or parole, training schools or community treatment need be discussed. Laws can be passed, experts hired, and public anxiety raised or lowered as appropriate. Crime is the 'servant problem' *par excellence*, and so much more manageable than any of the problems we have with our neighbours, our enemies or our masters. Juvenile delinquency is an eminently sensible problem for almost any contemporary society. It can be discussed anywhere with impunity, for juvenile delinquents, unlike multinational corporations, do not advertise or make political contributions.

THE ROLE OF SOCIOLOGY

Social scientists are by no means the worst culprits as far as these priorities are concerned, but they do contribute in a supporting capacity. Social scientists serve on government boards and commissions studying crime, draft legislation and design correctional programmes. Large numbers are involved directly in social control agencies, do consulting work or contract research for them. Even those in academe are inevitably involved in training social control practitioners and administrators. Supposedly academic courses in 'deviance' typically attract large numbers of students with career interests in social control and crime repression work, and many universities provide courses expressly for police officers, prison guards, probation and parole workers. Sociological textbooks in criminology, research monographs, journals and conferences all lend an aura of intellectual respectability to the social control enterprise.

CRITICAL SOCIOLOGY AND THE CONFLICT APPROACH

This is not the whole story, of course, and therein lies the contradiction central to our task. Alongside the official, consensus-oriented sociology of deviance has grown a critical sociology, of smaller dimensions, but very much alive and fighting. This includes a distinct theoretical approach, 'conflict theory', and a body of empirical knowledge supporting it. The quality of work in the conflict orientation, moreover, has been rather better, as often happens when an unpopular case has to be defended. The theoretical work has tended to be more sophisticated, for conflict theorists have had to take into account consensus-oriented work much more than the converse.

Some of the best empirical studies in the social control field, from the point of view of methodology, have been those debunking the whole social problem approach. There is now a whole literature showing that rehabilitation programmes do not rehabilitate,[1] and prevention programmes do not prevent.[2] Phenomenologists have challenged consensus sociology in their own way. Their descriptions of how juvenile courts operate, for example, have shown how factors, quite apart from either the offence or the supposed causes of delinquency, affect chances of conviction and sentence. Empirical evidence to this effect is accumulating,[3] and theoretical work attempting to account for it grows in proportion.

My own early work on crime rates in Canada gave further cause for suspicion. The analysis showed official rates of crime not to be rising in the post-war period, so long as serious indicators of crime were used. Traffic offences, especially parking tickets, did increase in this period, but this is hardly what the Minister of Justice means when talking about a crime wave. Other research with Canadian data has yielded similar conclusions,[4] yet the general belief in 'rising

1. Wilkins, Bailey, Barlow, McDonald (1972), Murphy, Waller.
2. McCord and McCord, Stratton and Terry, Powers and Witmer.
3. Wolfgang, Chiricos, Terry, Piliavin and Briar, Black and Reiss, Goldman, LeBlanc.
4. Hogarth, Canadian Committee on Corrections, Giffen. My own work is further discussed in Ch. 7.

crime' has not diminished. It is this tenacity of belief in the face of contradictory evidence that makes one wonder whether crime is 'really' increasing at all. It could be, one dares to imagine, that the crime rate is not rising anywhere; perhaps there is no more basis for it than the emperor's new clothes.

There is a persuasive example to this effect in the case of beliefs about rehabilitation. The more optimistic the findings of treatment success, it has been shown, the more deficient the methods used in the evaluation.[1] Yet the evidence for the rising crime rate has never been as strong as that for rehabilitation. Rather, the belief has been so much assumed to be true that it has not seemed necessary to prove it. Typically, holders of the belief have simply stated it as a fact, citing isolated statistics to dramatize the point. Nor has there ever been any lack of statistics to show trends in any direction wanted; so long as one chooses the years of comparison carefully, there will always be something rising.

The defects of the consensus literature have been much discussed by opponents of the approach. Conflict supporters for over a hundred years now have pointed out the tautological nature of the research findings, and the weaknesses of various theories. They have argued instead for profoundly different causal processes, based ultimately on the effects of the holders of political and economic power, variously defined, affecting the nature of crime through criminal legislation and its enforcement. In the early theories poverty and inequality were the main causal factors, and these were usually blamed on private property. More recently the emphasis has been on the capacity of official agencies to shape criminality through some process of labelling.

Much of the argument for these theories, however, falls into the same difficulty as that for the conventional approach. The assertions made lack the *naïveté* of the social problem theories, but there is the same exclusion of fundamentally different alternatives. There has been almost no attempt to *test* propositions from either theory relative to the other. Each side criticizes the other, points out its failings, and cites data gathered in support of its own propositions. Almost never is evidence produced from actual *tests*, in which propositions from both approaches have been considered.

The bulk of the literature in the deviance field can be seen as a debate over particular theories within the dominant, consensus

1. Bailey.

approach. Crime is assumed to be the result of some kind of social or psychological problem, and the debate concerns what particular problems are the crucial ones. There have been debates, then, between sociologists, psychologists, biologists and economists, over the relative merits of the psyche, the family, class, peer group, or the total society as causes of crime. Missing has been an honest consideration of radically different alternatives. There has been discussion, then, of what *type* of problem was the more important cause of crime, without consideration of the possibility that the whole social problem approach might be wrong.

The massive empirical literature ostensibly supporting these theories is, as well, of highly questionable value. Empirical studies were typically designed so that the influences of different social or psychological problems could be compared, but with factors outside the problem perspective excluded. Often the data sources were so inappropriate that the findings bear little relation to the question posed. Prisoners, for example, have been compared with free citizens, and the differences between them said to be what distinguishes criminals from non-criminals. The unfavourable characteristics of the criminals are then supposed to be what led them into crime.

Yet, doubtful as the merits of the consensus approach seemed, I was not prepared to go along with all the criticisms of it. I could not accept some of the doctrinaire attacks, for example, that the consensus social problem approach was wrong because it was contrary to the teaching of Marx. Nor did I agree with the romantic view: that consensus theory was not respectful of human dignity and should therefore be rejected. It was better not to assume, I thought, that beauty was truth, and truth beauty. Rather, I had begun to suspect that the consensus approach was bad theory and, if it were, it would be shown to be wrong on proper empirical investigation.

I have never believed that statistics necessarily lie, or that quantitative results are necessarily any more supportive of the *status quo* than the results of any other kind of analysis. There was no reason, then, to avoid or fear empirical work. I had no confidence that clear and consistent answers would emerge, and any piece of research I could envisage promised to be lengthy and difficult. Nevertheless, a project of empirical work seemed to be what was in order. After criticizing colleagues for using theories without comparative testing, I could hardly exempt myself from such an exercise.

Phenomenology was another alternative as an approach, avoiding certain pitfalls of both conflict and consensus work. This, however, did not seem the right answer, for it would have led us away from certain theoretical concerns. What the phenomenologists do is change the level of inquiry. It is not just that they do their research in a different way, but they ask different sorts of questions—*how* social control agencies work, *how* officials and the public interact, as opposed to *who* becomes a client of such an agency in the first place and *why*. Insights gained from phenomenological work have a bearing on who and why, but they do not answer those questions directly. Phenomenological work, then, can add considerable perspective to our concerns, but without speaking to the validity of either the conflict or consensus approaches as such. Questions as to why certain societies have high crime rates and full prisons, and others do not, cannot be addressed with phenomenology, and this is the sort of question I wished to entertain. Knowledge as to how children are treated by the police does not tell us why so many of them are working class, black, Indian or whatever.

The study envisaged was a study within the limits of conventional social science, with all its advantages and disadvantages. The assumptions of an objective, real world, at least partially knowable, were accepted, as were conventional criteria for assessing validity of propositions. I used conventional research tools, drawing on census data, official statistics, secondary analysis of other researchers' material and survey results. I do not believe that social science need be confined to investigating what is trivial but true, or profound but false. Rather I would argue that serious questions can be dealt with within the limits imposed by conventional, 'positivistic' assumptions, and hope to demonstrate this here. Later several basic philosophical and methodological issues will be taken up. This is best left, however, until after what can be done within conventional limits has been shown.

THE ELEMENTS OF THEORY: NORMS, SANCTIONS AND BEHAVIOUR

Theory is to be dealt with here in terms of three components to be explained: norms, sanctions and behaviour. Norms have been restricted to official, criminal norms, the criminal law. They include the content of a society's criminal code, and any other norms outside it, similarly enforced with punitive measures, by official agents of the society. The definition of sanctions was similarly restricted to the official level, punishments meted out, in the name of society, in the intention of enforcing the criminal law. Official sanctions include all punitive measures, whether the actual sentence, or conviction, arrest, provisional detention, police record, fingerprinting—for all involve some amount of suffering, inconvenience and unpleasantness to the subject. Criminal behaviour was defined as behaviour thought to be contrary to a criminal norm, whether resulting in an official sanction or not. Note that there is no suggestion that any behaviour is by its nature criminal, or deviant or immoral. Rather, criminality is something attributed to behaviour, if not by offenders themselves, by the police, prosecutor or other members of society.

Norms, sanctions and behaviour are quite distinct elements. No assumption is made that norms are necessarily enforced, or that the imposition of sanctions necessarily implies criminal behaviour has taken place. Rather the extent to which each is related to the other is a part of the theory, to be explored as much as their relationships with other social, economic, and political factors.

THE ROLE OF POWER AS AN EXPLANATORY FACTOR
The vast number of accounts of the origin and development of law, sanctions and behaviour are the theories of deviance and social control of the study. Among them, two orientations are distinguished—conflict and consensus—the crucial point of differentiation being the role of power in the explanation. Conflict theories are those theories in which the factor of power is given prominence in the explanation. Consensus theories are those in which any other factor is dominant—social or economic conditions, psychological factors or biological. Power may be a consideration in the case of consensus theory, as a secondary influence, or as a factor itself acted on. Any number of social and economic factors, as well, may be included in conflict theory, so long as they are treated as being affected by the distribution of power.

Power should be understood in the same sense as used by Weber, implying the probability of being able to secure one's own ends in a relationship, even against opposition. Conflicting interests are, then, assumed, with only one or other side, in any particular instance, being able to secure theirs. In any ongoing conflict, different sides may win different particular struggles, hence power may be seen as a variable. A group having more power than another would be one which more frequently secured its ends in particular encounters than the other.

The notions of 'conflict' and 'consensus' are used in a number of ways, so that certain distinctions should be made before we proceed. At the most general level, they refer to broad approaches, traditions or orientations, terms which will be used interchangeably. These include assumptions, facts and findings, hypotheses and full-scale theories or sets of propositions. Particular theorists can be identified as belonging to one or other tradition—for example, Durkheim to the consensus and Marx to the conflict. Studies can be identified as supporting the theories of one or other orientation. Particular theories can be seen as reflecting the concerns of one or other approach.

CONFLICT AND CONSENSUS SETS OF ASSUMPTIONS

The two approaches have often been dealt with as broad sets of assumptions within which particular theories have been framed. Most of the empirical literature indeed can be seen as a debate over particular theories all based on consensus assumptions. Similarly, disputes among conflict theorists may be seen as disputes over particular theories within the conflict tradition. Our concern, however, is with the dispute *between* the two approaches, at the level of theory. The two present strongly differing views of reality, and the object is to test them, against each other, as to the validity of their propositions. The desirability of using either approach as a set of assumptions will, after this testing, again be broached.

The theories in the two traditions included everything from carefully elaborated sets of propositions to isolated sets of hypotheses and conjectures. There were some theories covering all three components of law, sanctions and behaviour, with the relationships between them described in detail. At the other extreme there were statements on only one or other of the elements, with no connection evident between them. Much of the modern literature on 'deviant behaviour' is of this sort. The clarity of the propositions, as well, varied considerably, so that both clarity and comprehensiveness presented problems of classification. It was for this reason that it was decided to make the role of power the definitive criterion for purposes of distinguishing between the two theory types.

The power definition fulfilled the requirement of being simple and relatively objective to use, while making the division between the two theory types in a meaningful way. Theories that were assigned to the conflict type, on the basis of the role of power theorized, seemed also to belong to it on the basis of any number of other reasons. Similarly, theories that seemed to belong together as consensus type, on the basis of these other characteristics, happened to be defined so formally with the use of the power criterion. Using this definition meant, then, that the great mass of the theories could be easily assigned to one or other of the theory types, and yet seem to belong to it as well in terms of their other propositions, tone, authorship and associated empirical work. Very few difficulties in assigning theories were actually encountered, and these arose chiefly in cases of incomplete theories, and among theorists who changed positions.

The two theory types could not be consistently distinguished from each other on the basis of the particular *variables* used in their propositions. Certain variables were associated with one or other tradition for certain periods of time, but not indefinitely. The variables of economic determinism, for example, distinguished the theories well until the late nineteenth century. Conflict theorists, such as William Godwin and Robert Owen, based their explanations of crime largely on poverty and its immediate social consequences. Consensus theorists, notably Durkheim and Tarde, argued strongly against the poverty thesis and related economic factors. For many years the conflict–consensus debate was a debate over 'economic determinism', and was actually called that. Even in recent years, some of the best known consensus advocates, such as Radzinowicz and Glueck and Glueck, have seen fit to continue the attack on economic variables. For most consensus advocates, however, economic explanations have become respectable. Relative deprivation, for example, is a part of differential opportunity theory, and the consequences of unemployment are treated in theories dealing with self-image.

The *level* or *type* of variable used in explanations did not serve, either, as a consistent means of distinguishing the two types of theory. Again, a certain pattern appeared, which is quite instructive. Individual problem explanations have been more characteristic of consensus theory than conflict, but that said, the situation becomes more complicated. Conflict theorists early began to incorporate individual disorders into their explanations as secondary factors, playing an intermediate role in a causal chain. Further, while some consensus theorists worked almost exclusively with individual characteristics (notably Lombroso and school) in time many came to give an appreciable role to social factors. A major school, the French sociological school, emerged in the nineteenth century, treating social factors as the main causal factors. In modern functionalist explanations, social factors have usually been the most important variables in the explanation.

It was not *which* precise variables were used, or *what type* of variable, but *how* they were treated that became the criterion for distinguishing the two types of theory. In particular, it was how the variables were treated relative to power that counted. For conflict theorists, the ultimate causal factor lay in the actions of the holders of power, variously defined, in the pursuit of their advantages. Inequalities in power, economic or political, were ultimately responsible for the nature of the criminal law established, its enforcement, and the pattern of criminal behaviour appearing. In the nineteenth century, poverty was an important part of this explanation, but it was itself explained in terms of inequalities in power, and especially in the power inherent in the ownership of private property. More recently, conflict theorists have preferred other explanations, such as the role of official agencies in labelling, but these were again linked to the influence of the holders of power. Individual problems incorporated into the explanations would typically be related to economic inequalities. Engels, for example, cited an array of individual and social problems as causes of crime—drunkenness, overcrowding, ill supervision of children, lack of education and so forth, but these were all related, through poverty, to the development of capitalism.

In consensus theory power has been accorded much less importance, or no importance whatsoever. The range of variables employed at various times has been vast, and some of the causal chains lengthy. Ultimately, however, they go back to some kind of problem at some level. This may be a problem of absolute deficiency—such as malnutrition, idiocy or illiteracy. Or it may involve a problem of distribution or malintegration in the system, as in differential opportunity theory and culture lag. Whether something lacking, or a bad connection, there was always a problem to blame. Thus, when poverty appeared as a cause of crime, the explanation did not go past poverty, or at least not past the 'idleness and ignorance', that caused it. Whether it was environment or distribution that was blamed, then, it was clearly not the holders of power, the ruling class, the owners of the means of production, or the ordinary rich.

The use of power as the basis for the distinction between conflict and consensus theories had one other important result. The theories so distinguished could also be seen to be characterized by different *structures*, different *relationships* between law, sanctions and behaviour. In consensus theory behaviour was typically paramount. Law and sanctions were seen as having developed in response to the problems posed by criminal behaviour. In conflict theory, on the other hand, law and sanctions acted *on* behaviour. The holders of power affected criminal behaviour through the laws they established and the sanctions they imposed, as well as through other social and economic conditions. In both approaches there was typically feedback in the opposite direction. Conflict theorists described how behaviour also affected the formulation of the law, and consensus theorists how law and sanctions affected behaviour. The nature of the *dominant* direction of influence, however, was seldom in doubt. This is depicted in the chart on page 24.

The relationships between crime, law and sanctions were a matter of some importance in eighteenth- and nineteenth-century sociology of deviance and social control. With growing specialization in the subject in the twentieth century, however, it seems that these connections were lost sight of. 'Deviance' became the study of 'deviant behaviour', while law and the administration of criminal justice moved to the law faculty. The relationship between them all effectively belonged nowhere. Concern to treat these relationships as an important point of focus, then, may be seen as an attempt to return to an older, European sociology. The deviance–social control field is here conceived as a basic and central part of sociology, as it was at the origin of the subject. The fundamental issues of social order are still the important issues of sociology. In the deviance–social control field, however, these issues are obscured with the compartmentalization of the subject, and it is only when the relationships *between* law, sanctions and behaviour are examined that they reappear.[1]

The association of the consensus position with policies of greater

1. This discussion may help to explain the repeated use of the tedious expression 'deviance–social control'. Clearly, the two are complementary; social control is about deviance, and deviance implies a social control standard against which deviance is judged. The use of 'deviance' alone, however, often signifies a theoretical position (consensus) that deviant behaviour is primordial, and social control a response to it. 'Social control', alone, less often has a theoretical significance, hence I have felt somewhat more free to use that expression.

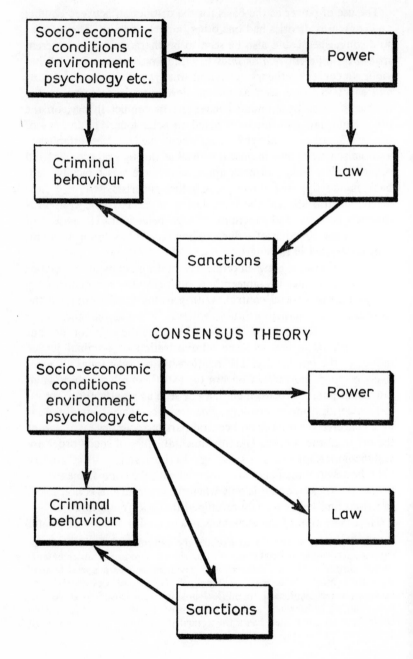

repression is made for good reason. Historically, consensus theorists have been more favourable to repressive measures than conflict, and the *enthusiasts* of severe repression have consistently been consensus-oriented. The relationship, however, was never one-to-one, and some consensus theorists even worked for the reduction of punishments. Nevertheless, it has been consensus theories, and empirical work supporting them, that have formed the intellectual basis to the law and order position. Advocates of greater repression have often used the consensus theory arguments of the day in making their case, and opponents have cited conflict explanations. In the nineteenth century, for example, those favouring harsher measures cited the born-criminal thesis—to show how deeply entrenched criminality was and how inefficacious lenient measures would be. Opponents stressed the prevailing conflict argument—that an improvement in economic conditions would reduce crime. The debate has since shifted, but the principle holds. Now social and economic problems are part of the consensus approach, and opponents argue labelling theory.

What is more telling about the relationship, however, is that when consensus theorists have used their theories to argue for leniency, the arguments have eventually been twisted. The early French psychiatrists, for example, used the insanity argument as a plea for leniency, and then found it adapted to social Darwinism. The same sort of thing has happened with modern consensus arguments. The various problems theorized to characterize criminals—and intended to elicit sympathy for them—become reasons for treating their criminality more seriously. Judges who accept a psychiatric problem approach have been found to sentence more severely than those with a more old-fashioned moralistic frame of reference. Probably few of the contemporary purveyors of consensus theory would want greater harshness in the law or its administration, although this is a consequence of their activities.

Chapter 2

THE ORIGINS OF THE CONFLICT–CONSENSUS DEBATE

The purpose of this chapter is to tell the story of the rise and fall of theories of crime, law and punishment. At the simplest level the objective was to account for the major particular theories that have appeared over the centuries in the field, focusing especially on those theories which relate the three components of law, enforcement and behaviour. The favour or disfavour the theories have received is described with an assessment of the weight of the empirical evidence for and against. In some cases theories continued to receive support even in the face of rather solid contradictory evidence and, when this happened, some suggestions as to why have been offered. Running through this account are indications as to how the theories have been used politically, as means to argue for greater or lesser repression. There are, then, several themes to follow in the unfolding of the story —the structure and content of the theories, the empirical evidence for and against them, their acceptance and political usefulness.

The discussion is organized around the conflict–consensus debate. The contrasting positions of the two theories at the various stages of development is described, along with the adjustments each made to the other. How phenomenological work has affected both conflict and consensus theories is indicated, including results which discredit the traditional approaches, and how theorists in both have incorporated insights from phenomenological work into the theories. The 'methodology' for this analysis, the sources sought in the literature search,[1] and the limits to it, are described in the Technical Note (pp. 291–3).

1. I have attempted to be comprehensive in citing sources, but without overburdening the text with footnotes. The exact references are confined to the reference section at the end of the book, and footnotes are used only

Certain ideas date back thousands of years before work in the social sciences began, appearing in historical accounts, myths, philosophy and religious treatises. Some of the ideas have remained virtually intact over this long period. The concept of criminal responsibility, for example, has changed very little since Aristotle. The account here, however, begins in earnest with the eighteenth century, for it was only then that recognizable theories began to appear. That is, explanations were stated without recourse to supernatural agents, and in a general fashion. There were, then, theories of *law*, as opposed to the description of the giving of *a* set of laws, as in the Ten Commandments. Similarly, there were theories of the causes of *crime*, and not only accounts of particular crimes, for example Cain killing Abel. And, although somewhat later, there were theories of punishment, in contrast with stories of particular people being punished for their misdeeds—Cain again, or Eve.

Montesquieu's *The Spirit of Laws* was the first account clearly to fulfil the necessary criteria, outlining a consensus theory of law with some peripheral attention to behaviour. The Scottish moral philosophers, Adam Smith and Adam Ferguson, were the next to add to the story, again to consensus theory. There were numerous expressions of conflict theory in this period, beginning with Beccaria's famous *Essay on Crimes and Punishments*, and including a number of the great French Enlightenment writers. Godwin, the English political theorist, provided a remarkable, thorough conflict account, developing theory on behaviour especially. By the end of the eighteenth century the essential components of conflict and consensus theories had been described. Moreover, the dispute between the two theories was explicit.

In the nineteenth century, sociology as an endeavour at the establishment of general laws, tested against real world data, began. Empirical studies, in which at least the rudiments of the scientific method were respected, are evident from the 1820s on. The basic

---

as a common sense guide to it. Footnotes are not then given when not needed to locate the work in question, for example when only one work by the author is referred to, or when the title or date of publication is also given in the text.

Page numbers in the text refer to the last work cited, and subsequent quotations not otherwise noted refer to the same page (this is to avoid frequent *loc. cit.* citations). Page references are to the English version unless otherwise noted.

methods used in the social sciences to date were developed in this period and, in terms of quantity, a massive amount of research was produced. There was a reawakening of interest in probability theory, although it was not until late in the century that statistical tests and measures of association were developed. The theories themselves grew prodigiously from the relatively sparse accounts of the eighteenth century. Distinctive schools, and subdivisions within schools, became recognizable. The development of consensus theory was especially great, particularly in theory of behaviour. This trend continued in the twentieth century, indeed to the extent that consensus theories of behaviour, and empirical work devoted to them, came to dominate the literature.

PRE-EIGHTEENTH CENTURY

The earliest surviving accounts of law and behaviour fall outside the criteria for theory immediately on grounds of their independent variables. They begin with seraphim and cherubim and move upwards in the spiritual hierarchy, while even the most timid deities and worldly prophets are quite beyond our powers of investigation. Moses' finding of the Ten Commandments on Mount Sinai is thus outside our account of theories of law, as is the serpent's temptation of Eve as the origin of deviant behaviour, and the punishment of Eve, Adam and Cain as the origin of sanctions. The same problem holds as well for impersonal supernatural forces, so that all kinds of accounts of innate good and evil have to be excluded. For this reason alone the writings of the first thousands of years in western societies fall outside our inquiry—the Old and New Testaments, the Sumerian and Babylonian laws, early Greek and Roman works.[1]

Human causes of deviance did appear in some of these accounts if peripherally. Poverty and lack of moral training in the family were frequently cited. These conditions, however, were treated rather as symptoms of another, spiritual cause, innate good or evil, greed, temptation of the devil, sin of the parents and so forth, and not as causal explanations in their own right.

The debate over economic conditions as causes of crime goes back at least to this early period, with Plato and Phalleas taking the

1. For good reviews of this early period see Bonger, 1905, and Van Kan. For a bibliography of sixteenth- to eighteenth-century work see Berriat-Saint-Prix.

equivalent of the conflict side and Aristotle the consensus. In *Politics*, Aristotle conceded economic need to be a cause of certain crimes, but not many, and not the most important. On this basis he opposed the equalization of property as a solution to crime. The remedy had to be sought in the improvement of the nature of individuals, to make people desire less rather than have more. This at least was the solution for those with 'nobler natures', while for the rest measures of repression had to be relied on (p. 1160).

There are crimes for which the motive is want; and for these Phalleas expects to find a cure in the equalization of property, which will take away from a man the temptation to be a highwayman, because he is hungry or cold. But want is not the sole incentive to crime; men also wish to enjoy themselves and not to be in a state of desire—they wish to cure some desire, going beyond the necessities of life (p. 1159).

Aristotle's thesis was the conservative one of the problem lying in the fundamental nature of the individual: 'It is in the nature of men not to be satisfied.' He differs from most consensus theorists, however, in the moderation and consistency of his stand. Ordinary property crime was not a serious enough problem to warrant social reform. 'The fact is that the greatest crimes are caused by excess and not by necessity. Men do not become tyrants in order that they may not suffer cold . . . hence great is the honour bestowed not on him who kills a thief, but on him who kills a tyrant' (p. 1160).

There was very little development of these early conceptualizations during most of the Christian era. Theologians wrote on many aspects of law, behaviour and sanctions, but very little on their origins. It seemed to suffice that God was the author of law and the overseer of punishments. Immoral behaviour was the working of some combination of the world, the flesh and the devil, precisely how not being of great consequence. This is quite clear even in writers like Augustine, who considered questions of law and behaviour at some length. Secular writers of the period, like Machiavelli, offered no more from the point of view of theory. Machiavelli discussed such crucial issues as the role of class struggle in changing governments, but he did not relate this directly to subsequent changes in law.

John of Salisbury, one of the great expounders of the organic analogy, is one of the most interesting medieval writers on the subject. In 1159, he described law as 'a discovery and a gift from God, a

precept of wise men, the corrector of excesses of the will, the bond
which knits together the fabric of the state, and the banisher of
crime' (p. 6). Law and punishment were effectively identified, in that
laws were assumed to be enforced, and whatever punishments were
actually meted out were lawful. Law was the 'punisher of violence
and all wrong doing' (p. 335). Law acted to prevent crime, but was
not always successful. What produced crime, apart from the 'will',
was not described.

It is, however, for the organic analogy that John of Salisbury is
deservedly famous. The prince was the head, the priesthood the
soul, and the senate the heart of the body. Officials and soldiers were
the hands, financial officers the stomach and intestines, and hus-
bandmen the feet. Law was important in the 'corporate political
body', as a 'bond of union and solidarity' (p. 335). It was fitting
that all should obey it for its qualities of promoting virtue, guarding
the public well-being and knitting together the fabric of the state.

The main precursors to theory in the conflict tradition were
Sir Thomas More, the first and last Chancellor of England to be
sainted, and Gerrard Winstanley, the leader of the Digger movement.
Both included social causes in their explanations of crime, notably
poverty, foreshadowing the great eighteenth- and nineteenth-century
debates over economic causes. Both as well blamed bad laws as
causal factors, again in a fashion very much in the conflict tradition.

More's account of the influence of law on criminal behaviour used
one of the standard arguments against severe laws in the conflict
tradition. Excessive severity he argued in *Utopia* provoked crime,
for a person who would be condemned for theft might as well kill
to keep his crime from being known. More's arguments on poverty as
a cause of crime involved an assessment of the causes of particular
types of poverty most conducive to crime. The practice of the rich
maintaining large numbers of servants for non-productive (status-
related) purposes, was one example. Such individuals might be kept
for a time, but a later heir might not be able to afford a large en-
tourage, and the servants would then be unfit for any useful work.
The decline of husbandry forced people to sell their possessions and
wander abroad, with eventually little else to do but steal (p. 33).
Others were forced into unemployment similarly for reasons beyond
their control. Sharp increases in the price of wool meant that people
who had previously earned their livelihood in wool-making no
longer could buy the necessary raw materials. Soldiers, injured and

sick after war, were unable to work, and were otherwise unprovided for.

In contrast with early consensus theory the causes lay in circumstances external to the persons ultimately committing crimes. The circumstances described included the most profoundly disturbing events of the time—war and the enclosure movement—and their effects on the lives of individual soldiers, shepherds and wool makers. The rich and powerful were certainly to blame, but so also were institutions. And, while More's discussion of causes was brief, the processes he described were complicated and these he presented with a careful, reasoned argument.

Winstanley was also passionately critical of the brutality of the law of his time. Like Thomas More he opposed capital punishment on the grounds that only God, the giver of life, had the right to take it away (p. 23). His non-religious argument is an excellent preview of modern conflict theory, relating the making of law to military conquest. It was the Normans who had introduced harsh laws, he argued, to subjugate the English. Those who supported those laws were supporting the Norman Conquest, and necessarily betraying England. Those who hanged their fellow Englishmen were 'traitors to England's freedom, upholders of the kingly murder power'. One of Winstanley's justifications for the Digger practice of illegally planting the common land was the prevention of crime. The basis for it was the simple one of poverty. Freedom to plant the land 'would prevent robbing, stealing and murdering, and prisons would not be so filled with prisoners' (p. 103).

Certain aspects of theological debate on law and immorality were important for their side effects. Disputes concerning what particular agents of divine will did were important in raising doubts, challenging evidence, and breaking the monopoly of prevailing doctrine. Consideration of *any* competing ideas, even between two religious doctrines, was a step towards consideration of *social* causes. Opposition to the doctrine of the divine right of kings was probably the most important source of competing ideas. The nature of the dispute, and the solution to it, varied profoundly across different societies, but throughout the issue provided a focus for fundamental re-examination of theory on law. The concepts of 'natural law' and 'natural justice' were similarly important in the development of legal theory. The concepts implied belief in divine will, but opened up the notion of competing sources of law, natural law being opposed to actual laws, and breaking the assumed connection between law as it was and should be.

HOBBES, SOCIAL AND DIVINE SOURCES OF LAW

The whole issue of the social origins of law was an extremely disquieting one to the writers who began to deal with it. Hobbes, writing in the seventeenth century, is a most instructive case. In his first published work, *The Elements of Law*, written apparently ten years before *Leviathan*, he stressed the divine origin of laws of nature. The individual was obliged to obey the law, for Scripture said so. In *Leviathan*, however, the obligation to obey the law lay in the social compact, the covenant made to end the war of all against all in nature. Yet the religious obligation was never entirely abandoned, leaving a profound contradiction in the work. Hobbes wrestled with the problem at great length, without resolving it. He was apparently unable to make the logically necessary step of settling on *either* divine decree, *or* the covenant as the basis for the obligation. The other problem in *Leviathan* is that the making of the covenant was a single event. The sovereign could be either an individual, aristocracy or assembly, but Hobbes did not state what sort of conditions determined change from one to another, or how actual laws would be affected by changes in the sovereign.

HENRY FIELDING

Henry Fielding, the novelist and magistrate, is the last of the pre-sociologists to discuss. His *Enquiry into the Causes of the Late Increase of Robbers* was a work with a message, dedicated to the Lord High Chancellor. The increase in robberies was evidently assumed not to need documenting, and Fielding concentrated instead on the causes for the increase, and his remedies, focusing on idleness and drunkenness. Habits and expectations changed, and the common people had become increasingly less willing to work for low wages, preferring theft and begging to honest employment. The civil power correspondingly lost its ability to control them, and changes in the law and its administration were needed to redress the balance (p. 344). These included tougher penalties in the law, lower requirements for proof of guilt, increases in prosecutions, less pity on the part of juries, fewer pardons, and more terrifying execution rites. Fielding's analysis of the balance of power between different sectors of society, and the interplay between economic forces, political and social was extremely interesting, but otherwise his contribution has been, in my view, over-rated.

EIGHTEENTH CENTURY

Sociological theory of law and behaviour began with the work of a number of eighteenth-century writers in France, Scotland and Italy. Montesquieu's *The Spirit of Laws* (1748) marks the first recognizable theory of law and, at least peripherally, of behaviour. The theory, in both cases, has to be extracted from much other, very disorganized historical commentary and philosophical argument, but the elements are unmistakably there—and have influenced work on the subject since. Adam Smith's *Theory of Moral Sentiments* appeared a decade later. It is a much more disciplined, indeed tightly argued work, notable for relating concrete laws with internalized norms, in fact in much the same way as in modern functionalism. Beccaria's very influential *Essay on Crimes and Punishments* appeared in 1764 and opened the debate with consensus theory. Beccaria took issue with Montesquieu in no uncertain terms, actually rebuking him in the book. The essential elements of the conflict-consensus dispute appear in this early argument.

MONTESQUIEU
Montesquieu's *The Spirit of Laws* is a work of some genius, although hopelessly confused and rambling. It was the product of twenty years' work, which no doubt helps to account for both its strengths and weaknesses. Among the anomalies in the work was recourse to the idea of the social compact and discussion of life in nature before it. Montesquieu, further, held to a belief in natural law, despite its inconsistency with the sociological theory he presented.

What makes *The Spirit of Laws* important is its treatment of law as a function of the type of society which produced it, and in turn having an effect on other social institutions, and criminal behaviour. Law was an important mechanism, capable of influencing criminal behaviour, and available to legislators to such an end. It was not the only determining factor and it could be counteracted by religion and mores. In societies with legitimate governments fewer repressive laws would be needed since love of one's country, honour and the like could be relied on to regulate social behaviour. In countries with despotic governments, by contrast, coercion would have to be used much more to obtain compliance. In support of this contention, Montesquieu noted that there had been a decline in severity of penalties in Europe as political liberties increased.

The classical argument for a utilitarian deterrence scheme was outlined in *The Spirit of Laws* some years before Bentham's much more precise formulation. Penalties should reflect the relative seriousness of the crimes to be deterred, for penalties out of proportion deterred the wrong crimes. Overly severe penalties upset the scheme, for one might as well hang for a sheep as a lamb (p. 89). Severe penalties did not necessarily deter crime at all, and positive means of inducing law-abiding behaviour should be considered (p. 82).

Apart from rational calculation relative to penalties, there were a number of other factors determining the nature and amount of criminal behaviour. Climatic conditions were important, through the effect climate had on individuals' physical and psychological constitutions. This was seen somewhat in terms of national character. People in cold climates, for example, were said to have greater vigour and confidence, and less sensibility than people in warm climates. The Japanese, as an extreme example, needed severe penalties to be kept in line, for they were a people of 'atrocious' character.[1] The inhabitants of the Indies, on the other hand, had 'soft, tender dispositions', so that little punishment was needed. Legislators were said to take these considerations into account in framing actual laws. In support of the idea itself, Montesquieu cited the available research of the day, on the relationship between temperature and sensibility. His statement of this problem is remarkably close to Eysenck's—to the effect that extraverts are more prone to become criminals because they are less conditionable.

Montesquieu's theory is as fundamentally conservative as modern functionalism. Montesquieu argued, for example, that legislators should not attempt to legislate contrary to the spirit of the society. Societies were complex entities whose workings were not well understood. Meddling might be dangerous, so it was probably best to leave well enough alone. Yet elsewhere he argued that law could be used to effect social change. Further, he believed some conflict

1. The Japanese themselves would seem to agree with this assessment. Of the forty countries in my study, they had the second highest rate of offenders reported to the police.

to be essential for societies, in that a tranquil society was a dead one. He was here effectively advocating a sharing of power between the executive, legislative and judicial branches, and was not advocating class conflict. Indeed he argued that the nobility, to which he belonged, should have considerable weight in government. The argument, then, is one really of the 'social functions of conflict' nature in the consensus tradition.

SCOTTISH MORAL PHILOSOPHERS

Adam Smith devoted a good portion of his life's work to the study of ethical questions, including the origins of law, sanctions and behaviour. He was writing on the subject at his death, but in his last years was dissatisfied with the results, feeling that his mental capacities had declined too much. For this, and presumably other reasons, Smith burned all his manuscripts shortly before he died. His most relevant surviving work was *The Theory of Moral Sentiments*, in which he introduced a social system type argument, relating actual laws to individual behaviour, through the moral sentiments. *The Theory of Moral Sentiments* was very influential in the years immediately following its publication but has seldom been treated as one of the classics since. Nor has it been given the credit it deserves as an early statement of functionalism. Smith's social system conceptualization was quite ingenious, anticipating Durkheim and Parsons very nicely.

Smith approached the subject by trying to answer the question 'By what means does it come to pass that the mind prefers one tenor of conduct to another?' He began with observations on the social nature of human beings, noting that even the selfish obtained pleasure in the happiness of others. People imagined themselves in others' situations, and thus identified with them. People judged other people's actions and their own, eventually developing common criteria for evaluation through a mechanism of identification. There was an important rational component in the evaluation, people considering the good or harm to society of the actions they evaluated. The rational component applied in decisions to apply sanctions as well as in conceptualizations of right or wrong. People were able to perceive that injustices were destructive to society and acted to stop them. Indeed they might be so strongly motivated to eliminate injustice as to use violence, including death. Sanctions meted out acted as a deterrent, by strengthening commitment to the moral sentiments in question. Smith explained as well how certain social conditions resulted in the corruption of moral sentiments. Servants, for example, were encouraged to develop their abilities to *please*, rather than to *serve*.

The connections between the cognitive, affective and evaluative components were not very explicit in Smith's theory. Nonetheless the rudiments were there, making Smith one of the earliest contributors to the social action concept. He was much more explicit on the relationship between individual personality and societal needs, giving a classic, if extreme, statement on the point. He was obviously very satisfied to conclude that this relationship was characterized by great harmony.

> Nature, indeed, seems to have so happily adjusted our sentiments of approbation and disapprobation, to the conveniency both of the individual and of the society, that after the strictest examination it will be found, I believe, that this is universally the case. (p. 219)

Clearly, the invisible hand could be relied on to regulate moral matters as well as economic.

Smith's explanation of criminal behaviour was based on the 'moral sentiments' or, rather, the lack thereof. The moral sentiments were what we would call internalized norms, so that where they were sufficiently strong criminal behaviour would not occur, and criminal behaviour necessarily implied some deficiency in their functioning. In *The Wealth of Nations* Smith gave a few indications as to how the moral sentiments might be negatively affected, but very little detail. The poor could be driven simply by want to commit property crimes, and the affluence of the rich could excite their indignation, making them yield to their baser sentiments (p. 319). Smith's sociological reasoning existed side by side with the familiar pre-sociological explanations of simple bad qualities. In the case of the rich these were avarice and ambition and, in the poor, hatred of labour and love of idleness. There were few sentiments that motivated injury to life or reputation, however, and these were rare— envy, malice and resentment.

Smith, in treating inequality and want as causes of crime did so in a fashion consistent with the consensus tradition. Inequality necessarily meant want, for, according to his calculations, there had to be 500 poor people for every rich one. Inequality itself was inextricably bound up with the division of labour, and the division of labour was a 'good', necessary for a high level of productivity.[1] The division of labour was a distinctive human creation, possibly the result of reasoning and language, although possibly also the product of instinct. The rich were entitled to their possessions for they had acquired them over long years, or even generations of work. Property and other possessions could not be maintained in large holdings without a system of law and the machinery for its administration. The establishment of civil government was then a necessary condition for the accumulation of property (p. 320).

Two other Scottish moral philosophers discussed aspects of consensus theory in the course of their work. David Hume was more a philosopher and psychologist than sociologist, but he did comment on the social origins of law in his *Enquiry Concerning the Principles of Morals*. The 'rules of equity and justice' depended entirely on the 'state and circumstances in which people found themselves' (p. 50). The origin of these rules lay in the utility resulting to society. Hume assumed that rules would be developed in accordance with the needs of society. He did not pay any attention to the mechanisms by which this was supposed to happen. He did, however, state that as conditions changed so did the nature of what constituted 'justice'. Justice could then be rendered 'unuseful' with changes in social conditions. There was no such confusion between what is and what ought to be in Adam Ferguson and for this, among other reasons, his work deserves to be part of the story. Ferguson did not add anything of substance to the theory of moral sentiments, but he said it all better. He began by stating certain propositions in the form of axioms— regarding self-preservation, sociability and so forth. He then derived his theoretical propositions, including those on morals, by making inferences from certain known facts and the axioms. There was no illusion that the individual–society relationship was harmonious. We are told that we *ought* to choose what is good for mankind (like the rest, Ferguson was a moral philosopher) but not that we do.[2]

Ferguson's example of separating sociology from theology was not followed by his contemporaries or the next generation of sociologists, at least not within the consensus orientation. Rather, throughout the rest of the eighteenth century, and for much of the nineteenth, theory was marked by mixed appeals to sociological

1. *Wealth of Nations*, p. 7.
2. *Institutes of Moral Philosophy*, p. 139.

principle and the more familiar gods. Patrick Colquhoun, a London
magistrate who wrote on the causes of crime, is an excellent example.
His theory was multi-causal within the sociological perspective,
and certain of the causes involved carefully specified sequences of
events. Crime had its origins in the 'vicious and immoral habits'
of the people (p. 32). Lack of education, to be more sociological
about it, played a role in the development of such habits, especially
the lack of education accorded 'the inferior orders' (p. 40). The
'superstitiousness of the Jews' was another cause, for the refusal of
Jewish parents to allow their sons to take on useful pursuits was a
source of 'depravity' (p. 40). Laxity in the law, the 'false mercies' of
juries, poor management of the police and lenient punishments
constituted other important causes of crime, as they have in much
consensus theory ever since (pp. 3, 27).

The magistrate clearly opposed the view that poverty was a cause
of crime, asserting that it was a *result* of 'extravagance, idleness,
profligacy, alcohol use and crime' (p. 34). The expansion of wealth
in England was, then, partially responsible for the increase in crime—
making Colquhoun one of the earliest theorists of 'good causing evil'.
Colquhoun was, however, more interested in causation at the individual level, and his account of how prosperity induced crime is one
of the earliest examples from the far right. The problem was that the
poor became accustomed to 'improvident and luxurious living' from
early infancy, which gave them false expectations and bad habits.

> The chief consumption of oysters, crabs, lobsters, pickled salmon
> and so forth, when first in season, and when the prices are high, is
> by the *lowest* class of people—the middle ranks, and those imme-
> diately under them abstain generally from such indulgences, until
> the prices are moderate. (p. 32)

The grocery list of the improvident poor has regrettably changed
in intervening years but, the reader is assured, the gist of the argument
will appear again and again.

In most consensus explanations, at any time, greater harshness in
dealing with criminals was urged. The exceptions are few, but there
was one even from the eighteenth century in *An Enquiry into the
Effects of Public Punishments*. Leniency was favoured in this argument and it was urged specifically that public punishments be
abolished. The grounds given were that public punishments des-
troyed the sense of shame in criminals, and the sense of shame

normally acted to produce virtuous conduct. Public punishments, by interfering with it, resulted in an increase in crime far from having the deterrent effect they were supposed to.

THE UTILITARIAN APPROACH

The utilitarian approach to crime and punishment involved a careful elaboration and systematization of certain earlier eighteenth-century ideas. The utility principle itself was not original, and rational calculation was a part, implicitly if not explicitly, of much eighteenth-century theorizing. Montesquieu and Beccaria had both used utility-type arguments, although only in rough outline. It was Bentham who worked out the application, characteristically in minute detail. Law, sanctions and behaviour were carefully interrelated in the theory, which was as general and comprehensive as any ever produced in the field.[1] Bentham was always much more a reformer than theorist, and his theoretical propositions formed only a small part of his work. These fall down, as do the proposals for reform based on them, on the premise of rational calculation. Probably never has a sociological theory had so little evidence in its favour, and so much against. Bentham's work on judicial reasoning, by contrast, was rather inspired.[2] He showed, with a comprehensive analysis of judicial decisions, that judicial reasoning was not consistent with the principles supposed to guide it. Thus, while the utility principle was contradictory to the doctrines of the time, these doctrines had, in effect, been abandoned anyway. A new approach to judicial decision-making was needed—the utility principle.

There was never any fundamental revision of the utilitarian position, so that as evidence against rational calculation accumulated, the theory was gradually abandoned. The theory served as a focus of dispute within the consensus orientation for many years, theories of psychological disturbance and so forth being compared with it. It still has some status in legal and professional circles, although it has not had a serious following in the social sciences for perhaps a hundred years. The contribution made by the utilitarians, however, is still not negligible. They did not resort to the social compact in accounting for law, or natural law or divine intervention. For Bentham's time this marks considerable progress, and even in Mill's these qualities could not be taken for granted.

1. *Fragment on Government.*
2. *Limits of Jurisprudence.*

COMPLETE AND RECOGNIZABLE CONFLICT THEORY FROM BECCARIA

Beccaria's essay was never intended to be a serious piece of scholarship, but was written for a radical discussion group whose members saw themselves as the Italian version of the Encyclopedists. Beccaria, aged twenty-six at the time, was otherwise occupied as an indolent noble. The book won immediate popular acceptance and has been cited in reform movements ever since. It has been credited with the abolition of many of the worst abuses of the criminal justice system, such as the systematic use of torture and secret hearings. Certainly Beccaria's humanitarian position was made clear throughout. The social world, as he saw it, was one of wretchedness for the mass of the population, with justice a luxury for the few. Montesquieu he took to task for lightly glossing over the corruption and cruelty of the day.[1] Two distinct classes were evident, one characterized by power and happiness and the other by misery and weakness. Laws were differentially enforced, the rich not being punished for their offences while the poor were punished brutally. Crimes against ordinary people were scarcely punished at all. The law, for the most part, was but the instrument of the passions of a small number (p. 2).

Beccaria's explanation of the origins of law was made largely in terms of interests, with common values as a secondary element. He used the social compact notion as a starting point, the compact giving the state the right to make, and enforce, laws in the common good. People were said to have given over their liberty to the total society, but only the least amount necessary to conserve public liberty (p. 10). This did not include power over one's own life, so capital punishment could not be a lawful penalty. The exercise of power beyond what was necessary was an abuse of power. Beccaria drew a clear line between justice and injustice, which was not based on natural law or some notion of divine will. This use of the social compact idea was not a conservative one. The compact accorded the state certain rights, but these were sharply limited and the influence of conflicting interests, illegitimate laws and unjust practices was stressed.

The role of common values in the explanation of law was subsidiary, but not inconsequential. Beccaria suggested that political morality was ultimately based on 'ineffable sentiments', which came from the heart. Laws not so established could not endure, and would

1. In the French edition, p. 6.

eventually be reversed—although this obviously might take some time. It would seem that Beccaria was thinking of the very distant future, for unjust laws did flourish, nor did he give any indication of expecting change in this respect in the foreseeable future.

Beccaria's conceptualization of crime as a defined phenomenon is remarkably similar to accounts which have recently become popular, notably in Quinney's *Social Reality of Crime*. He conceded that there was what might be described as a hard core of 'real crime', but the rest was a matter of definition on the part of the authorities. For every motive that influenced a person to commit a crime there were a thousand that influenced one into committing indifferent actions (p. 156). The probability that crime would be committed was then proportional to the number of motives that influenced one to commit crime, and the number of crimes so defined. To increase the sphere of criminality was to increase crime.

Two distinct types of causes of crime were discussed—economic conditions, together with their social consequences, and bad laws. Property crimes were committed mainly by the poor, out of necessity. A related cause was fear of other people; fear of the law, by contrast, had a salutary effect. Slaves, on account of their greater fear of other people, were more debauched and cruel than free persons, and thus more prone to commit crimes. Laws could affect crime in several ways. Too severe a penalty for a particular crime could deter someone from committing it by making another crime more attractive by comparison. For that reason, penalties should be fixed to reflect the relative harmfulness of crimes to be deterred. The punishment for any offence needed to be only severe enough to outweigh the good accomplished by the offence. Beccaria's utilitarian position was similar to Montesquieu's, but Beccaria went even further to argue, as a general principle, that laws *should* be established so as to achieve the greatest good for the greatest number.

Cruel laws could also promote crime, through their effect on the human spirit. This, like the fear argument, was effectively an argument of legitimacy. In an illegitimate society violence had to be used to control the population, debasing it as a consequence, and discouraging positive motivations to social behaviour. Education could have an important, edifying effect, although this was not so easily done as said. Few coercive laws would be needed in the ideal society since positive commitment to society would ensure that there would be little motivation to commit crime. Beccaria also argued for positive inducements to virtue, by way of real compensation for socially desirable behaviour.

FRENCH ENLIGHTENMENT WRITERS

Despite the name, Holbach's *Système Social* was as strongly conflict in orientation as Beccaria's *Essay*. There was the same portrayal of different laws for the rich and the poor, in practice, contrasted with what should happen in an ideal social system. Laws should reflect the will and interests of all, as opposed to particular interests, passions and caprices. Private property was the base of the conflict between rich and poor; religion was an invention of the first legislators to make the people docile. Holbach's statements on crime were much less well elaborated than Beccaria's. He did add one point, however, on the hypothesis that bad laws caused crime. He stated that people were often pushed into crime by their being unable to obtain justice, in other words being forced to obtain justice for themselves. Holbach displayed a strong concern for justice as the foundation of all social virtues. Equality, however, was a different matter; ranking was a natural phenomenon entirely consistent with justice (p. 140).

Holbach's treatment of the human individual is in line with mainstream social science. People were neither good nor bad by nature but acted in self-interest to seek happiness. Education of all kinds was based on imitation, so that vice was learned in the same way as virtue (p. 15). Crime, in other words, was a normal learned phenomenon. Holbach's denunciation of private property and religion as the opiate of the people was clearly radical. Nevertheless, there is a resounding conservative strain in *Système Social* as well. Law was the rule of justice, to direct the conduct of all, and justice was the platonic justice of all being in their proper place. One feels that life in Holbach's ideal society would be virtuous, well-ordered and monotonous. Under-socialization would not be a problem. The fit between societal needs and individual desire would be effectively perfect, so that individuals would genuinely experience the greatest happiness in contributing to the welfare of the social whole.

Mably stressed the extent of existing injustices at least as strongly as Holbach in his theory, which was similarly based on class interests. Mably's views on equality were sharply contradictory to those of the earlier writers, however, and it is this that made his theory of crime original. Equality was an essential source of legitimacy. To the extent that laws established greater equality they would be dear to the citizens, tempering the passions and bringing out the forces of reason (p. 88). The forces of reason, in turn, could be depended on to prevent injustices, including crime. Equality, then, was not only a good in and of itself, but it served to prevent crime. If people were bad, Mably was persuaded, it was ultimately the fault of the law (p. 83). Justice he defined in unusually concrete terms; it included, for example, not taking advantage of one's inferiors (p. 1). Mably's work, as his life, is immensely interesting in many ways extraneous to the discussion of conflict theory. He wrote extensively, largely on history and philosophy. His originality extends to having refused membership to that distinguished men's club, the French Academy.

GODWIN: CONDITIONS AND PROCESSES IN THEORY

Godwin is probably the most overlooked, underestimated theorist in the deviance–social control field. His *Enquiry Concerning Political Justice* included all the essential components of an integrated theory of law, sanctions and behaviour, making it one of the first comprehensive theories of social control The *Enquiry* was directed to many other subjects besides, but the theory was explicit, requiring no excess of scholarly zeal to extract it from its broader setting. The theory, clearly eighteenth century in style, is disarmingly contemporary in content. It began, as did the earlier versions, with the role of property in creating two distinctive classes, the rich and the poor. The rich used legislation to institutionalize their privileges. They were 'directly or indirectly the legislators of the state; and of consequence perpetually reducing oppression into a system' (p. 19). They designed laws, such as on monopolies and patents, to protect their own interests, but made criminal the equivalent institutions of workers—trade unions. The offences with the most severe penalties, capital crimes, were the offences they had no temptation to commit, like robbery (p. 21). Further it was the rich who controlled the enforcement of the law, a point Godwin argued forcefully. He conceded criminal trials were generally administered with great impartiality, at least in England. But the rich had recourse to numerous loopholes, notably pardons, which, over all, gave them decided advantages (p. 22).

The same inequalities of power that affected the nature of the law and its enforcement also affected criminal behaviour. In some instances the effect was direct, as in property crimes being motivated by extreme poverty (p. 462). More often, however, the effects were indirect, through the socialization of children. Private property taught children from an early age that greed and violence were well rewarded. The ostentation of the rich made the lot of the poor more difficult; human beings could accept hardships with cheerfulness if they were impartially shared (p. 17). It was not only absolute poverty, but relative deprivation, that affected the commission of crimes.

Godwin stressed that external circumstances made their effect on ultimate behaviour through a reasoning process. There was no simple, mechanistic connection between cause and effect, as so often charged by critics of conflict theory. Most behaviour was voluntary, and it depended not on 'direct and immediate impulses' but 'decisions of understanding' (p. 26). People loved justice and were desirous of helping one another, to the extent that it was difficult even for the very poor to commit a crime. Whether this was the result of instinct implanted by nature, or for some other cause, was not clear. Whatever the explanation, there was a strong commitment to the reasonableness of helping one another. To overcome this, the would-be criminal had to invent some 'sophistry', some 'palliation' to justify the crime. This is the process referred to in later sociological work as 'neutralization'. Conditions of real poverty were important in the causal sequence by furnishing valid justifications to the individual's conscience. In one place Godwin even went so far as to assert that it was only when crime was motivated by necessity that the reconciliation could be effected. Godwin was also one of the earliest theorists to make a distinction between behaviour and sanctions, and the factors that affected them. Conditions of inequality and oppression were major factors that affected both. The illegitimacy of certain institutions, however, was said to act particularly on sanctions. The more these institutions contradicted the 'general sentiments' of the human mind, the greater the severity required to avenge their violation (p. 381).

There were many other expressions of theory in the eighteenth century just as solidly in the conflict tradition, but with much less detail. Several of these will be noted briefly, simply to round out the picture. Morelly, in 1755, theorized property to be the cause of all 'evil, disorder, crime and depravity' (p. 79). The causal process by which this occurred, however, was not discussed, but rather the author then gave his views as to what the laws should be. Linguet, in a much more extensive account, gave a bitter description of the origin of criminal law, in the collusion of the most successfully violent to protect their gains. They authorized only their own 'common thievery', punishing severely those outside their ranks (p. 298). Those who dared to attempt restitution were punished as offenders against society (p. 300). Brissot de Warville blamed government above all in accounting for the causes of crime. Human beings were not born enemies of society, but only circumstances— indigence and misfortune—made them 'trouble the tranquillity' of society, and for these government institutions were responsible (p. 40). Morals were better, in general, in the lower classes, but the better-off had a greater capacity to control themselves. They had more to lose from breaking the law and, as well, had the benefit of education 'to tame the spirit' (p. 64). Prisons were said to increase crime rather than decrease it.

Chapter 3

THE DEBATE IN THE NINETEENTH CENTURY

In the nineteeth century the fundamental propositions of both conflict theory and consensus underwent considerable elaboration, with numerous branches of theory appearing for each. The theories, as they were inherited from the eighteenth century were sparsely stated, with little attention to nuances in relationships between causal links. Often causal propositions were part of a larger work, basically reformist in intention, the theoretical work included to defend a principle. In some cases the purpose of the work was theoretical, but the theoretical task was a broader one, only touching on law or behaviour peripherally. Documentation for the theories was, without exception, meagre. Authors made reasoned arguments, citing observations and anecdotes consistent with their position. They criticized the reasoning of competing theorists, suggesting alternative interpretations of their observations. There was some use of quantitative data, but only in a limited way. Lists of numbers of prisoners for various crimes would be given, for example, and estimates made of the numbers of various crimes and criminals.

By the end of the nineteenth century all this had changed. A number of original theories appeared, on law, behaviour and sanctions, in both the conflict and consensus orientations. Other theories were considerably elaborated and refined. There was immense growth and differentiation within the consensus orientation especially, so that several distinctive schools can be seen to emerge. The great disputes within the consensus orientation, which dominate twentieth-century sociology of deviance, began in this period. Specialization within conflict theory was, by comparison, minor. Rather, for theory of both law and behaviour, theorists added to the work of earlier writers, so that a basic continuity was maintained. Empirical work in sociology began in the nineteenth century, and some of it was of considerably better quality than commonly believed. The principal research methods used in sociology at all to date were developed by the end of the century. This includes systematic interviewing, secondary analysis of case records, the use of psychological tests, and the measurement of physical characteristics and physiological responses. The data would be presented in tables, often multivariate, and charts and graphs were prepared with rates and percentages. The use of probability theory in data analysis began in the middle of the century, although conventions for tests of statistical significance and measures of association were not developed until later. There was considerable use of aggregated data, both census records and institutional statistics collected by government agencies. Again, there was much use of secondary analysis. Many levels of aggregation were used: city, region and nation, both for cross-sectional studies, and time series.

At the same time it should be noted that much of the empirical work was, with the benefit of hindsight, ill conceived. Much of my criticism of nineteenth-century work concerns methodological errors. Empirical work was used for theory testing purposes, but not in a very satisfactory way. Many theorists were past using isolated statistics and anecdotes as supportive 'data' for their propositions, but their use of empirical studies was not qualitatively different. The dispute between competing schools was carried on with the use of empirical studies. Mutually exclusive propositions would be stated at the same congresses and appear in the same journals, in both cases with copious documentation. Since, typically, different research methods were used in the two orientations, and often different levels of analysis, this could easily be done. Proponents of the various schools for the most part talked past each other.

The debate between conflict and consensus theories was centred on economic factors in the nineteenth century as in the eighteenth. In conflict theory of crime, poverty was typically treated as the main causal factor, with lack of education and excessive use of alcohol often as its consequences, and these in turn leading to criminal behaviour. In most of these theories as well, there was some notion of law affecting behaviour, either particular 'bad' laws, or law in general. Conflict theorists, when they commented on severity of laws, consistently supported less harsh penalties.[1] Many of them

1. Pecqueur, Ducpétiaux (1827), Morgan, Carpenter.

opposed capital punishment,[1] transportation, long prison sentences and, especially, prison for children. Prison as a school for crime was a familiar theme, for reasons suggestive of later labelling theory.

Consensus theorists, by contrast, in general opposed economic arguments, and especially the basic one of poverty.[2] Some argued that poverty was a *consequence* of crime, rather than its cause.[3] A few theorists accepted poverty as an auxiliary factor or, more often, as a symptom of some other, underlying cause, along the lines of idleness and intemperance, or physical or mental defects. The ultimate causes cited in consensus theory in the nineteenth century can be divided roughly into two main schools—one based on social explanations, apart from economic, and the other on individual, biologically based factors. This is effectively a heredity versus environment argument, and it was often discussed in just those terms. There were theorists who admitted both,[4] but typically one or other type of cause was treated as the more important. It does not seem that either school can properly be treated as being prior to the other or, accordingly, either as a reaction to the other. Both have very obvious roots in the explanations of moral failing of the pre-sociological period. Those who began to give a social interpretation to such failings became social theorists, while those who gave a biological interpretation became biological theorists. The former stressed the moral training aspects of the earlier explanations, while the latter began to see immoral qualities in terms of congenital defects, epilepsy and so forth.

In the early part of the century social explanations were centred on lack of education, intemperance and unemployment, all suggestive of lack of moral fibre.[5] Other social explanations were gradually introduced, especially on the theme of lack of *moral* education. Problems in the family had an effect through inhibiting moral training. Age, sex, religion and ethnic differences were used in explanations to reflect related social circumstances. Urbanization, rapid population increase, the breakdown of traditional social bonds dominated in the later explanations. Durkheim's anomie conceptualization, the last of the original notions produced in the school, drew on this whole line of thought. There was considerably less

1. Tristan, Ducpétiaux, de Villiers, Sampson.
2. Tarde (1901), Durkheim, Giddings, Garofalo (1895).
3. Mirehouse.   4. Ferri (1881), Lacassagne, Vuacheux.
5. Rawson, Fletcher, Cargill, Mayhew.

concern over harshness of sentences in the consensus school than in the conflict. It would be admitted, for example, that prisons had a deleterious effect on their inmates, but this was typically accepted with resignation. Some consensus theorists actually argued for harsher penalties, and many favoured swifter and more certain ones. Some supported capital punishment and some even argued for transportation as a useful deterrent.[1] Where pleas for leniency occurred, these were usually confined to children.[2]

Opposition to economic determinism was just as strong in the biological school, proponents often opposing *all* kinds of social factors as causes of crime. It would be pointed out that not everybody who was poor or ignorant became criminal, so that the determining factor could not be poverty or ignorance, but some individual defect. There had been no reduction in crime rates with either the general decline of poverty or expansion of schooling, fairly conclusive evidence against economic determinism theories for the biological theorists. In terms of severity of punishment, the proponents of biological theories ran the gamut. Some, especially the early French psychiatrists, were committed opponents of cruel punishments. They argued that punishment did not have the intended effect for certain kinds of disturbance, and that treatment should be used instead.[3] Lombroso, the leading Italian school exponent, was a humanitarian in many respects, although he approved of capital punishment. More often, however, biological theorists supported harsh penalties, and some argued even for increased severity.[4] The 'born criminal' notion justified punishment, there being no hope of reform for such cases. If crime were indeed a disease, society had a responsibility to stamp it out before it spread.[5]

CONFLICT THEORY

ROBERT OWEN

Robert Owen elaborated conflict theory considerably from its eighteenth-century base. Bad government, and particularly unequal distribution of power, was at the heart of the explanation. Bad laws were the result of bad government, and these produced crime. There was then a vicious circle, for governments would have to

1. Mirehouse.   2. Waugh.
3. Pinel, Lauvergne, Sampson, Voisin.
4. Galton, Bonneville, van Hamel.   5. Drahms.

respond to the rise in crime with still more laws and greater repression. Owen's interest in law and behaviour arose in his practical concerns in the experiment to create a utopian society. Ideally, law would not be needed at all, but it would be required for some time even in a 'rational' society, until new attitudes took hold.[1] Bad law and bad government had their effect on crime in many direct and indirect ways. The very poor became criminals simply out of necessity, for food and clothing. Most of the British population (three-quarters of it) were brought up without adequate education, moral training or guidance. Such people, in Owen's terms, were 'trained to vice and misery', even to the point of being dangerous.[2] Education was completely lacking for the lower classes, and for the others it was of the wrong kind, promoting an egoistic spirit. Owen's explanation of crime included the same variables of idleness and ignorance that were typical of early consensus theory, but there is no mistaking his theory with any of the others. The crucial difference between the two approaches lay in conflicting interests and the power of the stronger group to defend itself. On this point, there could be no ambiguity; bad government was to blame for poverty, ignorance and associated ills. More precisely, it was government based on inequalities in ownership of property that was at fault.

Owen influenced the rest of the conflict theorists of the century, notably Engels, who acknowledged the debt in many places, later differences notwithstanding. In *Socialism Utopian and Scientific*, he described Owen's New Lanark experiment in glowing terms, claiming it to be so successful that no prisons, trials or police were needed. The reader is given to believe that crime had been completely eliminated (p. 10). A more disciple-like follower, William Thompson, incorporated Owen's propositions unchanged in his *Enquiry into the Principles of the Distribution of Wealth Most Conducive to Human Happiness*. The notion of education promoting selfish attitudes, conducive to crime, was repeated by all the major succeeding conflict theorists.

DUCPÉTIAUX: THE BEGINNING OF EMPIRICAL WORK
The next contribution to conflict theory also marks the beginning of empirical work on the subject, or at least the first such work I was able to find. It is a short paper by a Belgian socialist Ducpétiaux, published in 1827. The fact of a radical theorist stooping to do

1. *Book of the New Moral World.*   2. *New View of Society*, p. 6.

empirical work perhaps bears comment, for it is supposed to be out of character. When one realizes just how much the conflict position was the out-group position, however, it makes sense. Consensus theorists did not have to do empirical work to prove their point. It was the conventional wisdom of the day, questioned only by a small and uninfluential group of upstarts. No more than casual observation was required to remind the reader of its essential soundness. Not until conflict theorists began to use empirical data in support of their arguments were consensus believers forced into the competition. This, in fact, did not take long. Quetelet, a contemporary of Ducpétiaux, and also a Belgian, published an empirical paper, in the consensus perspective, as early as 1827 and the avalanche began.[1]

Ducpétiaux was something of a political activist when he published this first paper. His thesis was the familiar one of misery and ignorance being the chief causes of crime, bad laws auxiliary, with prisons playing a 'school for crime' role. In support of this he showed that the crime rate was higher in countries with higher proportions of poor people, for which he used numbers on relief rather than average income or wealth. England had more poverty than France, using this indicator, and a higher crime rate, consistent with his hypothesis.[2] Crime rates were further shown, for several societies, to be greater in poorer regions. In England the rates were higher in the more industrialized regions which, despite their greater total wealth, were the areas of the greatest economic fluctuations and, hence, real misery. Ducpétiaux also argued that changes in crime rates between 1816 and 1817 supported his thesis, or a mini-time series analysis. There was greater misery in 1817 than 1816, which corresponded with an increase in the crime rate. Most of the increase was, moreover, in property crimes.

Ducpétiaux's data on education were confined to regional level comparisons within countries. He admitted that crime rates were higher in the parts of France with the most extensive education, but argued that this was, in effect, a spurious relationship, due to the

1. Quetelet is often acknowledged as the first to have done empirical research on this subject, which would seem to be wrong. Quetelet, moreover, knew Ducpétiaux and his work. Ducpétiaux is also cited in Rawson's first publications on crime, in the *Journal of the Statistical Society* and in de Candolle's publications in the *Bibliothèque Universelle de Genève*.
2. *Justice de Prévoyance*, p. 13.

greater availability of riches to steal. When 'real' crime, or violent crime, was considered, his propositions were supported (p. 20). Ducpétiaux also made some casual observations on crime without hard data to back them up, with unlucky results. He remarked on the rarity of both crime and poverty in the United States, suggesting a causal relationship in accordance with conflict theory.

From the point of view of conflict theory, it is unfortunate that Ducpétiaux did not continue research on the lines of his 1827 publication. He can be excused for not pursuing the subject immediately, for he spent the next year in prison, on a sedition charge. This experience was evidently to stand him in good stead, for he subsequently became Inspector-General of prisons in Belgium and, while his later writings are those of the scrupulously careful civil servant, they continue to betray a passion not usually found in the publications of Inspectors-General of prisons. For whatever reason, he became more interested in applied problems after this first foray into crime data, working on law reform, poverty and the condition of the working class. He did publish some further material on crime rates, but only the bare statistics, without any text.

FLORA TRISTAN

Flora Tristan's *Promenades dans Londres* was at the opposite extreme methodologically. Essentially a description of the condition of life of the ordinary people of London, crime and prison belonged for the obvious reason that they were very much a part of this existence. Along with a great deal of descriptive material, Tristan included as well a number of theoretical statements on the causes of crime and the effects of prisons. The material was collected in the course of four trips to London, over a fifteen-year period. The widening of the gap between rich and poor was described, with its implications in ever-increasing luxuries for the rich and misery for the mass of the poor (p. 149). Economic conditions were the main factors cited as causes of crime. But Tristan, unlike other writers, showed how women were affected as well as men. The exclusion of women from most lawful employment, she argued, was responsible for a good deal of women's crimes, especially infanticide, prostitution and theft. Tristan subscribed to the 'prison as school for crime' thesis, stressing the effect of a prison sentence on employment opportunities on release. The prison experience was especially bad for children, for lazy habits, acquired in prison, made lawful employment less feasible. Unlike

almost all the conflict theorists Tristan accepted biological explanations of crime, as well as economic and social. She gave greater
prominence to economic explanations, but evidently saw congenital
defects as playing a role, roughly suggesting that it was the weakest,
or most defective who were the most vulnerable to economic pressures to commit crimes (p. 157).

There is such a peculiar combination of qualities in Tristan's
work that it was very difficult to place her methodologically and
philosophically. Closer to Owen than anyone else, she was not bound
by any philosophical system. She was open and eclectic theoretically,
so that she could accept biological explanations decades before they
became popular, and decades before other conflict theorists would
touch them. She was a socialist, feminist, and political organizer
above all. She was committed to massive societal change, through
proletarian organization, at the time Marx was still a social democrat. The purpose of *Promenades dans Londres* was observation,
and in this she sought to be comprehensive and fair. Unlike Owen
and Engels, however, she approached her task as something of an
insider. She was a Frenchwoman, of course, and so a foreigner in
England, but she had been poor, and she had worked for her living.
There was not the distance between herself and her subjects that one
finds in Engels, especially, yet she had certain aspirations of scientific carefulness and fairness, if not impartiality. In considering
Tristan, in short, we are confronted with the major dilemmas of the
current methodological debate on the relationship between researcher
and subject, and the place of theory in guiding research. Tristan's
solution to them was original, and probably one that should be given
a great deal more thought.

MARX

It is difficult to discuss Marx on law and crime for there is at once
too much and too little to say. Marx's influence on the whole course
of theorizing on the subject was great, yet he actually wrote little
directly bearing on it. His remarks on law were brief, although
highly general. Otherwise there are only tangential statements
about law, specific punishments and, more rarely, criminal behaviour.
Why Marx should have had so little to say has very much to do with
what he had to say. Law was one of the elements of superstructure,
itself to be explained in terms of material conditions, the system of
production and exchange, and its social and cultural ramifications.

To understand law it was necessary to understand this material base, and this itself was a major undertaking. Criminal behaviour was of less interest, for ordinary criminals belonged neither to the bourgeoisie nor to the proletariat, and so stood outside the dominant class struggle of capitalist society.

Marx apparently arrived at his theory of law by 1844, and did not change it significantly afterwards. Law, like other elements of superstructure, had its roots in the conditions of material existence. It could not be explained by itself, in the sense of by other legal phenomena, or by the evolution of the human spirit. Individuals entered into social relations to exist; these then affected all other relations and their view of the surrounding world.[1] They had no choice, but rather these relations were 'indispensable and independent' of their will (p. 11). The nature of the social relations of production corresponded to the degree of development of the material productive forces. This was the economic base of society, and on it rested the juridical and political superstructure. It was not 'the consciousness of men that determines their existence but, on the contrary, their social existence determines their consciousness'.

Marx's statement differed from those of eighteenth-century writers in several important respects. There are no longer only two classes, a rich and a poor, or the owners and non-owners of property. Instead the number and nature of the classes depended on the stage of development of the society. The motivation of the rich was not simply that of moral failing, greed or avarice, but was itself explained with the same laws of dialectical materialism.

In *The German Ideology*, Marx indulged in discussion of the functions of crime in capitalist society. He also wrote a denunciation of capital punishment and some commentaries on official crime statistics. The material on crime statistics, written for the *New York Daily Tribune*, is of interest mainly to show that Marx was committed to quantitative analysis, a fact which so many mid-twentieth-century disciples prefer to ignore[2]. The annual publication of crime statistics from the 1830s provoked debate between conflict and consensus advocates, and Marx took part in it. It is to Engels, however, that one must turn for a comprehensive treatment of crime statistics, and for a detailed statement of the Marxian position on crime and social control.

1. *Critique of Political Economy.*
2. This will be discussed much more fully in Ch. 8.

ENGELS

The Condition of the Working Class in England shows very much the influence of Owen, but Engels's analysis went further in several important respects. Engels began by showing how the living and working conditions of the working class were conducive to crime. He subscribed to the familiar hypothesis that a certain amount of crime was committed directly and immediately for sheer survival. This was documented with data on the relationship between rates of unemployment and crime. He incorporated numerous other factors as well into the explanation, especially to explain the large share of crimes committed by children. The link was in the family, poor living and working conditions demoralizing the family and resulting in child neglect. The family was seldom together, for the father had a long working day, and often the mother and older children had to work as well. Living conditions were squalid and domestic quarrels frequent in those hours parents were home. Recourse to the pub was understandable, but added to the demoralized atmosphere at home. Children were often left to their own devices, and moral education in the schools, which might have made up for neglect at home, was lacking.

To explain crime among adults, Engels resorted to a notion of 'loss of will'. This was a product of brutal treatment, which was itself a function of the stage of development of the social relations of production. In advanced capitalism brutality was well advanced. Workers were left to follow blindly the law of nature, turning into criminals as inevitably as water into a stream (p. 146). Engels's determinism was never more apparent than it is here, but his reasoning was never simplistic or mechanistic. The links in the causal chain were social ones, and these were made plain throughout.

Crime could be seen as the first manifestation of the war of all against all, eventually leading to proper, organized revolt. It was to be expected that crime would be higher in England than elsewhere for England was the most industrialized society in the world, and the ripest for revolution. Engels's argument on this point was similar to Ducpétiaux's, and crime rates were, in fact, higher in England than in the less industrialized countries, which supported this point. Further, crime rates were increasing over time, with industrialization.

PLINT: EARLY COMPARATIVE TESTING

One of those rare pieces of research—serious, comparative theory testing—appeared soon after Engels's *Condition of the Working*

Class. This was a study by Plint, of English crime rates over the first half of the nineteenth century. The purpose of the research was to investigate what were effectively the conflict and consensus theses of the day. The consensus view Plint described as crime reflecting the 'moral condition' of the people. The conflict view was economic determinism, and especially the effect of industrial organization. The findings were both unfavourable to the consensus view and favourable to the conflict. Against the moral condition thesis Plint showed that crime rates did not reflect changes in the availability of education. There had been gradual increases in numbers attending school, while the crime rate fluctuated in waves. Crime was, by contrast, positively related to the price of food, rising as food prices rose, or as people became poorer in real terms. Crime rates were greater in the manufacturing regions than in the more traditional areas. It was not the industrial workers, however, who were mainly responsible for crime, but unemployed labourers and predatory vagrants, attracted to manufacturing areas.

Plint's study seems to have had very little effect, then or now, so that it was astonishing to discover that he was right. Indeed, it was only with the corroboration of Thomas's study in 1938 and Gatrell and Hadden in 1972 that I was personally convinced. Plint's study must be commended as well for competence demonstrated in handling data problems. Plint discussed, for example, the effect of the size of the unit of analysis on results, noting problems that occur with units too large and heterogeneous. The problem of the effect of age distribution was related, as well, and again the sophistication of Plint's approach was such that one could well wish it emulated today.

MINOR CONFLICT THEORISTS

Three other English publications from the same period, all of a theoretical nature, also deserve at least brief mention.

Hall's work reflected the concerns of a practising doctor, and claimed neither sophistication in analysis nor generality in theory. Hall presented himself rather as a person in a position to observe a considerable range of human society. His theoretical position was strongly conflict, although he would probably not have liked the company into which that put him. This theory related criminal behaviour to the psychological consequences of poverty. Poverty, in turn, was related to inequalities of power which, in most societies, were said to reflect accumulated wealth.

Mary Carpenter gave a similar explanation of behaviour, applied to juveniles particularly, and again the tone was reformist rather than revolutionary. The discussion of causation was centred on a typology, which included both moral and economic conditions, the economic conditions clearly placing the theory in the conflict camp. Carpenter as well made some observations on inequalities in law. She pointed out, for example, the differences in punishment suffered by the starving orphan for a trivial offence, and the gentlemanly swindler guilty of much worse. The third work was by a humanitarian prison inspector, Hill, and reflects the concerns one would expect. Moral and economic conditions were, again, both causes of crime. The work is especially interesting as an early description of the labelling process. This appeared in Hill's tracing the 'career of a young delinquent'. The initial force towards crime was poverty, and a prison term was the necessary consequence. Prison had the effect of increasing criminal tendencies, and eliminating opportunities for legitimate employment afterwards.

PROUDHON

Proudhon left a few general remarks on the social causes of crime in his writing, and a few more detailed comments on the effects of financial speculation. His most general statement on crime reflects a rather firm determinism, although a 'more or less' qualification was included:

> Crime is never isolated, but always more or less caused, provoked, encouraged, tolerated and permitted by the system of relations, more or less exact and equitable, which form society, and it is for society to search in what it can have been guilty towards the delinquent.[1]

Financial institutions were partially responsible for crime. Speculation meant unearned income and luxurious living for some, which was deleterious for public morals.[2] Proudhon argued that the development of fraud and theft could be traced ultimately to the mentality promoted by speculation, through deterioration of moral training in the family, among other things.

1. *Justice dans la Révolution*, p. 521.
2. *Speculateur de la Bourse*, p. 160.

COLAJANNI

The Italian conflict theorist, Colajanni, is the last of the period to be discussed. He is of interest for insights both at the macro and micro levels, and is generally a good representative of the conflict position reached towards the end of the century. Colajanni strongly opposed the physical explanations of crime prevailing by then, especially in Italy, arguing for clearly social explanations in their place.[1] He was one of the few theorists who tried to answer the argument that 'not all who are poor become criminal'. It was true, Colajanni admitted, for some of the poor deteriorated into a stupor and others emigrated or committed suicide instead. At the societal level, Colajanni argued that socialist politics provided an alternative to crime to the poor—the argument of the collective versus the individual solution. He reported data showing lower rates of crime in countries with higher rates of socialist voting. Elsewhere he argued along the same lines, that socialist propaganda did not result in increases in crime rates, as charged by opponents to conflict theory. Again, data were reported to show lower crime rates in societies with socialist agitation than without it.[2]

ACCEPTANCE OF CONFLICT THEORY

Support for the conflict position grew throughout Europe over the century, and roughly up to World War I, although the theory never attained the support of biological theories, or of sociological in the consensus orientation. One of the five international congresses was devoted to the 'economic determinism' debate, which indicates fairly well the relative strengths of the two sides. The theory was most strongly supported in England, Belgium, Holland, Italy and France.[3] It attracted very little support or even interest either in the United States or Russia, where biological theories predominated.

The debate was never noteworthy for its quality of discussion. Opponents claimed that published crime statistics at the nation-state level were largely disconfirming of simple, poverty explanations.[4] This was true, so far as the simple poverty explanation was concerned, for crime rates were higher in the more industrialized,

---

1. *Revue Socialiste.*
2. 'Socialisme et sa propagande'.
3. See also work by Denis, Pecqueur, Proal, Guénoud, Cavaglieri and Florian.
4. Tarde, Garofalo (1885), Rostand, Giddings.

prosperous countries most of the time. Conflict theory, however, never depended on this simplistic notion, and to treat such results as disconfirming of economic explanations in general is naïve. Even as early as the eighteenth century *relative deprivation* was an important part of the explanation, and the data which disconfirmed the simple poverty explanation often supported relative deprivation. Ducpétiaux, in 1827, for example, treated fluctuations in the economy as the indicator of misery, rather than absolute poverty. Another major criticism of the theory has been based on a misconception of the theory as a single cause explanation. In fact, the single cause criticism is valid, in general, only for theorists prior to 1750 (and then excluding Thomas More) and otherwise only for a small number of isolated, peripheral writers since.

Vast numbers of studies were published both for and against the theory, so that a verdict on the evidence of the time would have to be inconclusive. With later empirical work, however, again with nineteenth-century data, credible support for the conflict position emerges. Dorothy Thomas's *Crime and the Business Cycle* is one important example, reaching a conclusion of moderate support for the theory. Based on British data, the analysis deals with several different periods, from the publication of the earliest statistics, in 1825, to 1913. Thomas found no consistent relationship between crime in general and the business cycle for the whole period, but the predicted relationships did appear for certain property offences for good parts of it. In the 1857–1913 period larceny increased with business failures. Further, considering data lagged one or two years, there were significant relationships between the business cycle and burglary, house- and shop-breaking. In the case of crime in general some results were favourable to the theory, for the early part of the series, 1825–40.

Considerably stronger evidence for the theory appears in the work of Tilly and colleagues, from a much larger study, but one directed primarily to collective violence (as in riots) rather than ordinary crime. The relevant findings from the study deal with changes in rates of crime in France from the first publication of national crime statistics to the end of the century. Roughly, the trend was of declining rates of crime with increasing prosperity. The rate varied across different types of crime, but the trend throughout was of decreases, gradual, and fairly substantial. There were fluctuations in economic conditions over the period, but again the overall trend was of increasing prosperity (p. 303). At the same time, there were gradual increases in the strength of the forces of order, so that it is not likely that declining crime rates could have been due to declining rates of apprehension or recording.

Recent work on British crime data by Gatrell and Hadden helps to put all these earlier, and more limited, studies into perspective. Their analysis shows increasing rates of property crime over the first half of the century, correlating positively with economic crises, measured by business failures. Economic deprivation had the effect of making criminals out of people who would not otherwise have committed crimes, and the rising crime rate over the period reflected the general trend of increasing misery for the poor, and the increasing gap between rich and poor.

> In nearly every decade of the nineteenth century, the year-to-year movements in the incidence of property offences were inversely correlated with the fluctuations of the trade cycle. They increased in times of depression and diminished in times of prosperity: more people stole in hard times than in good (p. 368).

Conditions began to change in the second half of the century, roughly from the 1840s and early 1850s, and the crime rate changed accordingly. Real income began to increase, economic crises became less frequent and less severe and the numbers of people living in desperate poverty began to decline. The rate of property crimes fell gradually through this same period. Its decline, moreover, cannot be accounted for as a figment of reporting changes. The size of the police force grew, as did public acceptance of it, so that one must expect the tendency to report crimes increased, and the probability of their being recorded. As well, with the decline in the use of the death penalty for property offences, reluctance to charge suspects probably weakened (p. 352). Thus, while there may be some doubt as to the basis in 'reality' for the increases in the early part of the century, there can be no doubt about the decreases in the later.[1]

Data on the characteristics of prisoners support this interpretation, although the argument is indirect. In the first half of the century, prisoners represented a much broader cross-section of the population than they did later. Despite the vast expansion of the

---

1. Some American data also show long-term declining rates, even despite substantial increases in population. This is discussed pp. 178–9.

school system in the latter half of the century, roughly the same high proportion of prisoners was illiterate as earlier. This suggests that they were increasingly being drawn from 'a criminal class', or that many honest people who earlier were forced into crime at times of acute need no longer were that desperate (p. 378).

The material altogether suggests that the early conflict theorists were right, from Thomas More, Godwin and Owen on. The early empirical studies, for all their sparseness of data, were clearly also on the right track; or, Ducpétiaux and Engels were also right. Tristan's more impressionistic work, of increasing misery and a widening gap between rich and poor, was also correct. Plint's analysis, the most elaborate, and with data up to 1850, again looks better and better with the accumulation of studies. What is extremely interesting to note about all this is that the conflict theorists whose hypotheses were substantiated were all from the early part of the century, from the period of increasing misery and an increasing crime rate.

That conflict theory was equally right for the latter half of the century presented difficulties to conflict theorists as much as consensus. For Marxists the problem is obvious—decreasing misery was contrary to other, more fundamental, predictions. There were other socialists and conflict theorists as well, to be sure, but for some reason these did not manage to put the picture together. Rather comparisons across societies were dealt with, or rates of crime among different sectors of the population, leaving aside the question of long-term trends.

Ironically, it was consensus theorists who took up the burden of explaining 'rising crime'—but by which time crime had begun to decline. At least, for the only two societies for which we have thorough analyses of trends over the whole of the period, Britain and France, crime rates were declining. The basic premise of most consensus scholarly work, in other words, was wrong. Italian school theorists turned to individualistic explanations, they said, because rising prosperity and expanded education had failed to reduce crime, proving that the explanation of economic determinism was wrong. A number of sociologists, and ultimately Durkheim, made a similar mistake, seeking a variety of other social factors *in lieu of* poverty. But this is to get ahead of the story.

NINETEENTH-CENTURY SOCIOLOGICAL EXPLANATIONS

The first sociological explanations of crime reflect very much their roots in taken-for-granted, moralistic accounts of earlier days. These early theories consisted of simple assertions as to the causes of crime, without any attempt to relate them to a more general explanatory scheme. The assumption seems to have been that the causes given were sufficiently obvious not to need much investigation. For similar reasons, presumably, there was only the barest reference to empirical observation. An English magistrate, Jackson, in 1828 accounted for the increase in crime with the multitude of gin shops, dissolute youth parading the streets, and lack of fear of punishment. An English clergyman, in 1840, cited poverty and poor physical environment as causes of crime, these by way of interfering with the development of morals.[1] A study of prison convicts concluded that lack of education, especially moral education, was the chief cause of crime.[2] In other early work the role of the press was emphasized as a cause of crime.[3] Lurid reporting of crime was supposed to induce imitation, or otherwise pervert the morals of readers. Lack of education was probably the most often cited cause of crime in this period, followed by intemperance, unemployment and overly lenient punishment. These were the preferred causes of crime in early American sociology, as well, which began to emerge later in the century.

Simple explanations still appear from time to time, of course, but in the academic literature they have been gradually replaced with more general explanations. Of these, two branches can be conveniently identified, a mainstream sociological school, and theory of evolution. I treat the mainstream explanation as beginning with the publication of Quetelet's *Physique Sociale* in 1835,[4] although it was not until later in the century that the school attained broad acceptance. Most of the theorists associated with it were French and, for this reason, the school has often been called the 'French sociolo-

1. Morgan.   2. Joseph.
3. Aubry, Despine, Minovici, Rostand, 1897.
4. The book was originally entitled *Sur l'Homme et le Développement de ses Facultés* with *Essai de la Physique Sociale* as a sub-title. In the 1869 edition the sub-title became the title, and this is how the work is usually known. In an abridged English version, 1842, it is called *A Treatise on Man and the Development of his Faculties*. Page references are to the second French edition. There are recent re-issues in both English and French.

gical school'. The evolution school dates from Spencer and Darwin. Evolutionary theory affected mainstream sociology as well, but the dissimilarities between the hard-core evolutionists and the others are great enough to warrant some distinction being drawn.

QUETELET

Quetelet was only a part-time sociologist, but the little work he did on the subject was methodologically ingenious, and altogether of impressive subtlety—making him one of the most important founders of the subject. His early training was in mathematics, and he was fortunate enough to discover a curve at the early age of twenty-three. This earned him a chair and established his reputation for life. He then moved on to more applied work, through astronomy and meteorology, and finally to sociology. Most of his work was in what we would call demography, on mortality and marriage rates. Towards the end of his career he became the head of the Belgian central statistical office, and Belgium became the most advanced country of the time in the collection and publication of official statistics.

Quetelet was a convinced positivist throughout his life, unashamedly confident that there were underlying laws which explained phenomena of all kinds, social as much as physical. It was the scientist's task to describe them as well as possible. Social phenomena were explicable ultimately in the same way as physical, although the difficulties in discovering social laws were greater. Quetelet was, again like so many nineteenth-century positivists, a man with an insistent conscience. He began with certain moral concerns which, in time, began to interest him as intellectual problems. A good part of his professional life was then spent in the scientific study of these problems or, in his terms, the application of probability to social and moral problems.

Quetelet's first work in the crime–social control field was a rather modest, descriptive study, reminiscent of Ducpétiaux's first paper on crime rates.[1] His *Physique Sociale* appeared soon afterwards, in 1835, a very impressive, systematic piece of work. It contains a defence of the assumptions and working rules of positivism, which will be discussed in Chapter 8. The theoretical task was the explanation of the *penchant au crime*, or the probability of a crime being committed. The answer Quetelet worked out, or rather

1. *Nombre des Crimes*; see also his papers of 1830 and 1831.

his structuring of the answer, can be identified as the foundation of mainstream sociology. The leaning to crime was to be explained by the conditions of everyday social life, the problems people faced, their temptations and the possibilities open to them to commit crimes. The underlying factors might never be properly understood, but certain observable aspects were available, which could serve to represent them. Quetelet then used what have since become 'the standard demographic variables' of social science research—age, sex, marital status, education, occupation, religion, race, and region. His contribution lay not in the choice of the variables—all had been used somewhere before—but in bringing them together, systematically, into a sociological theory.

Quetelet's position on economic determinism was worked out with the same principles. What was most important was how people assessed their lot in relation to others. It was relative deprivation that led to crime, not absolute, and the data he reported supported this conclusion. Crime rates were high where there were great inequalities in wealth, or where poverty would be less tolerable, in the light of others' ease. Sudden changes in conditions had the same effect. People accustomed to better conditions reacted to misery more acutely than those who had known no other life.[1]

From the methodological point of view, Quetelet was far better than his predecessors and, it is regrettable to say, of most subsequent sociologists. He was one of the first researchers to analyse the influence of a particular variable while controlling for the influence of another, related, one. He showed, for example, that the effect of climate on crime was inconsequential when race was taken into account. Similarly, differences in crime rates by sex declined substantially when education was controlled for. Quetelet was one of the first writers to discuss the fundamental problem of crime statistics, the effect of police and courts on rates supposed to be indicators of behaviour. He pointed out the gap between data on 'known and judged offences' and what they were intended to represent—'committed offences'. He could offer no general solution to the problem, but stressed that one had to be able to justify using data on known offences for the unknown, real rates. In the case of his analysis, justification did exist, for it could be reasonably assumed that known offences were a constant proportion of actual, committed offences. He then carefully spelled out the ground for this assumption.

1. *Physique Sociale*, p. 315.

THE SPREAD OF EMPIRICAL WORK

In succeeding decades a great deal of empirical work on the lines initiated by Ducpétiaux and Quetelet appeared. Guerry, a French statistician, appears to be the next person to have published in the field. Moreover, since his work appeared so soon after Quetelet's, he has often been credited with 'founding' the statistical school— Ducpétiaux being ignored in such observations. It was apparently Guerry who first depicted crime rates in the form of maps, a method which was much used in European sociology throughout the nineteenth century, and taken up again much later by the Chicago school.[1] De Candolle reviewed a number of the earliest studies in the *Bibliothèque Universelle de Genève*, adding and commenting on certain Swiss data at the same time. English studies began to appear with the first volume of the *Journal of the Statistical Society*, in 1838, and were published frequently as well in *The Economist*.[2] Fletcher and Rawson are the most notable contributors from this early period. Mayhew and Binny produced more popularly oriented work somewhat later, in 1867. The extensive *London Life and Labour* studies, by Booth and colleagues, included material on crime and prisoners among other subjects.

Over time the number of cited causes grew, although very much along the same lines as initiated by Quetelet. Statistical analyses became correspondingly lengthier, although changing little in style. By the end of the century very lengthy lists of causes became frequent. Morrison's *Crime and its Causes* is one of the better later examples, drawing largely on sociological writers, but also entering into debate with the biological. The inclusion of both biological and social causes also became common towards the end of the century. Since this most often meant biological theorists adding social causes, this development will be discussed later, as an adjustment of biological theorists to adverse criticism.

A small amount of social cause theorizing appeared in the United States in the nineteenth century, far outshadowed by biological work. The bibliographies compiled by Fink on biological theories and by Guillot on social show this in persuasive detail. Methodologically the sociological studies tended to be behind those of European of the same period. Substantively, they were similar. Lack of educa-

1. Other French writers who did similar work were d'Angeville, Frégier, Guégo and Moreau-Christophe. See also G. de Greef.
2. Cargill, Clay.

tion was by far the most popular cause, typically discussed in a 'lack of moral fibre' context.[1] One of the late nineteenth-century American texts, by Wines, was an extremely thorough and sophisticated account of crime, quite above the usual standard of the time. Social arguments, in so far as they were accepted, usually excluded economic factors. Giddings, for example, argued that crime varied with the 'strains of progress', but was independent of poverty. Serious crimes were not more frequent in poor countries than rich.[2]

My evaluation of the sociological–statistical approach has to be mixed. Supportive data can be found for a great variety of propositions if one looks hard enough for it. The amount of data published by governments from censuses, official agencies and so forth was immense, even as early as the 1830s, and no theorist had difficulty in finding some statistics to support any particular point at issue. The dominant findings, at the aggregate level, were opposed to simple poverty and ignorance explanations, a point discussed earlier. Studies of individual offenders, on the other hand, continued to show disproportionate representation of the poor and uneducated, the only thoroughly consistent results to appear. Findings on other variables, notably region, race and religion, were very mixed. There was, then, sufficient confusion in the results for them to be used for many purposes. Later it will be shown how they were used even to discredit the whole statistical approach. In terms of theoretical contribution the work of the statisticians after Quetelet is simple to evaluate: there was effectively no advance, or change, in theory. The next contributions to theory did not appear until the publications of Darwin and Spencer, which precipitated much activity in theory, and which is the next subject to discuss.

THEORY OF EVOLUTION

CHARLES DARWIN

Darwin's theory of evolution was, among other things, a brilliant solution to a problem left unresolved in Adam Smith's *Theory of Moral Sentiments*. Smith, to re-cap briefly, had used the notion of the moral instinct, which was said to determine the morality or immorality of behaviour at the individual level and which, over the ages, became generalized into actual laws. It was Darwin's genius to explain the link between the two levels, to suggest how individual

1. Eaton.   2. *Democracy and Empire*, p. 91.

norms ultimately generated concrete laws, and how laws affected individual norms and behaviour. The theory is recounted in the second volume of *The Origin of Species*.

To explain the development of the moral sense one has to begin with the more general social instinct, from which the moral sense arose. Briefly, the social instinct meant the tendency to feel pleasure in the company of one's fellows. It was probably an extension of parental or filial affection, and this could be explained by the principle of natural selection. The social instinct led to social action, logically enough—the provision of services, and co-operation in food gathering and defence. The better the co-operative practices developed, thanks to the social instinct, the greater the chances of survival for the family, tribe or species, in question. Groups which did not develop a social instinct would in time disappear, failing to find food in time of scarcity, or being killed off by stronger, better organized competition.

The development of the social instinct could be explained by natural selection, but its refinement to the level of self-sacrifice obviously could not, for the self-sacrificing might not reproduce in large numbers. Nor, Darwin thought, was it even likely that benevolent parents would succeed in bringing up more offspring than non-benevolent. The influence of self-sacrifice, and other moral qualities, was made rather in two other ways. Firstly, instances of self-denial or self-sacrifice elicited praise from others, and there was a tendency for praised actions to be imitated. Secondly, co-operative actions of all kinds tended to be reciprocated. Even the selfish, then, could acquire desirable habits if for the wrong reasons. The doctrine of the inheritance of acquired characteristics was then introduced, somewhat hesitantly, into the explanation. Darwin suggested that 'habits probably tend to be inherited' (p. 201), one of the first theses of evolution theory to be abandoned.

At the individual level the social instinct involved the notion of sympathy, the ability to appreciate the point of view of others, exactly as used by Smith and Ferguson. Through sympathy, feelings of approval or disapproval could be generalized, individuals perceiving reactions of their fellows to their own behaviour, and sensing how others interacted. As intellectual faculties developed, images of past actions and motives would pass through the brain, producing feelings of satisfaction or misery as the case might be. The possibility of reflection emerged as people began to make comparisons of other people's reactions and their own feelings in response (p. 171). People learned to respond to the approval expressed by their fellows, or otherwise perceived. This became a habit of 'self-command' in time, and, since habits were probably inherited, it, too, was probably passed on to succeeding generations (p. 177).

Darwin drew a strong contrast between his version of moral development and the utilitarian. Individuals in responding to approval were not, in his view, acting out of selfishness. People, he insisted, often acted without consciousness of pleasure, as did the lower animals. The social instincts could be said to have been developed for the general *good*, rather than general happiness (p. 185). Darwin oversimplified the utilitarian position on this point, for in the theory general happiness was ultimately related to the general good.

HERBERT SPENCER

The next evolutionist, Herbert Spencer, was considerably more faithful to the theory and the theorist than most of those to follow. Spencer defended Darwin when the bitter debate on evolution erupted. Later in life Spencer became a social Darwinist, milder than some, but a genuine one. He argued against social welfare provisions, for example, on the grounds that these would favour the survival of the unfit (his example, the drunken Irish) at the expense of the better elements of society (the sober Scots).[1] Spencer had actually used the evolution concept before Darwin, in *Social Statistics*, but in a much simpler form, along with his much misunderstood society-organism analogy. With the publication of *The Origin of Species*, however, Spencer re-grouped. He elaborated his theory considerably, introducing the doctrines of natural selection and the inheritance of acquired characteristics. It is the later, improved model that will be discussed here, published in *The Principles of Sociology*.

Law and custom, Spencer argued, evolved in accordance with the nature of society, so that as societies grew and became increasingly differentiated laws and customs changed. Law itself emerged out of custom, and the two remained closely enough related that the differences need not concern us. As the nature of society changed, as new problems emerged, new laws would emerge in response to them. The adjustment could take a long time to be accomplished,

1. In *The Man Versus the State*.

but the direction of the relationship was never in doubt. The time factor was typically great, so that law could be called 'the rule of the dead over the living'. Spencer did not have in mind the literary metaphor here, but rather the doctrine of the inheritance of acquired characteristics. Ideas, including norms, beliefs, values and attitudes, were transmitted from the past to the present in the form of inherited habits. In the early stages of societal evolution, there was no distinction between sacred law and secular. Law in the Pentateuch, for example, included beliefs about God, ritual, rules for all kinds of social relations, diet, work, marriage and child-rearing. The identification of law with the sacred was important, for it was through it that the law acquired stability. Crime in the early stages was punished cruelly. Later, the quasi-religious sanctions were dropped, to be replaced by those determined by the 'predominant man'. Finally, sanctions were determined by the will of the public, through some kind of governing agency. The type of sanctions that predominated, like the type of law, conformed to the nature of the society. Sentiments appropriate to the prevailing sanctions would emerge, and these obscured sentiments appropriate to other kinds.

Spencer used the terms 'status' and 'contract' in describing the evolution from early to later stages of society. Status was associated with early, personal rule, and contract with later, impersonal—a somewhat different conceptualization from Durkheim's. The status regime, with compulsion the basis for compliance, was made necessary by unequal social relations, which Spencer associated with early social life. The contract regime presupposed relatively equal relations, which Spencer believed to characterize nineteenth-century European societies. He went so far as to discuss 'equality before the law' as an actual fact, asserting modern law to be based substantially on the consensus of individual interests.[1] Evolution between the two types of society and legal systems by no means implied a simple, linear progression. Spencer allowed for various kinds of growth and change, including reversals to more primitive types of relations and morals. His comments on criminal behaviour *per se*

1. In a later, polemic work, Spencer identified the regime of status with the kinds of social relations advocated by the Conservative Party in Britain, in contrast with those advocated by the Liberals. He then argued that the Liberal Party should not support compulsory factory legislation, 'the factory acts', for these were inconsistent with the individualistic, voluntaristic type of social organization the Liberals stood for.

were very sparse. In a relatively late work, *The Study of Sociology*, he referred to crime as reflecting 'inferior original nature', but did not elaborate (p. 300). Nor did he discuss the relationship between law and sanctions.

MAINE: ANCIENT LAW

Only two years after the publication of *The Origin of Species* Maine's very important *Ancient Law* appeared. It stimulated a great deal of sociological work with evolutionary concepts, but in quite different way. There was no reliance on the theory of natural selection, inheritance of acquired characteristics, or analogies with biological organisms in Maine. Rather he can be seen as elaborating the much simpler evolutionary notions of Montesquieu, without the aid of biology. Maine's principal concern lay in the relationship between social structure and law, and particularly the relative proportions of criminal and civil law in written codes. The level of generality aimed at was much more modest than the biologically oriented theorists. *Ancient Law* is a 'first' in several important respects. It was the first full-scale work attempting a social science explanation of law, and the first written by a real professional.

Maine observed the preponderance of criminal to civil measures in the early history of the Teutonic code, from which he generalized 'the more archaic the code the fuller and minuter is its penal legislation' (p. 368). The reasons for this, he argued, could be discovered in other aspects of social structure. This was very much a matter of common sense. Disputes could not occur over rights that did not exist, and much of the law in contemporary societies involved rights that did not exist in earlier times. When there was family ownership of property, for example, there could be little law on succession. Similarly, when a patriarch held rights over the whole family, there would be little for the rest of the members to dispute among themselves. Nevertheless, Maine pointed out, much of what was formally penal legislation was not enforced by penal sanctions. The penal law of ancient communities was a law of torts, with civil sanctions and civil procedures (p. 370). It was only offences that were seen as affronts to the state or the total society that drew harsh sanctions.

The distinction between the content of the norms (whether criminal or civil) and the nature of the sanctions (harsh, penal sanctions or civil payments) was crucial in Maine's theory. The two dimensions were affected by quite different matters. In the first case, social relations, property and family institutions were the determining factors, as noted above. As to the type of sanctions used, it was the perception of who was the victim that was crucial, whether the state or a mere individual. The distinction, important as it was to the theory, seems often to have been lost. Later writers who observed a lack of repressive sanctions in a society concluded it had no criminal law. When criminal norms were seen to dominate in a society's laws, it was assumed that repressive sanctions also predominated, which need not be the case and was not in the societies Maine studied. Theorists who wished to prove ethical progress could do so by showing how there were fewer criminal norms now than in earlier days. To argue that 'society was going to the dogs' was equally simple. One had only to show how civil procedures and sanctions were used in earlier days, while brutal, criminal punishments came to predominate later.

Maine discussed barriers to the establishment of *systematic* criminal law as well, in reference to the development of early Roman law. At one stage an offence was seen as so great an affront to the state that actual *legislation* was needed to deal with it. It was necessary for this over-reaction of the state to be tempered before criminal law as such could emerge. Eventually legislatures stopped waiting for crimes to be committed to deal with them, establishing commissions with delegated authority for those purposes. Permanent bodies were the next step, and with them recourse to the courts became routine.[1]

DURKHEIM

Durkheim was, first and last, a student of the conditions of social cohesion. His interest in methodology amounted to more than dabbling, to be sure, but the great bulk of his life's work was on the central issues of social order. He began with a study of a concrete problem, on individualism and socialism, then moved to a more general level, at which he stayed. Much of what Durkheim wrote has, then, a direct bearing on our subject. He published one paper on theory of law, 'Deux lois de l'évolution pénale', and was working on an extensive manuscript on morality at the time of his death.[2]

1. For other work on the evolution of law and morals see Sutherland, and Dicey.
2. This was published posthumously as an article, 'Introduction à la Morale'.

There are relevant points in numerous of his books, collections of lecture notes, and shorter critical commentaries. The book reviews in the early years of *L'Année Sociologique* are especially good sources, for both Durkheim and his collaborators reviewed books on deviance in terms of agreement or disagreement with the master's views. There is a good deal of theoretical work and some data analysis to be found, but it has to be pieced together from these many sources. The result is an original theory of criminal behaviour, the famous theory of anomie, and a development of evolutionary theory of law and sanctions from Spencer, Darwin and Maine.

It seems best to begin with the theory of law and broach this through Durkheim's views on morality (*la morale*) and what we now call norms (*mœurs*). Morality referred to a system of ideas, of a general nature, regarding moral behaviour. Norms were particular moral notions sufficiently accepted to produce or inhibit the behaviour in question. Norms constituted a part of a collectivity's morality, and morality was a part of the collective conscience. For both morality and behaviour Durkheim focused on the collective level much more than the individual. Morality was essentially a collective phenomenon, having a correspondence at the individual level, but this being of little interest. Individual morality was but a reflection of collective. It varied among individuals, for the collective conscience varied in the success it had imposing itself on different members of society.

Questions of individual motivation were not of importance to Durkheim, or rather he defined them out of existence. Norms were moral ideas that were effective, hence what was problematic was, as for Darwin and Smith, the nature of those norms. The relationship between morality, as a system of ideas, and concrete laws was similarly not an issue. Durkheim appears to have assumed a close relationship between the two, so that, for practical purposes no distinction has to be made between morality and law. In effect he again defined the problem out of existence. Law reflected the morality of the collectivity, and the possibility of there being divergent norms within the collectivity was not admitted. The problem of the conflict theorists, as to whose norms would become law, cannot be discussed in Durkheim's framework.

Durkheim's theory of law began with the same fundamental position of the earlier consensus theorists that law and morality reflected the mentality, temperament and conditions of life of a society, being the product of the society's whole history.[1] Morality varied in time and place, accordingly, as these factors varied. The most profound variation was the transition, over the centuries, from criminal-repressive law to civil-restitutive. It was on studying this change, primarily in Europe, that Durkheim framed his general views. These were expressed as universal, sociological laws, although with an apology for the grossness of the generalizations.[2]

Severity of punishment was the subject of the first law. The explanation, or at least its main proposition, was grounded in the mechanical–organic solidarity dimension. The greater the degree of social organization and differentiation, the less severe punishments would be. A low degree of social organization implied cohesion of the mechanical solidarity fashion, which implied, in turn, a preponderance of norms concerning the collectivity—its religion, morality and traditions.[3] A high degree of social organization implied organic solidarity, and a preponderance of norms protecting individual interests. The gradual diminution of punishments over time did not necessarily indicate any tendency to complacency with crime, but rather a change in the nature of the norms violated. Neither did the reduction in punishments reflect a growing sympathy with the victim, a point Durkheim had suggested earlier, but subsequently rejected.[4] The suffering of the punished offender could never elicit the same sympathy as that of the victim.[5] Growing concern for individuals, as such, then must imply growing concern for innocent victims. If this were the instrumental factor punishments would have increased, which they had not. To understand the evolution of punishment it was necessary to understand the evolution of crime, for the type of the punishment reflected the type of the crimes committed.

The nature of the power held by the central government was the next component of the first law. Whether the government held absolute power or not was the crucial factor. With absolute power a government would be held in awe by its citizens as a god—the difference in power between the people and the government being similar to that between themselves and their god (p. 93).

1. 'Introduction à la Morale', See also work by Mauss, Richard, and Tarde (1893).
2. 'Deux Lois', p. 65.
3. 'Deux Lois', pp. 65–92; *Division du Travail*, pp. 44–80.
4. *Leçons de Sociologie*, p. 133.
5. 'Deux Lois', p. 85.

Affronts to the government would then be felt as affronts to a deity, and deserving of appropriately severe punishment. Durkheim added as well that, in so far as offences were *seen* as affronts to the collectivity, rather than of individual interests, they would elicit punishment of a repressive nature. The point was not developed, but it would appear that *perceptions* of offences would have an effect on the severity of punishment as well as the structural factors explicitly dealt with.

The second law involved a functionalist argument in the narrowest sense, and can be dealt with briefly. It was directed to explaining variation in the use of prisons among societies. Effectively Durkheim argued that it was only with the development of cities that prisons had become functional. It was, consequently, only in societies with cities that prisons began to be used in punishment.

Given Durkheim's definition of norms (for which, in effect, if deviant behaviour occurs, norms must have been absent) some notion akin to anomie had to be the chief cause of crime. What was problematic was the successful internalization and ongoing effectiveness of norms, and anomie signifies precisely 'normlessness'. At the collective level anomie meant the collective conscience was weak, fragmented and ineffective. From the point of view of the individual, anomie implied a confusion between right and wrong, possibly divided loyalties as to the source of guidance on such questions, and perhaps a lack of commitment to, or an abandonment of, the cultural values and norms of a previous age. Periods of major social change, as in revolution, war and religious conflict, were powerful causes of anomie and, consequently, of crime. The nineteenth century was a major period of upheaval in France and other European countries, and the increases in crime throughout that period, Durkheim argued (erroneously), reflected that. Declining acceptance of traditional religious beliefs was especially critical, given that no other source of morality appeared to replace it.

Durkheim discussed other causes as well for murder, although always by way of similarity with, or contrast to, causes of suicide. Anomie was still an important cause for both, for Durkheim believed it had a similar effect on each. Whether the strain of anomie pushed an individual into murder or suicide depended on the strength of the person's norms.[1] In effect, the better socialized citizens did it to themselves, rather than to their fellows. The same conditions that

1. *Le Suicide*, p. 408.

determined altruistic suicide were also held to affect murder, chiefly a strong passion for life. In this case, again, the choice between murder or suicide was a matter of degree; it required greater altruism to commit suicide than murder. Vendettas were an example of altruistic motives for murder, and the decline of vendettas a sign of declining commitment to the collectivity, The fact of the murder rate being higher in Catholic countries than Protestant was explained in similar fashion. Collective life was richer in Catholic societies, according to Durkheim, thanks to reinforcement by ritual. Finally, the murder rate was theorized to vary inversely with the third type of suicide, egoistic. Where individualism was weak there would be insufficient passion to kill oneself or another. In this respect altruism and individualism were treated neither as mutually exclusive sentiments, nor as different reflections of a common underlying sentiment. Rather they were distinctive sentiments within the collective conscience, positively related. The pressures that induced an individual to commit murder, suicide or, by extension, any other crime, were discussed in terms of the individual's everyday social situation. Durkheim took up Quetelet's standard sociological variables, and indeed his work marks the first real advance in such analysis from Quetelet. The variables of age, sex, marital status, occupation, religion, and so forth were given a careful sociological interpretation. The social situation—pressures, temptations and inhibitions to commit crime—differed between young and old, men and women, married and single and, accordingly, age, sex and marital status could account for differences in rates of crime committed. Durkheim argued forcefully against Lombroso and the criminal anthropologists of his day, making *L'Année Sociologique* the vehicle of some of the most scathing attacks on the school.

Durkheim's understanding of what murder rates meant was profoundly different from the common view of his time, or ours for that matter. The fact of the murder rate declining throughout Europe over the nineteenth century signified ethical progress to evolutionary-oriented writers. For Durkheim, there could be no such consolation. The cost of progress was great: declining bonds of altruism. The decline in murder signified weakening bonds, and a profound threat to social solidarity.

This raises the last point to be made on Durkheim, his much misinterpreted conceptualization of the normality of crime. Durkheim went much further than many of his contemporaries who were not prepared for more than the *predictability* of crime. Durkheim insisted that a certain amount of crime was essential for the survival of a society. Crime should be considered abnormal only in excess. An absence of crime would indicate too strong and successful a collective conscience, and a collective conscience of that power would inhibit all change in morals and values. Without change a society would stagnate and die.

Morality was too intimately bound up with the life of the collectivity for Durkheim to allow any compromise on this point. A change in morals affected other aspects of social life, the economy, and vice versa. There could be no minor fiddling with a society's morals, but any change in morals would have serious and widespread consequences. Attempts to change morals indeed were met with appropriate resistance. The great reformers sought to change the morality of their day, suffered and died for the interference.

The theory of anomie is one of the great success stories in sociology. It has been adapted to explain drug use, juvenile delinquency, mental illness and numerous other particular kinds of deviance, and still appears as an explanation of suicide. It enjoys immense popularity, despite considerable empirical evidence to the contrary, both with respect to crime in general and the various particular applications. Perhaps the most important disconfirmation of the theory is Tilly's study of French crime rates in the nineteenth century, being based on the same data as Durkheim used, but a longer series.[1] The results of the time series analysis of property crime have already been referred to as supporting the economic deprivation hypothesis, for the beginning of the case against anomie. The results of the cross-sectional analysis, of rates across eighty-six administrative units of France, for each of the census years between 1831 and 1861, are even more pertinent. These indicate *no* relationship between property crime, violent crime and collective violence, hence neither a common response to strain nor any complementarity between three major forms of response. Property crime was strongly, positively correlated with level of urbanism and the rate of urbanization. The rate of urbanization was also positively related to property crime, but less strongly, and it is rate of change that is crucial to the anomie explanation. The relationship between level of urbanism and property crime simply reflects that urban settings are more conducive to property crime than rural (more to steal in cities). The results were

1. Lodhi and Tilly.

incompatible with *tension*-type explanations or the explanation of the anomie approach. Rather they were supportive of *structural* explanations along the lines indicated in the case of property crime and urbanism, concerning structural opportunities for crime.

AMERICAN SOCIOLOGY OF LAW

The early sociological work on law in the United States reflects the influence of Spencer more than anyone else. Certainly most of it was based on evolutionary concepts, and all of it, until well into the twentieth century, was consensus in orientation. There was the same interest in the transition from custom to law as in Europe. Sumner's *Folkways* marks probably the best development along these lines.

Confidence in the adjustment of law to societal needs was typically expressed with little doubt. According to Ross, 'Law expresses the will of the entire group so that there can be no clashing of jurisdictions,' a view excluding the possibility of conflict by definition, as in Durkheim.[1] Giddings allowed for force in his account of the origins of law, but it was the force of the population at large, not that of a ruling minority. Conceding that there was a tendency for the strong to kill off the weak, he believed this to be offset by the fact that even the very strong could be killed off by the average, if in numbers. Hence there was a tendency to harmonious co-operation, and even equilibrium.[2]

NATURE OVER NURTURE: BIOLOGICAL THEORIES OF CRIME

The great search for physical causes of behaviour can be seen in the vast number of biological theories of crime developed in the nineteenth century. The theory of evolution had a profound effect on the course of theory, we shall see, but the roots of biological theories go back long before evolution, to the physiognomy and phrenology of classical Greece and Rome and the Middle Ages. The underlying thesis was that physical characteristics, such as head size and shape were reliable indicators of intellectual and moral qualities. In earlier times this was discussed in terms of general moral faculties, with very little specific reference to crime.[3] In the nineteenth century, the

1. *American Journal of Sociology*, vol. I.
2. *Principles of Sociology*, p. 113.
3. della Porta.

theories were elaborated considerably, to include specific propositions about crime. Analogies with animals were made as well, reflecting the nineteenth-century revival of comparative anatomy.
Criminals and the insane were described as being closer to the lower
animals than the law-abiding and healthy,[1] with photographs and
sketches supplied in illustration. Gradually, alongside the bumps on
the head, the shifty eyes and the animal expressions, other physical
indicators began to be added. Lesions of the brain, notably, were
studied for their effects on behaviour, and it is in this sort of approach
that the foundations of mainstream psychiatry can be found. Organic
diseases, epilepsy and, in time, developmental problems and purely
psychic disorders began to become important as causes, eventually
eclipsing, but never eradicating, the phrenological.

There was, then, a vast proliferation of theories of causes and
several trends to be sorted out. In mainstream psychiatry the causes
based on external signs began to lose favour, and psychic problems,
and later even social, replaced them. In the criminal anthropological,
or Italian school, external signs remained critical. This was the school
of the born criminal *par excellence*, with the slanted forehead, heavy
jaw and crooked ears to prove it. It was here, we shall see, that
evolution theory left its mark, through the doctrine of atavism. The
actual branching of the Italian school from the mainstream dates from
the publication of the first part of Lombroso's *Criminal Man* in 1871.

THE EMERGENCE OF PSYCHIATRY

Theorizing, for our purposes, begins with the work of Philippe Pinel
at the turn of the century. Pinel was a French physician and author of
several general medical treatises before turning to psychiatry. His
text on 'mental alienation' was one of the first comprehensive texts
on mental disorders. The five-fold classification he outlined became
the basis for the next stage of work—the elaboration of actual
psychiatric theories of criminality. What was important about
Pinel's classification was that it distinguished *degrees* of disturbance,
a necessary condition for the emergence of theory on crime. The all-
or-nothing conceptualization excluded insanity as a cause of crime,
for insanity implied inability to form a guilty intention, an essential
element in most western definitions of crime.

Pinel's classification was succeeded by many and grander schemes,

1. Lombroso, *Criminal Man*; Maudsley, *Crime et Folie*; Lacassange.

involving complications quite unnecessary for us to entertain; the nineteenth century was, after all, a great period for classification. The earliest examples were important for the same reasons as Pinel's, in breaking down the simplistic sane–insane dichotomy. Esquirol's classification was one of the most important, based on types of partial insanity, or monomania. Thus there was homicidal monomania, suicidal, erotic and so forth, all named relative to whatever the partial insanity focused on. Prichard elaborated on one of Pinel's types of disorder, 'mania without delusions'. He observed that the malady was often periodic, giving a description of what later became known as 'manic depression'. Prichard gave this the unfortunate term of 'moral insanity', which has caused it to be confused with early versions of psychopathy.

Gall's six-volume treatise on the functions of the brain, published in 1822, is one of the more interesting transitional works. It was very influential in nineteenth-century psychiatry, including those sections which can only be described as pure physiognomy. Gall theorized, for example, unequal development of particular 'organs' or parts of the brain as the cause of criminal behaviour of all kinds. Elsewhere, his analysis is remarkably modern. He pointed out the wide variation in senses and abilities, including moral qualities, among individuals. This meant, he argued, that some would be saints and heroes and others would be evil, just as some people were musical geniuses and others totally insensitive to music. The same held for the quality of love of property, which Gall believed to be innate. For most individuals, this would be developed in normal proportions, while for some it would be exaggerated into greed. Similarly, the instinct of self-defence would operate normally for most people, but in excess would mean murder. The extent to which these various senses were developed would not necessarily be visible in the size of the organ or in a protuberance. Only in instances of extreme development, it was suggested, would direct observation be possible.

Gall also considered social factors as causes of criminal behaviour, especially poverty and lack of education. Where these were the determining factors, he believed rehabilitation to be possible, but when the cause was internal, repentance was rare. This is a clear expression of the born versus occasional criminal notion, although these terms were not used. Gall pointed out that education, religion, prison and forced labour had not been successful in extirpating crime, which suggested that the predominant cause must be internal, and not susceptible to change. Gall also introduced, briefly, the notion of psychopathy, in discussing the condition of 'not having a conscience'. Ordinary educational means could not be used with such individuals, for these depended on an appeal to conscience. Conscience could be developed only by 'artificial' means, which were not elaborated. Physical organization of the brain remained a cause of crime in Lauvergne's theory but now with social factors playing a much more important role. The theory indeed seems to be the first in which physical and social factors were *integrated* in explanation. Organization of the brain was a cause of crime for its effect on the development of 'all moral and intellectual instincts'. External circumstances were critical as factors encouraging or discouraging 'innate dispositions'. In the case of property offenders, social factors were actually the *chief* causes of crime, especially lack of parents, poor education and otherwise bad upbringing (xi). A professor and doctor, Lauvergne worked out his theory in the course of his practice with convict forced labourers. He included descriptions of the convicts in an appendix, as supporting documentation for his thesis. The tone of discussion throughout was remarkably sympathetic. Lauvergne was opposed to prisons, on the grounds that they promoted crime. Alternative means were needed, he argued, which would improve criminals by good examples, and prevent the deterioration of their innate bad qualities (vi).

Psychopathy as a concept dates back at least to Aristotle's description of the vice of the non-existence of the faculty of moral choice. 'Brutality' was the original name for the condition and it was under this name that Mayo wrote about it in 1838. The concept itself, however, was described in precisely the same terms as are still used. Brutality, or psychopathy, meant an incapacity to make moral choices, or a destitution of the moral faculties. It was analogous to the lack of sense of smell or, more seriously, to idiocy. The condition was not a type of insanity in Mayo's view, although equally a 'disease of the mind'. Rather, insanity involved a disturbance that interfered with the conscience, so that the conscience would not be heard. With 'brutality' there was effectively no conscience to hear. Mayo further emphasized the distinction between the moral and intellectual faculties, which again helped to break down the all-or-nothing approach of earlier conceptualizations. The two faculties were similar in that both varied by degrees, but they were different dimensions, and brutality applied only to the moral.

THE BORN CRIMINAL

Much of the search for physical causes of crime was focused on the theme of the born criminal. This was true before the Italian school added its special conceptualization of atavism and before the concept became popular. The rudiments of the idea were worked out well before Lombroso and the idea seems to have had quite broad acceptance before then. Two of the major contributors to the theory were actually Britons: Thomson, a Scottish prison doctor and the famous psychiatrist, Henry Maudsley. Thomson, in 1870, described criminals as constituting a distinct 'caste'. They were said to have certain psychological characteristics in common, a 'low physique' (indicating physical degeneracy), a low state of intelligence, and 'moral instinct', and serious liability to 'insanity with brain diseases', including epilepsy (p. 348). Criminals were more vulnerable to diseases than normal persons, which was 'proof' of their degeneracy. Living in vice, and the hardships of prison, were contributory factors, but heredity was the chief cause (p. 330). Thomson's propositions were supported by observations on some 6,000 prisoners. Data were reported on race, hair and eye colour, height and weight, although with the admission that it was not altogether clear to what use such information could be put. The Italian school was soon to provide answers on all these points.

Darwin was referred to in the argument, along with a lesson drawn from plant breeding, to show why criminals should not be allowed to propagate. Further, Thomson argued, criminals were retrograding from generation to generation (p. 327). They could be seen as a separate tribe, like the Ishmaelites, actively opposed to civilized life. The paper, for all its loose, racist allusions, was not without scientific aspirations. Conclusions were stated in the form of general propositions, and the role of empirical work stressed. Thomson criticized certain of the earlier French writers for their lack of practical knowledge on the subject, claiming credibility for his views on the grounds of their having been based on observation.

Maudsley elaborated the born criminal thesis considerably, drawing on Thomson's empirical observations as documentation.[1] He described three classes of criminals, one affected by external circumstances, an intermediate group, and the born criminals, who were said to be generally lacking in intelligence, and disproportionately given to physical anomalies and epilepsy. The physical

1. *Body and Mind*, p. 66; *Crime et Folie*, p. 31.

basis of born criminality was the same as insanity, and both were explicable in terms of the same physiological laws. Yet Maudsley also described crime and insanity as different types of a more general degeneracy. Further, he claimed that insanity often led to criminality in the next generation and vice versa.[1] Maudsley believed in the inheritance of acquired characteristics, which would make possible this sort of interaction. Later, however, he began to emphasize the differences between criminality and insanity. At one point he even allowed that, if one had the misfortune to be a criminal, one would at least be spared madness, and if mad, one escaped crime. The confusion was not resolved in either direction. Maudsley continued to cite cases in which both madness and criminality were present, and suggested there was a neutral zone between them, in which it was difficult to judge.

By the 1860s, a distinctive psychiatric school can be seen to have been established, and by the 1880s, it was well established. A great deal of research was done, and there were numerous learned meetings to discuss it. Journals devoted exclusively to mental disorders began to appear. Psychiatric theorizing was even a prestigious activity. The leading members of the school held high status in the medical profession as a whole, to a much greater extent than the case today. Texts for medical students and lawyers began to be published, diffusing theories and research results to ever wider audiences. The general public was not left far behind. Popular versions began to appear in modest numbers, a century later to become the industry of paperback psychiatry.

The school spread from France and Britain, through Europe, and, by the end of the century, to the rest of the European-oriented world.[2] It became strong in the United States, although not as successful as criminal anthropology itself. The school was characterized by concern with practical matters perhaps more than theoretical. Psychiatrists were much involved as expert witnesses and consultants, and by far the bulk of the psychiatric literature concerns the use of insanity pleas, criteria for determining responsibility and the like. The quality of research in the field has been notoriously low. Much of the documentation for theories was based on case analyses, with partisans of the theory making the diagnosis and assessments. We

1. *Crime et Folie*, p. 30.
2. See also Georget, Lucas, Morel, Johnstone, Ray, Baldwin, Baudin, Buckham, Down, Hoffbauer Meyer.

shall see that, for this reason, the school lost ground to the socio-logical—but that is a story for the next instalment. By the end of the century, psychiatric theory was a very important school within the consensus tradition. It no longer holds quite this status but remains of importance itself, and as a source of explanation for mixed-cause theories.

CRIMINAL ANTHROPOLOGY

The Italian school has been so much misrepresented that it is per-haps best to begin with what it did not do.

It was not, as already shown, the originator of the born criminal concept, nor of most of the ideas associated with it—race, physical degeneracy, mental defectiveness, epilepsy, insanity, alcoholism or inherited predispositions. Methodologically, its claims have been even more erroneous. The use of head and body measurements was pioneered by Broca and other physical anthropologists in the 1850s. The use of large samples has to be credited to Thomson, and case histories at least to Lauvergne.

The frequent reference to Lombroso as the 'founder of scientific criminology' is especially unjustified. It is not only that the school was wrong—a judgement of hindsight—but its work can be judged wanting by the methodological knowledge of the day. The funda-mental mistakes made in the Italian school concern problems dis-cussed, sometimes thoroughly, decades earlier. Quetelet alone warned against the most serious mistakes as early as 1835.

The basis of Lombroso's legitimate claim to fame lies in his atavism concept, a most ingenious application of evolution theory to the explanation of criminality. Given the perception of the problem, the concept represents a brilliant solution (but the premise is wrong). Briefly, the problem arises in the view of evolution as involving ever greater refinement of the moral instinct. For, if morality were indeed ever improving, how was it that crime continued to exist and, less understandable still, that the crime rate was everywhere in-creasing. Of course crime was not everywhere increasing, and perhaps it was not anywhere, short term fluctuations aside. As shown earlier (pp. 59–60), for Britain and France, official crime rates had entered a steady decline, despite increases in police force size and changes in law that might reasonably have made the reporting and recording of crime easier.

Nevertheless, given the misperception (and something could always be found to be rising, at least some years, to nourish it), there was a dilemma—and atavism solved it neatly. The atavist, a type of born criminal, was a throwback to an earlier period when the moral instinct was less developed. The crime rate could then be increasing (thanks to an increasing number of throwbacks) and the moral instinct improving at the same time. Further, with a belief in the inheritance of acquired characteristics, crime which appeared at any one time, for any reason, could explain later crime, as having been inherited.

Lombroso's initial scheme involved only two types of criminal, the true or born criminal (only one-third of the criminal population) and occasional criminals, or any other type. For the latter type, the causes of crime were forces which prevented the moral instinct from operating. This included physical diseases of various sorts, epilepsy, insanity, feeble-mindedness, and social and economic factors. As criticism mounted, Lombroso was forced to pay more attention to social and economic causes, and he expanded his typology accordingly. For political offenders, social factors were actually given prominence, and even patriotism and honour could be causes. Eventually, vast lists of factors were cited for the various types of crime, including fertility of the soil, barometric pressure, meteors, diverse social and economic conditions and, in incredible detail, biological make-up. Social aspects of physical conditions were discussed to some extent, for example the effect of the climate on social life.

Still, there is some ambiguity as to Lombroso's position on social and economic factors. In *Criminal Man*, for example, his coverage of social factors was extensive: gang membership, tattooing and use of argot, among others. These were discussed, however, as *signs* of criminality rather than causes. Criminals were said to band together for mutual help and encouragement, which they needed because they were living outside the law.

Lombroso paid scant attention to law in his work, but other members of the Italian school did. None of them, however, went past the position of the earlier evolutionists. Letourneau, in an introduction to *Criminal Man*,[1] described the progress of justice from the vaguely felt sentiments held by 'our savage ancestors'. These sentiments

1. The second French edition.

began at the level of an eye-for-eye retaliation, to be gradually refined into the written law.

Garofalo, one of the most hawkish of the Italian school, provided scarcely more detail.[1] He emphasized the doctrine of the inheritance of acquired characteristics, repeating both Darwin's and Spencer's arguments in it. Thus, whether decided on through reasoning, as in Spencer, or by sentiment, as in Darwin, norms were passed on to later generations. The sentiments of 'pity' and 'probity' were important in deciding what went into these norms. When average sentiments in the community were injured in either pity or probity, Garofalo argued, the act in question came to be defined as criminal. Ferri's early description of the evolution of law was similar in substance, although a little more sophisticated and less enthusiastic.[2]

The story of the Italian school was very much a success story. From its inception it quickly became the dominant school of criminology, and the one to which all the others addressed themselves. Lombroso was himself by all accounts an impressive and charming man, maintaining a vast network of colleague relationships. His daughter, also a doctor, kept his work to the forefront some years after his death, appearing at conferences and publishing his last work posthumously, as well as publishing on juvenile delinquency herself. The school was especially strong in Russia[3] and the United States, but had a substantial following throughout Europe, and some in the Third World.[4]

It is curious that the United States should have been so receptive to the born criminal concept, since work on crime there has been typically very pragmatic and reform-oriented from its beginning. However unlikely the born criminal concept was, though, it had many other advantages—fitting in well with the American preference for individualistic explanations. Hofstadter has argued that material showing the influence of social and economic factors was routinely

1. *Criminology.*   2. *Criminal Sociology.*
3. Tarnowsky, a prominent Russian member, was one of the first of Lombroso's disciples to publish results against the theory. Other contributors were Drill, Tschisch, and Roukavichnikoff.
4. Other contributors were, in France: Féré, Corre, David, Bournet, Laurent, St. Aubin, Soury; Germany: Drahms; Belgium: Thiry, Dallemagne, Piepers; Spain: Macedo; Britain: Nicholson, Galton, Ellis; Romania,: Minovici. Minor contributors from Italy were Taverni and Magnan, Frigerio and Ottolenghi, Tamburimi, Ottolenghi and Rossi, Taladriz; United States: Star, Talbot.

interpreted in terms of physical. Certainly the great bulk of the work in crime in the United States reflected Italian school assumptions although this was not always made explicit. Even Lester Ward accepted the view that crimes were 'diseases of society', mental in character. He, though, used this as an argument for greater *leniency*.[1]

Arthur MacDonald was one of the more prominent and hard-line members of the school. As well as producing one of the more comprehensive accounts of Italian school work, he campaigned actively for the cause. He urged the federal government to adopt the philosophy full scale. Laboratories were to be attached to all prisons to insure that the necessary work was done—a recommendation not followed.[2]

Frances Kellor was responsible for one of the more persuasive presentations of the theory. She argued, in effect, that crime arose through misperceptions and inappropriate responses in everyday social functioning. Individuals not able to adjust to others, on account of defects in the 'senses, perceptive co-ordinating faculties' were particularly susceptible to becoming criminals. Kellor listed numerous social and economic conditions as influential in addition to physical defects. Her conceptualization of law was typically Italian school, and very similar to that of the American sociologists of the same time. 'Criminal law had its origin in the necessity for preserving peace and harmony as civilization progressed and social life became complicated.'

The theory attracted serious criticism from the start, both on the part of opponents, and partisans who sought certain modifications.[3] Some theorists dropped certain aspects of the theory, notably epilepsy, but the basic elements remained unscathed for decades. In much of the debate advocates and critics simply talked past each other. The sociologists would demonstrate an association of various social conditions with crime, with data at the aggregate level, the criminal anthropologists an association between physical factors and crime at the individual.

The main result of sociological criticism, conflict and consensus, was the incorporation of social and economic causes along with the biological, into various types of mixed-cause theories. This would be

1. *Dynamic Sociology*, vol. 2, p. 366.
2. See *Abnormal Man* for the academic discussion, *Plan for the Study of Man* for the polemics.
3. Naecke, Jelgersma, Benelli, Minovici, Morrison, Francotte, Gross.

done often by specifying biological causes for certain kinds of crime (violent) or certain kinds of criminals (the mentally ill or the born criminal), allowing social causes for property crimes and 'occasional criminals' respectively. Lacassagne was the leader of one of the most important mixed-cause approaches, centred in Lyon. In his work a wide variety of social factors was included in the causal explanation, but biological factors were still given the major role.[1]

DISTURBED SEXUALITY AS A CAUSE OF CRIME

An offshoot of Italian school work was an interest in disturbed sexuality as a cause of crime. Italian school theorists had too many other causes on their hands to do justice to sexuality, but they did raise the issue, in a rudimentary way, and begin to investigate it. One early suggestion came in a case study investigation by a leading American member, Arthur MacDonald. The problem posed was to find a motive for apparently motiveless crimes. In the case of a fifteen-year-old boy, guilty of cruelty to other children, the explanation offered was sexual excitement. In the case of an adult murderer, the motive diagnosed was a mixing of the sexual and cruelty instincts.[2]

A modest theory of pubertal development was worked out by Marro, a prominent Italian member of the school. Marro's thesis centred on the relative sizes of the head and body. In childhood, he pointed out, the head was relatively large for the body, and the offences of childhood reflected this rather civilized state of affairs. Seldom were they worse than lying or cheating. Offences of violence, in particular, were almost entirely lacking among children under fifteen. At puberty this changed. The skeleton grew rapidly, so that the head lost its relative advantage. Crimes of violence began to appear at this stage and soon reached their peak (p. 197). The documentation for the study was quite thorough. Marro compared rates of conduct by pubescence, between children in ordinary schools and correctional institutions, holding age constant. Among younger boys, early puberty was associated with bad conduct, while among older boys sexual immaturity was. Among girls, the onset of menstruation was consistently associated with bad conduct.

1. Other writers adding social factors were Laschi, von Liszt, Maliarewsky, Alimena.
2. *Le Criminel Type.*

CONVERGENCE OF CONFLICT AND CONSENSUS THEORY

The reader who is suspicious that so many theorists can be classified unambiguously as conflict or consensus will be relieved to find out that this was not always the case. The exceptions are rare, but they exist, and the next theorist, Ferri, was a major example. So far, the two camps have been rigidly divided. Theorists who took a conflict position on law and sanctions, seeing them as being determined largely by the interests of the powerful, continued this line of reasoning on behaviour. Criminal behaviour, too, was influenced by the decisions of the holders of power, directly or indirectly. Those who took the consensus view, that any other factors were more important, again did so consistently. If biological factors were what determined criminal behaviour, they continued to have their effect on law and sanctions, for legal institutions developed in response to the problems posed by crime. Logically, of course, other combinations of causal factors could exist. One could, for example, be a conflict theorist on law and sanctions, but credit biological factors with determining crime. Or, one could refuse to choose between biological and economic factors and give equal weight to both.

Ferri is immensely interesting as a theorist who began as a humble member of the Italian school, eventually to produce a complicated theory integrating conflict and consensus perspectives. The theory was a determined endeavour at the reconciliation of Marxism and evolution theory and drew the wrath of Marxists and evolutionists alike. The theory was not all that far from what became the standard socialist explanation of crime, but it was condemned, none the less, by the major socialist theorists. Consensus theorists rather tended to ignore it, citing Ferri in his earlier work, which was unmistakably consensus in orientation. The reception accorded the theory perhaps demonstrates just how firm the line of division was between the perspectives. It is telling that the only enthusiastic support Ferri won for his efforts was from an anarchist, Kropotkin.

Ferri began his career as a reconciler with a more modest project, the integration of social and economic factors with biological, *within* the consensus framework. This was the theme of his *Criminal Sociology*, published in 1881, and the book that established his reputation. The dominant influence in that work was Lombroso, whose *Criminal Man* had appeared only some ten years earlier.

Lombroso was deferred to as the founder of scientific criminology, and biological factors were described as the main causes of several types of crime. Ferri departed from Lombroso in emphasizing social factors in the explanation of occasional crime, especially of property offences. He argued against Garofalo's contention that economic conditions were *not* causal factors. The book otherwise portrayed the school's philosophy faithfully. It gave, as the overriding goal of the school, the reduction of crime itself, and not the mere reduction of harsh punishments as in the classical school.

The school's concrete objectives were described in some detail. Recommended criteria for sentencing were established, in accordance with its causal theories. In the case of mentally disturbed criminals, it was argued that treatment should completely replace punishment. Professionals clearly had, in Ferri's view, the necessary expertise to make the right decisions. He criticized the penitentiary system on grounds of psychological theory. The single cell philosophy presupposed rational processes of motivation, consistent with the classical position, but not the Italian school. Moreover, for an Italian, accustomed to sunshine, to be put in a cell was to be buried alive. Capital punishment was a legitimate punishment in that death was a natural occurrence in the struggle for survival. Species and tribes had to kill to defend themselves, and a modern society had this right as much as they. Later, however, Ferri argued that modern societies did not *need* capital punishment.

Very soon after *Criminal Sociology*, Ferri published another work, *Socialismo e criminalità*, in which he expanded considerably on the social and economic factors affecting criminal behaviour. This book, unfortunately, is available only in Italian, and I have had to use instead a summary of its thesis. This appears in *Socialism and Positive Science*, the book in which the Darwin–Marx reconciliation was argued. It was in *Socialism and Positive Science* as well that Ferri explained how his own position had evolved. He stated flatly that he had not been a 'militant socialist' at the time of writing *Criminal Sociology*, and presumably his position would have been different if he had been (p. 94).

Ferri's interest in the reconciliation was the defence of socialism from the charge of being unscientific. The theory of evolution had made socialism out of date, by showing how competition was in the nature of things. Co-operative, collective action was hopelessly romantic, in this view. Ferri's reaction was to attempt to prove that the incompatibility was a misunderstanding; social Darwinists had distorted the theory of evolution, and it was only with this distorted view that the incompatibility existed. Ferri then devoted a good part of the book to showing where the social Darwinists went wrong. He disputed their rugged individualism interpretation, drawing extensively on Kropotkin's *Mutual Aid*.

It was no longer the case, Ferri argued, that the struggle for survival insured the survival of the fittest, but social conditions transformed the game to 'survival of the best adapted'. Military service, for example, meant that it was unhealthy rejects from the army who married youngest and reproduced the most. The dowry system favoured rich unhealthy women over poorer but sturdier. Socialist philosophy, in any event, did not deny inequalities among individuals, which would have been unrealistic. It was, indeed, well aware of them, and took them into account in seeking to provide an equal start to all. There would still be struggle for survival under socialism, but an intellectual one in which co-operative practices were developed.

The means of existence could be insured to all who worked, which made the struggle to death a thing of the past.

Social and economic factors were emphasized in Ferri's final position on crime. Nevertheless, he still accorded a fairly substantial role to biological factors, more so than did the main conflict theorists. Crime would diminish substantially with socialism, but Ferri imagined rather more lingering and less withering than these others. He moved considerably from his Italian school origins, but still felt it necessary to list numerous physical and psychic disorders that would account for a fair number of crimes, even under ideal social and economic conditions. It seems that Ferri's keenness to see law reform along the lines of the Italian school led him eventually to support Mussolini.[1] Certainly he made complimentary remarks about Mussolini to this effect in 1926. Ferri died in 1929.

Ferri evidently never took up the question of long-term trends in economic conditions and criminality. Hence, despite having a foot in both camps, he never discovered the faulty premise that misinformed so much consensus work. Nor did he realize the extent to which the early conflict theorists were right, or begin to explore the implications of that point. Rather the faulty premise continued unchallenged well into the twentieth century and exchanges in the conflict–consensus debate suffered accordingly.

1. See the essay on Ferri in Mannheim, *Pioneers in Criminology*.

Chapter 4

TWENTIETH-CENTURY RESOLUTIONS

If the last two chapters have succeeded in making any point, it should be that much that passes for recent discovery has ancient origins. Twentieth-century work is characterized more by quantity than by originality, so much so that the whole approach to discussing theory and research had to be changed. The quantity of research was especially great, but even in the case of theory a highly abbreviated presentation had to be settled on. The aim now is to report main trends: the few new ideas emerging, the disappearance of others, and the convergence and evolution of still others.

Some original theory appeared in the period, thanks to Freud and the psychoanalysts. There was much work on integrating social and psychological explanations, and theory of anomie and alienation boomed. Consensus theory was extended to something of a logical extreme by Parsons. Conflict theory and consensus theory both changed radically, conflict to give up its stress on economic factors, and consensus theory, if not to welcome them, at least to admit them as respectable explanations.

An important development, theory and research began to appear explicitly on *sanctions*, as opposed to law. Theorists earlier had paid little attention to the differences between the two—laws were assumed to be enforced and the application of sanctions assumed violation of the law. Now conditions affecting enforcement were discussed and empirical work on social control agencies, especially in the United States, was done. The police and juvenile courts were favourite targets. It became possible to theorize why certain laws were not enforced, or enforced more against certain types of people than others.

Another important development was the focus on *process*, both on law enforcement and criminal behaviour. Differential association theory, conceptualizations of crime as normal, learned behaviour and, finally, labelling theory mark the stages of progression of these ideas. Research problems were raised on *how* delinquency was created: how delinquents were selected and processed and labels made to apply.

The two world wars, the Russian Revolution, the rise of fascism and the decline of European imperialism all had profound effects on the course of theorizing, in some ways directly, and otherwise through changes they effected in universities and intellectual life more generally. Research results contrary to consensus theory continued to appear, but what was different now was that there was so little *for*. Standards of research were improving in sociology and this was felt in the social control area as well. Criteria for accepting hypotheses became tougher, sufficiently so that research intended to be supportive of the school proved not to be. Propositions were gradually abandoned, or reduced to a shadow of their former selves. This did not mean the total abandonment of the search for physical causes, for new hypotheses continued to emerge. The great attractiveness of the message was, however, now a thing of the past, and perhaps World War I was as responsible as anything else. The war made the central theme of the theory implausible—the gradual perfecting of the moral instinct. Certain of those who had believed this were dead, as were opponents to the theory, and the incoming generation could never be persuaded.

From the strictly academic point of view, it was Goring's famous *English Convict* that closed the case on criminal anthropology. A massive work, published in 1913, it soon became the standard source for opponents to the theory. Methodologically, the study was impressive, although it was still based on the comparison of prisoners, as representing criminals, and free citizens as non-criminals. Karl Pearson was the statistical adviser, and the analysis was thorough and sophisticated. The study itself involved numerous tests, in which 3,000 inmates were compared with different samples of the non-criminal population. These latter included Oxford and Cambridge students (whose head measurements proved not to differ significantly from those of criminals), royal engineers and soldiers.[1]

It took some time before the negative studies, and even Goring's,

1. For other work opposing the school see Spaulding and Healy, Holmes, P. Parsons, Mensbrugghe.

had their effect. Some loyal supporters continued to publish as if nothing had happened.[1] One typical example is that of a Chicago sociologist, Henderson, who argued a multi-causal theory very similar to that of the late nineteenth-century Italian school. The explanation included climate, the seasons, and electrical storms, as well as defects in body, intellect and will, along with alcoholism, sexual excesses and epilepsy. Another writer, Grimberg, actually referred to 'evolutionary backstroke' in a study of delinquent girls, claiming organic inferiority and dullness to be causes of delinquency, along with alcoholism and disorganized family life.

More often, however, writers accepting the basic propositions of the Italian school also included some social factors, following the example of Ferri's *Criminal Sociology*.[2] There were numerous other variants as well. The 'anatomy as destiny' hypothesis was dismissed in one theory, in favour of a hypothesis amounting to 'chemistry as destiny'.[3] The cranial deformities of the original Italian school constituted only an intermediate explanation, it was said. They were themselves the product of chemical abnormalities which might, as well, have other effects on crime more directly. There were then 'born criminals', but their deformities could be traced to defects in the mother's blood and lymph system in pregnancy (p. 70); Lombroso was wrong only in the details. In another study, notable for its respectful references to Lombroso, feeble-mindedness, epilepsy, insanity and psychopathy were all included as causes of crime.[4] Lombroso was right and Goring wrong in yet another publication although what Goring's errors were was not specified.[5] The work took up one of Lombroso's later interests, the relationship between genius and criminality, both as manifestations of abnormality.

Studies on crime differences among various racial and ethnic groups in the United States were used to discredit criminal anthropological theory. The evidence tended to show that race as such was not important in explaining crime. The social and economic circumstances faced by the different waves of immigrants varied, and it was

1. This is evident in comparing studies from the first part of the century to those after Goring; examples of supporting publications appear as recently as 1973: Hollander, Renda and Squillace, Lydston, Grapin, Goddard, Mosby, Ellwood, Pinatel, A. Wilson, 910 Varma, Carrava.
2. Maxwell, Michon, de Greef, Belby, Laignel-Lavastine, Aschaffenburg.
3. This work, by Schlapp and Smith, has the provocative title of *The New Criminology.*,
4. Hoag and Williams.   5. Rhodes.

these that affected propensity to crime.[1] Similarly, studies of crime rates in Australia served to discredit the theory.[2] If crime was inherited, it was argued, Australia should have a higher crime rate than Britain, for Australia had acquired much of England's criminal class, and now had their offspring as well. Yet crime rates in the Australian colonies were lower than in Britain. Throughout the period the only evidence of reasonable quality favourable to Lombrosian theory was Lange's study of twins. He found identical twins more similar with respect to criminal behaviour (that is, either both twins criminal or neither) than fraternal twins. Since the social environment was the same for both types he concluded that it was physical inheritance that accounted for the difference.

The hangers-on to full-scale, undiluted criminal anthropology theory were few. Most of the distinctive propositions, such as atavism, degeneracy and the principle of inherited criminality, were abandoned. What was left was a very simple statement of some kinds of physical and mental deficiency being factors predisposing to crime. Goring was especially influential in this revision, for he found English inmates to be disproportionately characterized by some such defects although properly this conclusion applies only to prisoners, not criminals. He stressed throughout, however, that there was no *one* type of defect, mental or physical, characteristic of criminals. This position, of *some* kind of defect, became a very popular cause of crime and delinquency, assuming, for a time, almost a conventional wisdom status.

The mental deficiency hypothesis was particularly well received and, indeed, was supported in numerous studies. It featured in academic explanations,[3] books by professionals, especially prison warders, and popular accounts, such as Clarence Darrow's. The studies of 'defective families', the notorious Kalikaks and Jukes, were based on this reasoning although, in fact, the data reported never suggested a strong association with crime, as opposed to mental illness.[4] A substantial number of studies have indicated criminals not to be less intelligent on average,[5] and the controversy continues. Chassell's extensive review of the literature on intelligence and crime concluded that empirical work, to 1935, was inconclusive, and there is no reason to think otherwise today. Most of the studies

1. Hourwich, Work.   2. Sutherland.
3. Pailthorpe, Miner, Ferguson, Hollander. 4. Galton, Goddard.
5. Murchison, Slawson, Young, Otterström.

supporting the hypothesis involved comparisons of incarcerated criminals and free citizens, and sometimes the prisoners had been incarcerated for many years.[1] Properly speaking, the studies only showed that criminals who had been caught and sentenced to prison were, on average, of lower intelligence, more likely to have a physical defect, and more liable to ill health, than the free population. Whether this is because criminals are less intelligent and do not run as fast, or only that the weaker and duller are caught is anybody's guess.[2] Warnings to this effect have been in the literature for many years, largely ignored. Augusta Bronner's very thorough assessment of the problem in 1914 similarly had little effect.

Theory based on body types was a more serious attempt at the revival of biological explanations of crime. Several such theories appeared in the twentieth century, and in all of them there were denials of association with the Italian school.[3] The resemblances were, nevertheless, strong, although they did not go so far as the atavism concept. Social factors were included as well, but as subsidiary. Rather, the dominant idea was that social factors had been *overstressed* in recent years and biological factors too much ignored.

Sheldon's *Varieties of Delinquent Types* was a frank attempt to revive biological theory, asserting that 'behaviour is a function of structure'. Psychoanalytic theories of crime, 'Freudianity', were strongly opposed, as were, with less vehemence, social. Assertions were based on case analyses, with no controls. In the Gluecks' analysis delinquents (all incarcerated) were compared with non-delinquents (free), and with matching that excluded consideration of certain important social factors. The findings of support for the theory, then, have to be considerably qualified. We do not know what effect physical appearance has in sentencing, but can hardly assume it to be negligible. One can well imagine a judge sentencing a strong, athletic-looking boy to a reform school, while sending the 'skinny weakling' bookworm home. That there are so many mesomorphs (the athletic type) in reform schools may reflect just that. Any effect that physical factors do have may, further, be made through social factors. Quinney, among others, has suggested that physical strength

1. Pailthorpe, Burt.
2. This is not even to raise the question of the effect of prison conditions on testing.
3. Hooton, Sheldon, Glueck and Glueck,.1956.

probably affects recruitment into gangs, and subsequent labelling as a troublemaker.

PSYCHIATRIC THEORIES

The psychological literature for the period ranges from psychoanalytic theories of an 'adult entertainment only' nature to any number of tedious combinations of psychological problems and social factors. Freud's influence was important, but indirect. He was not himself much interested in criminal behaviour, but rather furnished the general ideas that colleagues subsequently applied. The central concept was unconscious guilt produced by the Oedipus complex. Freud observed cases of patients experiencing guilt *before* committing an offence, which suggested that it was guilt which had driven them to the act. The application to actual criminal behaviour was only briefly suggested. Freud also wrote some of the early theory on alcoholism and morphinism but not in the context of its being criminal behaviour.[1]

Theory based on the psychoanalytic stages of development—oral, anal and genital—has occasionally been used in explanations of crime, including general crime. The argument was developed initially as an explanation of alcoholism and then extended to the use of opiate narcotics, seen to be similar in function. The explanation is still used more for illegal drug use than regular crime. Numerous types of disturbances have been described, such as 'oral fixation', 'regression back to the oral stage', 'archaic oral longings', 'desire to return to the womb' and so forth. Many of these explanations included heightened sex drive at puberty as a precipitating factor. The fact of high recorded crime rates at adolescence then became strong prima facie evidence of support for the theory. Sex drive problems at other stages of life have also been used as explanations, especially for sex offences.

Much of the work in the psychoanalytic school was framed around the concept of 'disturbed ego development'. Aichhorn, in a book introduced by Freud, gave one of the first and most well-known accounts, although insisting that his work was not an attempt at theory. He described delinquency as a problem of imbalance between

1. Other sources on psychoanals are Smith, Alexander and Staub, Karpman and Horney. Drawing more marginally on the concepts were Thomas, and Healy. Reich apparently worked out a similar explanation some time after Freud, but independently (Alexander and Selsnick, p. 373).

the pleasure and the reality principles. The imbalance could arise from an excess of love or severity in early childhood and, in either case, it resulted in an incapacity to defer gratification for future pleasure (p. 198). This conceptualization of the delinquent as an immature person, unable to defer gratification, has been immensely popular and much used in treatment programmes. Aichhorn's work is important also for moving the focus from unconscious sexual disturbances, to the external conditions thought to produce them. In his own work he stressed conditions in the family in the early upbringing of the child.

Kate Friedlander wrote perhaps the classic application of psycho-analytic theory to delinquent behaviour, and one much used both in practice and academe. The explanation of delinquency began with the domination of the ego by the pleasure principle, with no independent superego. This, however, only explained 'latent', or potential, delinquency and it was social factors that determined whether or not the latent delinquency became manifest (p. 14). The explanation represents one of the more careful attempts at integrating social and psychological factors. It is interesting as well in stressing that the differences between the delinquent and non-delinquent were quantitative rather than qualitative. Friedlander also suggested that the real problem to explain was not 'why delinquency', but why individuals became socially adjusted, or a return to the earlier formulation, of why the moral instinct.[1]

Empirical work on psychoanalytic theory has largely been a story of negative results. The more concrete, sexual aspects of the theory have particularly failed in testing. Andry, for example, found no relationship between stages of development and delinquency, although he did find a positive association between delinquency and disturbed relationships with the father, consistent with the Oedipal guilt argument. Some of the work initially held to be supportive of the theory, notably Bowlby's controversial work on 'maternal deprivation', has since had to be re-interpreted, less favourably. The evidence in the one area I have examined comprehensively, illegal opiates use, was strongly and consistently contradictory.[2] Moreover, evidence supportive of the theory, as in the case of the Italian school, has been almost entirely confined to studies of dubious value. In

1. Others with work along roughly similar lines are Rubenfeld, Glover, Fyvel, Bandura and Walters.
2. *Causes of Non-Medical Drug Use and Dependence.*

most cases the data consisted of comparisons between incarcerated delinquents or criminals and a free control group, and often the diagnoses of disorder, neurotic conflict or whatever, had been made by a partisan of the theory. Given that assessments of personality leave much more to the imagination than skull measurements, the scope for believers to confirm their theories has been considerable. The facts of broken home or disturbed relations between parents are themselves considerations in sentencing, especially for juveniles. In extreme cases, problems in the family preclude anything but an institutional disposition. That is, children are sent to an institution *because* of the home situation, a practice that becomes common as community services for such children are scarce. As well, there is the problem of the self-fulfilling prophecy. The more judges send children to institutions 'because they need the treatment' the less valid are findings in which institutionalized children are compared with those outside. Theories of disturbance are, in fact, widely believed, so that research results not based on very careful work have to be held suspect.

As psychoanalytic theories gradually lost favour they were more than replaced with other kinds of theories of psychological distur- bance. The focus remained on conditions in the family in early childhood, but now poor conditions were said to produce some sort of disturbed personality or defects in functioning, ultimately resulting in crime or delinquency. Many theorists included social factors as well, although simple poverty explanations were still resisted. Typical examples of causal combinations would be emotional disturbance, immaturity, and insecurity, with bad housing, school and neigh- bourhood as the social causes. Some theorists, such as Friedlander, organized their theories around psychological causes, with social factors playing a subsidiary role, or being introduced as precipitating factors. Other theorists, such as Alexander and Healy, centred their explanations at the social level, with psychological disturbances acting as the precipitating factors. Very much the same conditions, however, appeared in both.

In Britain, Burt's *The Young Delinquent* was one of the most in- fluential explanations, although based on extrapolation from only one case history. Van Waters offered a simpler account, centred on family and school factors. Trasler's *Explanation of Criminality* was a more recent, middle-of-the-road account. Harriet Wilson's *Delinquency and Child Neglect* concentrated on family problems, also of the same period. One of the earliest American examples was Schoff's *Wayward Child,* which hypothesized family, school and employment factors as causes of delinquency, in that order. The author suggested discrimination against women as an indirect cause, on the grounds that the exclusion of women from responsible positions in education had an unfavourable effect on quality. Healy and Lathrop's *The Individual Delinquent* listed a vast number of causal factors, with numerous complicated causal chains connecting them. The study was based on cases, the authors imputing the causes of delinquency for each case in turn. Other American contributions from the same period were Slawson's *The Delinquent Boy* and P. Parsons's text *Crime and the Criminal.* Probably the most important of the American examples, however, has been the Gluecks' *Unravelling Delinquency.* It was directed expressly to prediction but, in the course of specifying predictive factors, outlined an underlying theory as well. It has been immensely influential throughout the western world, despite serious attacks on its methodology.[1]

One of the results of the work of the psychoanalysts was a stimulation of interest in psychopathy. The psychoanalysts did not change the substance of the theory from its early nineteenth-century formulation, but rather reinterpreted it in psychoanalytic terms—the psychopath becoming a person with a defective superego. Debate was then centred on what was responsible for the defects. This was, in effect, a debate over causes of crime, for the relationship between defective superego and criminal behaviour was assumed to be close. As for the other types of psychoanalytic explanation, the hypothesized causes stressed early upbringing.[2]

The psychopathy explanation was used a great deal in the twentieth century, mostly in reference to serious crime—'habitual offenders', sex offenders and users of illegal opiates. Preventive detention laws for the 'criminal sexual psychopath' indicate how seriously the theory was taken by the medical and legal professions. The empirical evidence on psychopathy has been mixed, which means much more positive support than for other explanations. The positive findings,

1. Texts arguing multi-cause theories roughly along the same lines have appeared in many countries: in India, Haikerwal, Rao, Saxena, Sethna; France: Hesnard; Turkey: Kunter; Egypt: Kolaly; Belgium: Debuyst; Sweden: Kinberg; Germany: Seelig; Tunisia: Bouhdiba; Canada: Szabo, Topping; United Kingdom: Walker; United States: Sutherland and Cressey.
2. McCord and McCord, East.

moreover, include some from studies with relatively acceptable research methods. On the other hand, there has also been considerable evidence to the contrary, and much of the material ostensibly favourable is suspect for the same reasons as outlined above on the other psychological theories.

Eysenck's theory of inadequate conditioning as the cause of crime may be seen as another development along these same lines. The thesis was that crime was a result of insufficient conditioning, which itself was affected by the dimension of extraversion–introversion. Extroverts condition less well than introverts, and Eysenck's evidence showed a disproportionate number of criminal extroverts. These findings could be used to explain why individuals exposed to similar conditioning, as members of the same family, could differ so much in subsequent behaviour. The research (and debate over it) goes on so that, at the moment, no conclusion can be drawn. One qualification does have to be made, though, in that Eysenck's criminal subjects were prisoners, hence the broader application to criminality is questionable.

SOCIAL THEORIES

One of the interesting theoretical developments of the period occurred when economic causes of crime, including genuine poverty, began to be accepted as explanations in consensus theory. The resistance of consensus theorists continued, especially to poverty itself,[1] but a substantial number came to accept various sorts of economic explanations. This is clear in Chicago school work, and in American adaptations of anomie theory.[2] Questions of *process* became increasingly important throughout the century. This can be seen initially in the studies of deviant subcultures, the notorious sociological field work of the whorehouse and the gay bar. Those less interested in entertainment began to do studies of social control agencies, opening up a much neglected dimension.

Phenomenologists then began to put the two together. The other important trend of the time has already been discussed, the convergence of social and psychological factors. This will become obvious

1. Glueck and Glueck (1956); Radzinowicz; Sorokin (1928), Glover, Holmes, Aschaffenberg, Henderson, Grimberg, Rao, Barnes and Teeters, Tobias.
2. Elkin, Samuel, Lander, Yen, Fernand.

again when Parsons's very general theory is discussed, for it subsumes psychological and social level causes.

The Chicago school marks the beginning of broad acceptance of *social* causes of crime in the United States and the entrance of economic. Its major works were widely read and, while remembered now more for what they led to than what they accomplished themselves, they are still read. The Chicago school itself is associated with social problems, and especially urban problems. There were actually few works on criminality, but these were immensely effective. Thrasher's *The Gang* described the social organization of a gang, establishing what is still an extremely popular research activity. Shaw's famous *Delinquency Areas* hypothesized delinquency to vary inversely from the centre of the city outwards. The book included a map of Chicago with concentric circles superimposed to illustrate the point. The mapping approach of course was not new—maps by region appeared in the 1830s—but the application to the city level was. In *Natural History of a Delinquent Career* social factors were examined, corresponding to those already described for cities, now from the point of view of a single delinquent's life history. The account is reminiscent of case studies, but now with social factors imputed as the causes. The 'career' concept itself dates back at least to 1853,[1] but it was Shaw's use of it that was taken up by labelling theorists. Further research on city organization was done in many other cities, often on related problems, like mental illness and suicide.

Twenty years after the first Chicago study the *magnum opus*, *Juvenile Delinquency in Urban Areas*, appeared, reporting data for a number of American cities, supportive of the theory. In time, however, data to the contrary accumulated sufficiently for the superficial aspects—distance from the city centre—to be abandoned.[2]

The explanation was never a mechanistic one, at any time, but rather distance from the city centre meant distance from the greatest social problems. It was the central downtown areas that were most affected by immigration, and migration of southern blacks, and it was there that social disorganization was greatest. Social disorganization signified the breakdown of norms, in precisely the same way as Durkheim's anomie. It seems that the Chicago school writers did not

1. Hill, *Crime: Its Amount, Causes and Remedies.*
2. See Morris, *The Criminal Area*, for a critical review of the ecological school.

realize how close they were to Durkheim, although in time other sociologists, notably Merton, did.

The work of the Chicago school affected all later theoretical developments in the United States, some way or another. Differential association theory was one of its earliest offspring, taking up the school's interest in *process*, and neglecting initial conditions. It stimulated a great deal of research on relationships among criminals and delinquents, and in people in the course of becoming criminal. This, in turn, affected differential opportunity theory and, later, labelling and phenomenology. It was Merton, however, who discovered the roots of the social disorganization problem and worked out the American version of anomie.

At one level, Merton's 'Social structure and anomie' was just that, an application of Durkheim's general theory to a particular case, American society in the twentieth century. But, of course, it did much more. Merton changed the focus of the social control field, moving it from the individual problem level to the social and cultural. The 'problem' leading to criminal behaviour was the disjunction between cultural goals and social structure. Individual problems remained, for it was individuals who felt and responded to frustration, and especially failure in the land of equality and opportunity. Individual problems, however, were carefully related to the level of structural faults. Cloward and Ohlin pursued certain structural problems further, in their application of anomie theory to juvenile delinquency in New York City.

Sellin's culture conflict represents quite a different explanation substantively, but again focusing at the structural level. The cause of crime lay in people acquiring norms in conflict with the dominant, legal norms of their society. This did not suggest any problem at the individual level. Rather, these individuals had acquired their norms as they were supposed to, but through migration, conquest or some major social change, found these no longer applied. The 'problem', then, lay at a higher structural level, the integration of different cultural systems. The similarity with differential association theory was strong, for in both 'criminal' norms were held to be learned in the same way as non-criminal norms—in ordinary primary group interaction. Culture conflict theory was more ambitious, however, in taking the explanation of delinquent behaviour back a step in the causal chain. While differential association explained only the *transmission* of delinquent behaviour already existing, culture conflict accounted for the existence of the initial delinquency itself, at least to the stage of different norms between societies at the time of migration or conquest.

The applicability of culture conflict theories, however, was always rather limited, and probably for this reason it never achieved the following of anomie. Typical examples of the sorts of crime to which it was applied were the murder of unfaithful wives and income tax fraud. The theory is of interest also in that it drew attention to the role of *law* in deviance, showing that behaviour defined as criminal in some legal systems was not in others, a much neglected point at the time.

The rise and fall of anomie theory were both unusually speedy happenings. The theory quickly became popular academically, and even was used as the underlying philosophy of some delinquency prevention programmes, notably the New York Opportunity for Youth programme. It seems that it never attained wide acceptance in professional circles. Practitioners outside the major American cities, for the most part, remained loyal to psychiatric disorder theories. The theory was, however, taken seriously in academe, and quickly became the subject of much empirical testing. So far as the results on crime and delinquency explanations are concerned, the results were largely negative.[1] Unfavourable evidence began to check the spread of the theory, probably before it reached its full potential audience.

Supporters of anomie theory tended to be people firmly attached to the consensus approach, but relatively open to new ideas, and rather more sympathetic to delinquents than is usually the case. The sociologists attracted to anomie theory, then, were the sort to be attracted to the phenomenological approach. Certain of the anomie explanations, in introducing notions of labelling, prepared the way. The support initially accorded anomie theory, it seems, before very long moved to phenomenology of some kind, and especially labelling theory.

LABELLING THEORY: SAFE AND UNTESTED

The most popular current theory in the consensus tradition is undoubtedly labelling, an explanation almost unsullied by empirical test. As a theory of *process*, labelling is not tied to any particular initial conditions, and so can be incorporated into any number of concrete

1. Clinard, Downes, Hirschi, and Martin and Webster.

theories. It will be viewed here first in relation to consensus theory. Later how it has been used in conflict theory, where it fits much better, will be shown. At its simplest, the labelling notion means a delinquent or criminal label being applied to a person, by official representatives of society, resulting in subsequent crime or delinquency. The type of official agency involved (police, court, school or prison) varies among particular theorists, as does the mechanism by which the label is applied, but the general idea is the same throughout. The early versions were rather simple. Respectable people rejected labelled criminals, in jobs and ordinary social contacts. Criminals, as a consequence, were forced into criminal gangs, for want of better company, and crime itself, for want of legal employment. Later, the process became more complicated, with effects on self-image being considered, and the structure of deviant groups and counter-institutions.

Becker is usually credited with introducing the expression 'labelling', in 1963, in his paper 'Labelling Outsiders'. This marks the first use of the term in contemporary work, but the general notion is very old. Many accounts of prison as a 'school for crime' stressed the effect of the convict label on employment. The term 'labelling' even has been used before, in the case analysis of a delinquent boy. The argument consisted of tracing the unfavourable effects of the label, in precisely the same way as the term is used today.

An American text, Tannenbaum's *Crime and the Community* gave an account of the labelling process in 1951, using the term 'tagging'. The book stressed the role of officials in the process, minimizing that of the individuals tagged, almost to the point of their being victims of circumstance. Lemert's *Social Pathology* appeared at the same time, describing a general theory of deviance, in which society was accorded the power to develop persistent deviance from even trivial misbehaviour. The process involved a 'primary deviation', or one not seeming to be immoral to the actor, resulting in penalties, which then instigated further deviance. Deviance and penalties would then alternate, escalating ultimately to the rejection of the deviant from normal society, and his or her acceptance of deviant social status. A number of studies in the 1950s and 1960s described processes more or less along these lines, for different kinds of deviance. Cohen in *Delinquent Boys* described the delinquent gang as a response to rejection on the part of official representatives of society, especially the school. Delinquency, often destructive, but trivial, and 'for no good reason', was a defence mechanism by which the rejectors were themselves rejected.

A short, but graphic, paper by Garfinkel, described the 'status degradation ceremony', or the initial stage of the labelling process. It was suggested that the ceremony, such as a court hearing, set off a process of re-interpretation of the individual's past history. Subjects of status degradation found their previously accepted qualities now suspect, for the new information showed what 'they had really been like all along'.

With Goffman's concept of the 'moral career', the whole process of status degradation was traced, from its beginning with 'mortification' to acceptance of a reduced status. The notion was applied initially only to inmates of total institutions, but has since been extended to a broad range of deviants.

There has been considerable empirical support for various aspects of labelling theory, although, to date, full-scale tests are lacking. The strongest support comes from studies of the effect of prison sentences on released inmates. A number of studies have shown a decline in occupational status on release.[1] There is evidence indicating that conviction alone, and even police investigation without a charge resulting, have a negative effect on employment opportunities.[2] The much discussed role of the school in the early stages of labelling has been documented to some extent empirically.[3]

PARSONS: CONSENSUS THEORY AT ITS GRANDEST

Parsons's formulation of deviance and social control is an impressive feat at two levels, as concrete theory explaining crime and social control, and as a framework of analysis for the whole consensus tradition.[4] It will be used later in the study as a concrete theory, but here, first, as a general orientation. Using it as a perspective all the existing theories and hypotheses on criminal behaviour can be brought together. Crime is theorized to be a response to strain, produced at some level, in some system. The great mass of theories of various problems inducing crime then become particular instances of strain within the framework. Theories of poverty and

1. Glaser, Murphy.
2. Schwartz and Skolnick.
3. Toby and Toby.
4. *The Social System.* See also Pitts, introduction to *Theories of Society.*

ignorance fall into place with theories of epilepsy and physical abnormality, at one extreme, and with anomie and culture conflict at the other. The nature and level of the strains produced vary, but all involve some kind of strain, eventually perceived by some actor in some role relationship, guided by some norms. All risk that a response to this strain will be a deviant one, and that some of these responses will be of sufficient importance to be treated as criminal.

Deviance is a response to strain which occurs when an actor's expectations are not fulfilled. To account for deviance, then, one must turn to expectations (their nature and level), and the conditions which determine the extent to which they will be fulfilled. It is non-fulfilment that is crucial, and whether this is seen as excessive expectation, or deficient fulfilment is not important. Absolute or objective needs are not recognized as such. Not even the worst poverty need necessarily cause crime, but only when there is an expectation of something better. Violation of expectations could be as basic as the expectation to eat. The source of the violation might occur at any level as well. Individual problems, such as defective intelligence and ill health could be causes, where expectations are greater than possible achievement. Societal level events, such as depression, mean large numbers of people subjected to deprivations for which they have not been prepared. Malintegration of subsystems, between ethnic groups, social classes and the two sexes, may be the cause of strain.

The malintegration may occur at the level of role-sets, a person having conflicting role obligations from different role-relationships. A boy may face conflicting demands, for example, in his relations with family, the parish priest and his friends at school. Ideally, there is a known, accepted hierarchy of role priorities, which would specify which should be acted on in any given conflict. In practice, however, the ordering may be ambiguous, and 'mistakes' are easily made. The more complex the system, of course, the greater the chances of error, so complexity itself is one of the factors affecting crime.

Parsons also used his concept of pattern variables, or dominant orientations in a society, for explaining nonfulfilment of expectations. Children, for example, may be socialized to high expectations of affection, but as adults be expected to relate in an 'affectively neutral' fashion. Expectations of achievement may be an unpleasant shock, after an upbringing in which ascribed status could be taken for granted. Or, a high value on achievement would necessarily cause strain in a society with meagre resources. Too little emphasis on affection could be incompatible with biologically given needs.

Parsons's definitions of deviance, at both the individual and sytem levels, were much broader than criminal behaviour. At the individual level deviance was the motivated tendency for an actor to behave in contravention of one or more institutionalized normative patterns.[1] Crime was but one type of deviance, although as the violation of the society's official norms, the most important. The content of these official norms reflected society's highest values. At the system level, deviance was the tendency for one or more component actors (individuals or groups) to behave in such a way as to disturb the equilibrium of the system. Any kind of behaviour, including failure to act, could be deviant if it had the effect of disturbing equilibrium. The definition is an instructive one, a forceful statement of the position that nothing is inherently deviant or normal. Conversely, it suggests that anything can be deviant. Killing is not necessarily deviant, for example, and indeed is institutionalized in war, execution, and the elimination of surplus children. Where it is not institutionalized, as in settling domestic disputes, it is disruptive, and especially so in societies placing a high value on ordinary human life. Hallucination, to take another example, is often institutionalized for religious activities, and certain forms of leisure and relaxation. Outside these spheres it may be disruptive, especially in societies placing a high value on purposeful, worldly activity.

Social control, consistent with the consensus tradition, was a response to deviance. At the individual level it referred to motivational processes, both in deviant actors and others, to counteract deviance, including internalized norms, attitudes, beliefs and values. At the system level, social control referred to all the re-equilibrating processes that re-integrate behaviour with previously institutionalized expectations. This included law, agencies of law enforcement, and all the agencies of socialization as prevention—in the family, school, religious and cultural institutions.

While any particular conditions or problems at any level could be subsumed into Parsons's scheme, all were not equally welcome. His own examples were middle-of-the-road social and economic problems and their psychological consequences. Poverty, overcrowding, rapid population increase and disruptions of various kinds could all be causes of crime through the strains they posed for the actor. Any

1. *The Social System*, p. 250.

conditions which cause undue strain to the family hindering the upbringing of children, would have to be suspect. Poor education, for similar reasons, could help to produce crime.

CONSENSUS THEORY OF LAW

As for criminal behaviour, the first work in law in the century was based on nineteenth-century materials, and nineteenth-century theoretical ideas, and is effectively indistinguishable from earlier work.[1] The break, when it came, however, was profound. Again, as for theory of behaviour, it was the abandonment of evolutionary theory that had the greatest effect. The main consensus theorists had depended on the evolution of the moral instinct for explaining the development of law, so that when the moral instinct lost credibility, much theory went with it. The view that acquired characteristics could be inherited was completely rejected. The theory of natural selection continued to be used by some theorists, notably Timasheff, but in a more limited fashion.

In a sense, a move away from evolution was a necessary condition for the development of any complex theory of law. Law was not an important part of evolutionary theory nor, when it was but an emanation of the moral instinct, could it be. Law was, in effect, so closely tied to the moral instinct that it did not need explanation in its own right.

With the growth of academic law there was a certain fragmentation of the field and, for a while, a narrowing of focus. Theorists did not keep pace with developments in each other's fields. More fundamentally, the links between the components of law, sanctions and behaviour were obscured. A lapse in the conflict-consensus debate was an inevitable result. A crucial element in the debate lay in the relationships among the components, and specialization meant that these were ignored. The links between law, behaviour and sanctions, in effect, fell *between* fields, to belong to none of them. Conflict and consensus theorists continued to present different points of view, to be sure, but the full extent of the differences, and the structural differences in particular, were not pursued. Even Sorokin and Timasheff, who discussed economic determinism, and knew the Marxist literature, did not get to the heart of the differences in approach.

1. See Ehrlich, *Sociology of Law* and, for Durkheimian work, Mead, J. Hall, Gurvitch, and Lévy-Bruhl. See also Stone for discussion.

There has since been a move back to a more integrated approach, but the fragmentation is still more the rule than the exception.

WESTERMARCK

Westermarck's *Origin and Development of the Moral Ideas* represents the culmination of nineteenth-century consensus work on law. Published in two volumes in 1904/06, it was based on nineteenth-century data and mainstream consensus concepts. Theoretically it was grounded in Adam Smith's moral sentiments, as was Darwin's and Spencer's work. Moral concepts, according to Westermarck, were developed from moral judgements elicited in everyday interaction. A process of generalization meant that habitual behaviour gradually acquired a moral component, or a notion of obligatoriness. What *was* done became what *must* be done. Sanctions emerged through a similar process of generalization.

Law was defined as expressly formulated rules enforced by a definite sanction (p. 165). Law reflected the custom of the time it was formulated and, thus, might lag behind custom. Despite the problem of lag, however, the norms of the criminal law generally reflect the moral judgements of the population as to what was wrong and what the punishment should be. 'The criminal law of society may thus, on the whole, be taken for a faithful exponent of the moral sentiments prevalent in that society at large' (p. 200). Confidence in the legitimacy of legal institutions was further expressed in the process of custom becoming law. A 'sense of justice' and the 'purpose of equity' were influential in the development of the law (p. 165).

Westermarck's exposition was well documented with comparative ethnographic materials. He limited his analysis of crime to murder, and on this did a comprehensive study. The propositions he developed were clearly directed to explanations of *why* certain norms appeared in certain societies and other norms in others.

HOBHOUSE

Hobhouse was a philosopher more than a sociologist, but there are several points on which his work is relevant. He, with Wheeler and Ginsberg, conducted a comparative analysis of preliterate societies, directed to testing economic determinism of 'social and moral development'. The study, *The Material Culture of the Simpler Peoples*, was one of the first to use quantified ethnographic data, which it did in an exemplary way. The results were supportive of economic determinism but in a consensus framework rather than a conflict. The work marks one of the earliest adaptations of the economic determinism argument to consensus theory. Hobhouse's work on law and ethics, like that of his student Ginsberg, was always in the consensus tradition in the extreme. Rights and duties, according to Hobhouse, were determined by the contribution they made to the harmony of life as a whole. Since human conduct was not naturally harmonious, repression was required and existed, however only for the fuller development of society. Hobhouse's influence in British sociology and social philosophy over the decades contributed to the wide acceptance of consensus theory of law. Ginsberg continued the same orientation for decades longer, bringing it further into mainstream British sociology.

POUND AND THE INTEREST THEORY

Roscoe Pound, Dean of the Harvard Law School for many years, was immensely influential in American academic law circles. He wrote extensively from the 1920s to the 1940s, although never fulfilled his early ambition to write a full-scale treatise on sociological jurisprudence. Pound was well versed in continental legal scholarship and served to bring much of this work to the attention of American scholars. As for legal scholars the world over, Pound's academic interests were very much intertwined with the practical and normative. Much that he discussed under the heading of 'theory' sociologists would regard as normative. To confuse matters more, he often failed utterly to distinguish between what the law *was* and what it *ought to be*. Pound was careful to define his work as 'sociological jurisprudence', as opposed to sociology, but the problem remains.

Interests were defined at three levels: individual, social and public. Individual interests were further subdivided into those of personality (physical and spiritual existence), domestic (the family) and substance (economic). Social interests pertained to the existence of the group as a whole, in the sense of the survival of civilized social life. Public interests were really a special type of social interest, concerning values. In any particular case, several conflicting individual interests might be involved, and one or more social or public. In divorce, for example, there would be individual interests of wife and husband (peace of mind, re-marriage), social interest in the upbringing of the children (adequate care), and public interest in the preservation of a valued institution (the family). The number and kinds of interests pressed would always be more than could be satisfied, and for this reason there would always be a need for law. This is made clear in the 'Survey of Social Interests':

> Looked at functionally, the law is an attempt to satisfy, to reconcile, to harmonize, to adjust these over-lapping and often conflicting claims and demands, either through securing certain individual interests, or through delimitations or compromises of individual interest, so as to give effect to the greatest total of interests, or to the interests that weigh most in our civilization, with the least sacrifice of the scheme of interests as a whole. (p. 39)

Pound thus held that law accorded priority to public, social and individual interests in that order, the same order as in Parsons's and the less explicit earlier consensus formulations. His confidence that public and social interests would be met ahead of individual place the theory solidly in the consensus tradition. Even the interests of the most powerful individuals of a society would be sacrificed in the interests of the good of society as a whole.

The nature of public and social interests would change, as social and economic conditions changed, but the principle remained. The trend in the United States, in Pound's view, was towards the 'socialization' of the law—the tendency to accord ever greater weight to public or social interests over private. For example, while previously it was deemed to be in the public interest to uphold individual property rights at any price now greater priority was given to overall costs and convenience. Modern examples would be expropriation laws and no fault insurance.

SOROKIN AND TIMASHEFF

Sorokin and Timasheff brought an extraordinary combination of qualities to the sociology of law. They not only brought European materials to the attention of American scholars (as did Pound and others), but managed to shift the focus of the field in a more theoretical direction. In this sense they delayed the 'Americanization' of the subject, keeping European sources relevant when this was no longer the case elsewhere in sociology. It was not until the 1950s that 'purely American' work on law began to be common. Both anti-Marxist, Sorokin and Timasheff were at least willing and able to discuss issues from the Marxist literature.

Sorokin's *Social and Cultural Dynamics* contains his vast, function-

alist theory of culture and social structure. The propositions on law
and ethics, part of this larger theory, were worked out with Timasheff.
The scheme was a simple, highly general one, asserting a tendency to
unification of the different components of culture. Systems of truth,
ethics and law fluctuated, with a fluctuation in any one affecting the
others.

The correspondence between ethics and law was close. The official,
actually enforced, code was the most authoritative, most accurate
reflection of the ethical mentality of the society.

> The gradation of the punishments is a fairly good indicator of the
> comparative gravity of the wrongfulness of the specified class of
> prohibited action, as it appears to the respective societies and
> culture mentalities. The greater the crime, the greater usually, the
> punishment. (p. 528)

Discrepancies between law and ethics existed, but should not be
exaggerated, especially for early periods. Law did not change
quickly, hence a discrepancy indicated change in socio-ethical mentality. The greater the discrepancy, indeed, the faster this change had
been (p. 526). When discrepancies became considerable, the relevant
code was revised or replaced.

The analysis on which the theory was based was extensive and,
from the point of view of method, interesting. Sorokin examined the
development of the legal codes of five societies—France, Austria,
Italy, Germany and Russia—from the earliest times until the present.
Various activities, 104 in all, were grouped into broad types of
crime—against the physical person, moral person, property, religion,
family, sex, evidence and documents, state and political order. The
inclusion and exclusion of particular activities was then traced
under these broad types. The same basic trends in all five societies
were found (p. 536).

Timasheff further worked on the theory, producing a superior
formulation of it, in my view, in his *Introduction to the Sociology of
Law*. Careful attention was paid to factors affecting sanctions, as
opposed to the *content* of official norms. Perhaps the most valuable
feature of the book was its discussion of the role of power. There
could be no mistaking the theory with the conflict approach, for the
nature of the power structure was itself explained in consensus terms.
Power structures, Timasheff asserted, could only survive if they were
in the best, long-term interests of a society. There were effective

limits constraining the holders of power in their exercise of power, and the interests of the community as a whole were more important ultimately than the interests of the powerful.

Timasheff attempted to account for differences in law between societies, incorporating theory of natural selection. Natural selection meant victory for those societies with the most efficacious ethical rules, or the rules most adequate to the true needs of the community (p. 235). Differences in law between societies reflected ultimately differences in needs. Natural selection meant that the true needs of the community would be met. At the extreme, those groups whose needs had not been met did not survive to be discussed at all. The fluctuations proposition was part of the explanation. Law was integrated with other elements of culture, for both were products of the society's historical development, and both had been affected externally by the same causes. Internally, there were the pressures of logical consistency, which similarly acted to insure integration of cultural elements (p. 326).

Power and ethics were both ultimately determined by the same criteria, for in both survival was the ultimate judge. It was, after all, the same individuals who were involved in both matters of power and ethics and, it followed, some kind of relationship between the two systems would be worked out. Antagonism between power and ethics was possible—but rare—and would normally be transitory. Neutrality was more likely, but also not frequent. The precise factors that affected changes in the power structure were discussed in some detail. Finally, a tendency for habit to be transformed into custom was described, what *is* becoming what *ought to be*, or 'the normative tendency of actuality' (p. 245).

Sanctions, in Timasheff's scheme, were divided between legal and extra-legal. The more highly developed the society, the greater would be the importance of legal sanctions. With a high degree of development, sanctions would be administered in a complex system, by officials acting on behalf of the 'corporate will', and guided by legal rules. Generally the degree of pain inflicted reflected what the individual merited in view of the socio-ethical convictions of the day. The infliction of punishment, moreover, restored the ideal order defined by law. Legal power showed its force in the application of sanctions and socio-ethical convictions were reinforced.

Where there was a strong correlation between socio-ethical conviction and legal powers a condition of 'legal equilibrium' held. In such circumstances motivation to obey law would be strong, and a tendency for the 'initial or normal' situation to be restored on violation (p. 269). Timasheff paid little attention to causes of crime. Law was a social force that acted on individuals to inhibit crime, but was not the only force, and not always the strongest (p. 354). The occurrence of crime meant that one or other of these other forces was stronger. Precisely what these other forces were, and how they acted, was not explained.

CONFLICT THEORY IN THE TWENTIETH CENTURY

Conflict theory followed quite a different course of development in the twentieth century. World War I and the Russian Revolution mark the critical break, as in the case of other intellectual work, but the break was even deeper. Conflict theory nearly disappeared in western societies after the war, while in the USSR it became *the* establishment theory. Biological and psychological theories were actually banned in the Soviet Union in the 1920s. Since then there has been a certain revival of 'bourgeois theory', at least to the extent of social psychology. In western Europe and the United States conflict theory was co-opted rather than banned. Parts of it, economic factors of various sorts, were absorbed into consensus explanations, but the theory as a whole lost favour. It was not until the 1960s that interest in conflict theory as such re-emerged.

The intellectual debate deteriorated as the ideological dispute became a matter of national boundaries and arms. There was always a formidable gulf between the two approaches, with both sides tending to dismiss the other after only a cursory examination. Now the examination became even more cursory and the dismissal firmer. Theorists in the Soviet Union took sufficient notice of western work to condemn it, but did not draw on the material seriously or reanalyse it, in contrast with nineteenth-century Marxists. In the west, Marxist sociology was simply ideology, and not reliable as a source of honest ideas.

BONGER

Bonger's *Criminality and Economic Conditions* represents nineteenth-century conflict work at its best. Published just after the turn of the century, the book includes both a comprehensive statement of theory and a valuable review of the major theorists and empirical work.

The theory was directed only to criminal behaviour, but in setting this in a conflict framework, Bonger examined law to some extent as well. The theoretical review was written initially for a competition at the university of Amsterdam on the economic determinism debate, winning second prize.[1] The work was then expanded into a doctoral thesis. Bonger subsequently pursued a conventional career as an academic lawyer, moving gradually in the consensus tradition, his intellectual position apparently following his politics. In 1936 he published a text quite indistinguishable from consensus work of the time. Bonger wrote extensively on political issues throughout this time, especially the threat of Nazism. His last work, published posthumously, reflects these concerns, dealing with the relationship between race and crime. A marked anti-Nazi, Bonger committed suicide on the invasion of Holland by the German army.

Criminality and Economic Conditions was at once too much to the right and the left. For Americans, it was Marxism, and suspect. Yet *Criminality* never became a model for work in the Soviet Union. Bonger was as respectful to Marx as any Marxist ever was, and the theory was close to what Soviet theorists later produced themselves. As Solomon has pointed out, though, Bonger was always a social democrat and, as such, no more acceptable to the Soviets than the Americans.

His theory of criminality begins with definitions of criminal norms and immorality, which amount to an abbreviated theory of law. A criminal act was one felt to be immoral, committed by a person in a social group, and punished by specialized organs of that group with something more than moral disapprobation (p. 381). Immorality was defined as that which was prejudicial to the interests of a group of people united on the basis of those interests (p. 279). The interests of the dominant class and the dominated were opposed, and it was the dominant class, for the most part, that had acts prejudicial to its interests defined as crimes. Some acts, like murder and rape, were contrary to the interests of both classes alike and, exceptionally, there might be cases of acts being defined as crimes which were prejudicial to the interests of the subordinate class—for it was not wholly without power. 'However, in every existing penal code hardly any act is punished if it does not injure the interest of the dominant class as well as the other' (p. 380).

1. The first prize went to Van Kan, whose work is also a very good source on the issue.

The explanation of criminal behaviour was framed in this broad context of morality and immorality. The question as to why one became a criminal became that of why one acted in one's own interests rather than those of the group. The reasons offered were grounded in the development of capitalism: poverty, inequality and alienation. Structurally, these were examined in terms of criminal tendencies or thoughts (or positive forcings towards immorality), forces opposing, and the particular circumstances occurring at the time of a potential crime. Substantively, Godwin, Owen and Engels were the main sources. People were born with a social instinct, Bonger argued, in the line of Godwin, which should inhibit criminal tendencies, and counteract them when they did appear. Systems of production and exchange to date, however, impeded the development of this social instinct. In the case of capitalism, the system of exchange set one person against another, isolating individuals and weakening what links existed among them. Workers forced to sell their labour had little chance to develop strong bonds with their society. The servility required of them was demoralizing, and they suffered, too, in seeing the rich live lives of luxury. Family life in advanced capitalism was disorganized and this was an important force toward criminality. The problem was a structural one, endemic to capitalism. Capitalists were as bound to it as the workers they were forced to exploit.

Child labour became necessary at certain stages of capitalism which both directly and indirectly helped to produce criminal behaviour. Child labour meant that children learned competitive attitudes early in life, rather than co-operative, stifling the development of social sentiments. Children early came into contact with people of low morals for, with lack of education and poor living conditions, general moral development was badly wanting in the working class (p. 407). Absolute want had very direct effects in motivating property crimes, committed in aid of mere survival. A host of mediating factors was cited, along the line of Engels. Alcoholism was an important cause, especially of sex crimes. Prisons had an unsavoury influence, making professionals out of simple occasional criminals. The role of the press in instigating crime was also discussed. Bonger stressed that the press was controlled by the capitalist class, and directed to making money rather than serving any social purpose. Lurid accounts of crime aroused tendencies to imitation—a point made by conflict and consensus theorists alike.

Bonger's statement on the nature of crime under communism was classic. Crime would virtually disappear on the establishment of communism, for the causes of crime would disappear. The nature of productive relations would be radically changed, and it was in these that the important causes of crime lay. Sentiments of altruism would flourish. Remaining as causes of crime would be only those rare instances of personal pathology. These would be dealt with medically, by professionals, and not as crimes.

Bonger did not take up the question of long-term trends, and accepted the rising crime thesis. Not challenging the basis of the consensus argument, he used comparisons of economic conditions across different societies and regions and short-term fluctuations. As well, he made much of data showing disproportionate criminality among the poor and badly educated, but which again leaves aside the question of *levels* of crime and social control. Despite the thoroughness of his analysis then, Bonger also failed to resolve the fundamental problem in the conflict–consensus debate. He has been criticized as not being a good Marxist, but possibly it was because he was *too* good a Marxist that he did not see the point. Later he moved to a consensus position, thereby escaping the contradiction.

KROPOTKIN: ANARCHY THEORY BREAKING THE RULES
Kropotkin's theory embraced as peculiar a combination of elements as ever appeared in the history of our subject, although no more unlikely than the circumstances of his own life. A Russian prince, Kropotkin was a page in the tsar's court, and later an official in Siberia, where he discovered the rivers did not flow in the direction St. Petersburg maps made them out to. It was through this work in Siberia that he became an evolutionist and worked out his principle of mutual aid. Severe climate and government incompetence were the influential factors. August snows and massive spring floods showed that environment was the effective check on over-multiplication— much more powerful than competition of individual against individual. Both animals and people developed co-operative practices in the face of common disasters, and through these survived. The government in St. Petersburg so mismanaged affairs that the essential role of local, mutual aid became even more evident.

Kropotkin's first work of concern was a pamphlet, *Prisons*, published after his own imprisonment in the Peter and Paul fortress. Along with comments as to the ineffectiveness of prisons as reform institutions, it contained several theoretical propositions. Kropotkin argued against the standard Italian school explanation of crime, although accepting its research findings; facts were facts. He accepted the hypotheses on climatic and other physical determinants of crime, for instance, but insisted they had their effect through social conditions. His interpretation of physical anomalies was different. While everybody in prison might indeed have one arm longer than the other, or some such asymmetry, it was bad environment that made anomalies effective in instigating crime. Biological and physical environment factors of all kinds had an effect on crime, but only indirectly, and their total effect would generally be weaker than psychological or social conditions.

In Kropotkin's two full-scale works the focus changed from *criminality* to *morality*. In *Mutual Aid* Kropotkin described the development of the moral instinct, as defined by Adam Smith and Darwin. The moral instinct was an inherited habit, developed over long years of evolution, appearing in animals before the emergence of the human species.

Instinct had been badly overpowered in higher civilization—by individualism—but had never totally disappeared. It was still evident in many surviving 'instincts', such as communal property in farming villages, and many co-operative practices, especially among the poor. It was much more alive than was apparent in written history, for historians gloried in wars and calamities, ignoring the lives and accomplishments of ordinary people (p. 91).

Kropotkin wrote *Mutual Aid* with the explicit purpose of countering the rugged individualism of Darwinian thought. Most of his criticism was directed at social Darwinists, notably Thomas Huxley, rather than Darwin himself. Darwin, however, was to blame for overestimating the importance of the individual struggle of all against all. Unfortunately, he had not completed his work on the struggle of species against the environment, which would have helped to correct the imbalance.

Kropotkin opposed the prevalent view of early human society being organized in small, isolated families, at war or at uneasy peace with each other. The picture he drew, based on findings from the Early Stone Age, was considerably more harmonious, of sizeable populations living in small communities in close proximity to one another. The original family organization was of loose communal marriage. The family with permanent and possessive relationships was a more recent invention. These points are important in Kropotkin's argument, for he theorized the social instinct to have first developed relative to bonds to a *whole* community, tribe or band—a unit larger than the family. Clan organization of some kind developed universally and, in time, village- or territory-based units evolved.

Kropotkin's substantive ideas on morality were most fully describ-ed in his *Ethics*, a work he never finished, and which was published, as far as it went, only after his death. His concept of morality, like Proudhon's, was based on justice. Without justice, there could be no morality, and without equality there could be no justice. Primitive notions of justice and morality developed in mammals, who often had more than one offspring, which meant that sharing had to be learned. Humans learned principles of morality, justice and equality from animals (p. 16). In primitive times, humans lived close to animals, as hunters following them, and later domesticating them. Ideas of good and bad were drawn from nature—as opposed to any supernatural or idealistic source. Spoken language stimulated the generalization of ideas.

Kropotkin defended his propositions largely with ethnographic materials. Fines and payments of retribution, common in primitive societies, demonstrated this notion of equality—the payment restor-ing the balance disturbed by an offence. Kropotkin intended his *Ethics* to be a positive source of morality and not only a study. A new source of morality was needed, he believed, for it was for lack of a credible moral system that the Russian revolution had not spread further.

JANE ADDAMS

Jane Addams was one of the few theorists difficult to place between conflict and consensus theory. Her theory of criminal behaviour was a thorough indictment of American urban, industrial society, but the role of the holders of power was not explicit. Her purpose in writing was not so much academic as practical, which is one explanation for the omission. Another is simply her isolation from relevant theoretical developments. Addams was too much a radical for the conservatives who dominated American sociology at the time, yet, as an American, she was isolated from conflict work in Europe. In any event, the alternative of assigning her to consensus theory appeared less desir-able. One could make her an example of the early accommodation of conflict ideas in consensus theory, but this would seem to miss the point.

The *Spirit of Youth and the City Streets* was a description of the alienating forces of city life which led to crime. The isolation of newcomers from the country was graphically depicted, the segregation of the young from the mature, the pressures of delayed age of marriage and, above all, the growing meaninglessness of life. With the Puritan work ethic, work was at least a means of self-expression. Now it was as exhausting as ever, but even duller and more conducive to strain. Much petty delinquency was simply a protest against monotony (p. 107). Genuine, restorative recreation was almost totally absent, which meant that needs unfulfilled at work went unfulfilled completely. At the material level, the lack of a welfare system was stressed. 'Commercial America' provided nothing to live for, either, spiritually. There were no historic bonds to act as restraint, no ideals to channel the quest for adventure.

Addams sketched out the ideas that others later expressed more formally. Much Chicago school work, and anomie, can be seen as elaboration of her initial ideas. She anticipated certain themes in city politics as well. In *Democracy and Social Ethics* she described networks integrating corrupt politicians with their local communities, later used in accounts of 'the functions of crime'. She was also one of the first writers to cite non-pathological causes of crime. The quest for adventure was one, and the more routine learning of petty crime through primary group associations another.

The work of the early twentieth-century conflict theorists was not well received. Kropotkin appears never to have been taken seriously as a theorist. Bonger's work had a certain prestige for its sheer size, as something to footnote when opposing conflict explanations. Glueck and Glueck, for example, dismissed it because they did not approve of 'single variable' explanations.[1] War, racism, revolution and emigration took their toll of the likely recruits to conflict theory in the next generation, and the damage done was never repaired. Examples to the contrary, in western Europe, are few.[2]

DAHRENDORF: THE REVIVAL AND REVISION OF CONFLICT THEORY

Dahrendorf appears to be the first western sociologist to return to the theory, publishing a paper on conflict theory of law in German in 1961, and in English in 1962. The paper reflects an awareness of the

1. *Physique and Delinquency*, p. 2.
2. Rozengart, Laski, A. Wilson (1908).

length and richness of the two contrasting orientations, and a number of pre-sociological writers, notably Rousseau, were discussed. Nevertheless, the omissions seem prodigious.

Yet even this much of a revival of the classics had very little effect. The paper was not cited in the American works next to appear, neither by major writers (like Quinney), nor in textbooks (such as Schur, Lofland or Rosenblum).[1] From these works, indeed, one would gather that conflict theory had a rather short history, emerging in reaction to the dominance of modern functionalism.

Dahrendorf has been much maligned for his revision of conflict theory, although more, perhaps, for his political career and official limousine than for what his theory said. The revision remains true to the essential elements of the conflict approach and is, altogether, a potentially very useful contribution. It was not worked out in detail however, for Dahrendorf's interest in deviance was only peripheral. His objective was to explain stratification, from earlier inequalities in power, and it happened that criminal law helped to make the connection.

The need for some such factor as law arose since Dahrendorf rejected the two traditional Marxian explanations of stratification, private property and the division of labour. Private property could no longer be blamed for inequalities, since its virtual abolition in many countries had clearly not resulted in the abolition of inequalities. The division of labour explanation failed on other grounds. There was no necessary relationship between differentiation of tasks by occupation and inequality in rewards accorded them. The solution to the problem Dahrendorf recommended referred back to the notion of moral community, but with a different definition from Durkheim and later functionalists.

A society had, by definition, a set of norms to which sanctions were attached (p. 167). The existence of a set of norms and enforcement procedures presupposed an already existing unequal distribution of power. Those who made and enforced the law (broadly defined, so as to include informal norms and sanctions) necessarily had more power than those against whom they were enforced. The number of

---

1. Ignorance of Dahrendorf's work is difficult to understand in that his earlier *Class and Class Conflict* is well known in the United States as well as western Europe. Curiously, this book has been much cited in works on deviance, while the paper on deviance has not. Again, this underscores the extent of the European–American break in sociology.

potential norms in a society was as great as the imagination of its members. The fact that only a small number were officially recognized indicated a selection process, with those holding most power having their particular norms established as the norms for the whole society. Enforcement of norms meant loss of status to those sanctioned. Every stratification system had, underlying it, inequalities of rank resulting from the imposition of sanctions. Societies might introduce other distinctions among their members, and many conditions might act to increase the complexity of the stratification system. But, argued Dahrendorf, the hard core of social inequality was sanctions (p. 167).

The value system of the moral community was universal only in the sense that it was universally obligatory. The extent to which it represented the consensus of a broader cross-section would vary, but it would certainly reflect the most important concerns of those in power. 'In the last analysis established norms are nothing but ruling norms, i.e., norms defended by the sanctioning agencies of society and those who control them' (p. 174). Those who were less favourably placed in society would strive to gain power so that they could establish norms that would raise their rank at the expense of those they overcame. Thus every stratification system generated its own opposition and bore the seed of its own destruction (p. 177).

The conditions which determined whether a person found it easy to conform with the norms, or difficult, or impossible, were themselves part of the social structure. These included age, sex, occupation and other group memberships. The likelihood of committing a crime, in other words, was at least partly determined by one's place in the social structure. Personal idiosyncrasies were allowed some effect, but were not relied on.

MINOR CONFLICT THEORISTS

Vold was one of the earliest American writers to use conflict theory, in his textbook *Theoretical Criminology*. He stressed the frequent political component of crime, arguing that 'crime' was often the result of fulfilling role obligations, on the part of members of a politically impotent group (for example picketers on picket duty). Crime was a form of political behaviour, the criminal a member of a 'minority group' (p. 202). His theory departed from the conflict model in relating the formulation of law to a legislative majority rather than a small group of power-holders. Further he stated that the theory should not 'be stretched too far', but applied to only certain types of crime (p. 219).

Comfort, a British psychiatrist, described the law as a compromise between the mores of the rulers and the ruled. In pre-industrial England law was contrary to popular mores in many respects, where it served to preserve the interests of the rulers (p. 4). But pressure groups outside the ruling class had little chance of having *their* particular mores adopted as law. What is original in the thesis was not that the holders of power used criminal law to further their interests, but that they were disproportionately likely to be pathologically aggressive people. Evidence for the point was drawn from psychiatry. The idea is useful for introducing an intervening mechanism—the recruitment of criminally aggressive persons—between the possession of power and its deployment.

Turk's *Criminality and Legal Order* represents a more systematic use of conflict theory in the explanation of crime.

The first stage of the theory dealt with relative probabilities of normative–legal conflict over various types of behaviour. The second concerned probabilities of criminalization within various social categories. The theory assumed some process, akin to labelling, which allowed authorities to operate criminal definition and sanctioning schemes.

Macnaughton-Smith's concept of the 'second code' is a potentially very useful contribution along these same lines. Actual enforcement practices may be rather poorly related to the ostensible legal code of a society, but violations of an unwritten, implicit code the real basis of enforcement. These may include statuses, such as low social class, membership in a racial minority, or other characteristics, such as looking suspicious. Research should be geared to events and circumstances that lead to someone being labelled in practice, or the contents of the second code.

Social histories of crime have been another source of stimulation to conflict theory. Hobsbawm is perhaps the best example, with a description of banditry in agrarian Europe, explained with the standard conflict argument of social and economic circumstances. Bandits were recruited from the surplus rural population, which grew in times of economic crisis (p. 13). Banditry decreased in spring and summer as work became available, increasing in the 'dead' season. These patterns occurred across national boundaries, which further indicated that it was basic economic factors, common to all agrarian societies, that were crucial.

Banditry in Hobsbawm's description was liberty. Most people were prisoners of their landlord and the work cycle, but the bandit had broken free. He was regarded as hero, champion, liberator, and settler of scores by the peasants, by the landlords, a simple outlaw. Banditry was not a social movement, although sometimes a precursor to revolt, and it symbolized revolt.

Conflict theory was used in case studies of legislation in the 1950s and 1960s. These attempted to account for the institution of a new law, or a major change in interpretation of an old, as a result of a new group gaining political power. The most notable are Jerome Hall's *Theft, Law and Society* and Jeffery's 'The Development of Crime in Early English Society'. Since these have been reviewed elsewhere (Quinney) I will discuss instead another example.

Cook's study was an analysis of Canadian narcotics legislation with the use of conflict theory. The penalties set for drug possession in the 1920s reflected very accurately the relative *power* of particular users, and not the objective *dangers* of the drugs. The most dangerous drugs were addicting patent medicines, largely used by the middle class. These were not included in the legislation, despite arguments by members of Parliament, who were themselves physicians, as to their dangers. The most severe penalties were for opium, which was used almost exclusively by Chinese, at that time not even citizens.

QUINNEY: CONTEMPORARY CONFLICT THEORY

Quinney's *Social Reality of Crime* is a comprehensive theory of crime and social control, and the main source of conflict theory to be used in this study. All the components of law, sanctions and behaviour were considered, indeed with roughly equal attention to each. The links between the components were carefully specified. Phenomenological work was used, along with more conventional social psychology, in making the connections. The role of power, in relation to conflicting interests, was stressed at each stage of the process in determining the nature of criminal law, overseeing its enforcement and ultimately in affecting behaviour patterns. Quinney as well worked on a fourth component, conceptualizations of deviance, showing how this, too, was affected by power. Numerous factors apart from power considerations were introduced at each stage, so that the joint effects of these factors and power could be assessed.

The theory was based on a notion of crime as defined behaviour, 'created by authorized agents in a politically organized society' (p. 15). Criminal definitions described behaviour that conflicted with the interests of the segments of society having the power to shape public policy.

The greater the conflict of interest between the segments of a society, the greater the probability that the power segments would formulate criminal definitions. The notion is sharply at odds with the consensus position, in which law reflects agreement over major values and, in functionalist versions, as well serves to reduce or mitigate conflict. Law changed in response to the interests of the powerful, and so in time was affected by the factors that determined them. Hence changing social conditions, emerging interests, increased demands that political, economic and religious interests be protected, and changing conceptions of public interests could all have an impact.

At the next stage, it was stated that criminal definitions were applied by segments of society having the power to shape the administration of the criminal law, hence the probability criminal definitions would be applied varied to the extent that behaviours conflicted with the interests of the power segment. The holders of power did not personally administer the law, but delegated its administration to authorized agents who represented them—the police, courts, and correctional agencies. To the extent that there was delegation there could be variation in interpretation. Community expectations of law enforcement, visibility of offences, public reporting of offences, and the ideology of legal agents themselves all could have an effect (p. 19). The probability of criminal definitions being applied in specific situations depended on evaluations made by those agents. Their views of 'criminal behaviour', in general, and their assessment of the situation at hand affected these decisions. Labelling theory was drawn on generously here, to explain criteria used.

Behaviour patterns were affected in two principal ways. Firstly, behaviour varied across the segments of society. The holders of power were more likely to define as criminal the behaviour of *other* segments. Hence members of unpowerful segments were more likely to commit criminal acts simply by following patterns normal to them. Secondly, people were affected by labelling. People had conceptions of themselves as social beings, anticipated consequences to their actions, and acted accordingly. People who were defined as criminal, then, began to see themselves as criminal, or to learn to play the role of the criminal (p. 22).

Conceptions of crime were the last component, bringing the scheme full circle. Individuals were said to create their own social reality, and then act in reference to it. Their conceptions reflected the communications they received personally, and through the mass media. Communications, in turn, and especially the mass media, were affected by the power segments. The more the power segments were concerned about criminality, which depended on conflicting interests, the greater the probability that criminal definitions would be created and behaviour patterned accordingly. Quinney's account began with the creation of and changes in the law, went on to law enforcement and then to actual behaviour and conceptualizations. Yet he stressed throughout that all other directions of influence were possible as well—behaviour affecting the formulation of law, conceptions of crime affecting enforcement and so forth.

Quinney's supporting arguments were based almost entirely on American material, and most of it fairly recent. The supporting evidence was of the case analysis type. Changes of legislation were accounted for in terms of new groups gaining power, pressing their interests successfully over others. Examples from the literature on enforcement showed how the interests of the powerful were translated into day to day decisions to enforce the law. The literature on labelling was used to show how individuals, on being sanctioned, began to acquire views of themselves as deviants, were cut off from contacts with the respectable world, and became increasingly identified with visible deviant subcultures.

Quinney's documentation was relatively extensive, but does not constitute empirical testing. In a literature as vast as deviance examples can be found to support virtually any argument and case analyses are particularly weak evidence. For any change in the law *some* kind of conflict of interest could be found which could be said to account for it. This, however, is not to say that the theory is untestable. Indeed, certain propositions will be tested from it in this study.

CONFLICT THEORY IN THE SOVIET UNION
My discussion of conflict theory in the Soviet Union is confined to secondary sources, and mainly Peter Solomon's *Soviet Criminology*. This very useful account includes a brief overview of developments from the revolution, with more detailed discussion of the chief later

writers. Soon after Soviet government was established, social factors began to replace biological and psychological as causes of crime. The change was a substantial one, for Russia had been one of the countries where the Italian school had been most successful. Psychological work before the revolution had been heavily physiological in orientation. Now biological theories were actively opposed, and psychological, as lying somewhere between social and biological, were a matter of dispute. Before long, psychological theories were rejected as well. In 1929 all psychological study of crime was banned, including social psychology (p. 29). A few years later, sociological study was banned as well. The only explanation permitted as a cause of crime was the role of enemy social classes.

De-Stalinization in the 1950s meant greater latitude in the study of crime. The ban on psychology continued, but social factors re-emerged as legitimate causes. In time, psychological factors, too, reappeared. A number of scholars began to revive them, stressing their role as mechanisms through which social conditions had their effect. Nevertheless, the enemy class theory did not disappear and capitalistic institutions remained as prominent factors in most explanations. Theorists differed as to what aspects of capitalism were the most conducive to crime, such as 'remnants' of pre-revolutionary institutions, the example of, or contact with, contemporary capitalist societies.

A. B. Sakharov's theory went further still, while not neglecting the remnants of capitalism, incorporating a wide range of social factors, and channelling the explanation through the individual. The genesis of crime lay ultimately in the individual, so that to understand causation one had to account, at some stage, for behaviour—people's attitudes, motives and temperament. Economic causes were important for their effect on individuals, but did not affect everyone equally. A comprehensive theory, including both individual factors, social problems, and the broad pressures of capitalistic institutions, was required to explain crime.

The theory was organized around two causal chains, one through objective circumstances affecting the likelihood of a criminal act, the other through subjective circumstances, including anti-social views on the part of the offender. Both were then extended back to broad economic, social, and cultural conditions, among which were the ever-present remnants. A number of objective circumstances were possible factors: administrative errors, bureaucratic organization of work and leisure, behaviour of others, alcoholism, the effects of legislation against crime, and practical measures in the fight against crime. At the subjective level, the gravity of the offence, anti-social views, psychological peculiarities and temperament were all factors. These were then said to be affected by processes of socialization, which involved another list of factors. Family conditioning and up-bringing, schooling, social work and the production collective, everyday surroundings, and general cultural and educational level were all influences to be considered. Behind both causal chains were several fundamental social-cultural factors. Consciousness could lag behind objective conditions so that, while a socialist society had been established, consciousness of this might not have fully permeated the population. The existence of the capitalist world was an ongoing cause, providing bad examples and opportunities for economic crimes and corrupting influences. Material inequities, which still existed, were another fundamental potential factor.

Sakharov's theory was attacked as crudely individualistic, biological-psychological. It is too early to say what the long-term outcome will be, but certainly the theory has survived initial criticism. Other work, on similar lines, is under way. Psychological study began again in 1965, largely oriented to social psychology. Sakharov's defence of psychological research, not so incidentally, was based on its usefulness for purposes of rehabilitative work. There does not seem to have been any explicit empirical testing of the theory, or any other. Very little data on crime and sanctions are published in the Soviet Union so there is little opportunity for outside researchers to do any actual data analysis. Some work has been published showing associations between official crime and social problems.[1]

The convergence of work between western and Soviet scholars has been much remarked on, notably the move to social systems conceptualizations among Soviet.[2] The move has indeed been so great in the case of theory on crime to raise doubts as to whether Soviet theory is still in the conflict orientation at all. Certainly their conceptualization of the criminal act, and the relationship between criminal behaviour and law depart considerably from those of the early Marxists. Crime now tends to be treated in the same fashion as in western consensus theory, signifying violation of a society's most

1. For other work in English see Connor, Shargorodski, Djekebaev, International Social Science Council and *Current Digest of the Soviet Press*.
2. Gouldner.

important norms. Agreement on these norms is effectively assumed to be universal and, accordingly, what is crime non-problematic. The remnants explanation is a conservative, culture lag explanation, and it remains important in the theory. The remnants are attributed to a factor of power, but it is the power held by the capitalists in the past that is crucial, and not the present.

Studies of changes in the criminal law since the Communists gained power have been strongly supportive of conflict theory. The changes themselves have been numerous and complicated, but the fundamental changes made reflect the changed interests of the holders of power. Economic crimes, crimes against currency and the black market were important when the government began to build a socialist society, and eradicate the capitalism of the tsarist past. Ordinary crime, like murder and rape, became, by comparison, less important. The most threatening offences were in the economic realm, hence the severest penalties were reserved for them. Ordinary murderers began to get relatively short prison terms and sentences to labour colonies, although this was later changed as a result of unfavourable public opinion.[1]

THE MAIN THEMES

Conflict theory emerged in the eighteenth century as the theory of economic determinism. Poverty was the central causal factor, often with unemployment, or as a result of unemployment. The two signified a lack of useful activity, resulting in general demoralization. Drunkenness might be an intermediate factor influencing criminal behaviour. Poverty and unemployment were clearly related to unjust, unequal distribution of power or accumulated wealth. Often the institution of private property was blamed, even in very early accounts. The holders of power, however defined, were said to use criminal law, among other things, to preserve their privileges. They formulated laws with this objective and insured that they were enforced to their own advantage.

Consensus theory seems to have been less precisely stated in this early period. As the theory of the conventional wisdom it needed neither precise formulation nor careful empirical work to be believed. As propositions to the contrary began to be entertained seriously,

1. Berman. For an account of changes in Chinese law see Cohen, *Criminal Process in China*.

however, consensus advocates had to compete with formulations of
their own. One can only speculate as to what motivated anyone at
any time, but certainly much of the early consensus theorizing was a
response to the economic determinism arguments of the conflict
writers. The pre-sociological themes of immorality, idleness and
ignorance evolved into sociological propositions. Lack of education,
and especially moral education, was typically the chief cause.
Idleness was a subsidiary cause, which implied unemployment, but
poverty itself was resisted as an explanation. Poverty was sometimes
described as a *result* of crime, or both were the consequences of a
more general idleness, seen as an inherent characteristic or vice.
Drunkenness, too, was often a related cause, again typically as a vice,
and not a product of poverty, or something to blame on the oppression of the rich or propertied.

Theory of law was even slower to be secularized than behaviour.
It began as something revealed by a western male deity, in time to
evolve into the workings of the 'moral instinct', which might or
might not have divine connections. Law, either way, functioned for
the common good. The relationship between behaviour and law was
typically seen as very close. Law was commonly conceived of as
a generalization of ethical behaviour. People saw the desirability
of good behaviour and made it obligatory. To account for the
nature of behaviour was eventually to explain the nature of the
law.

Conflict theory was further elaborated in the nineteenth century,
but very much on the same lines. Many intermediate variables were
added, and a variety of causal chains linking inequalities in power to
ultimate behaviour was carefully specified. The basic Marxian
explanation of law was formulated at mid-century. Law was an
element of superstructure, reflecting the nature of the social relations
of production of the time.

Differentiation and elaboration within consensus theory was
prodigious. Distinctive schools emerged, based on the relative
weight given individual and social level pathologies. Numerous social
and economic problems were included in the sociological school,
although there was still a reluctance to admit the central economic
variable of poverty. Problems at the level of the total society—
industrialization, urbanization, religious crises and associated anomie
—became important late in the century as explanations of crime.
Common to all these approaches was the assumption that the crime

rate continued to increase, despite growing prosperity—hence the concentration on non-economic factors.

There was a vast growth of biological theory, at the same time, so that explanations came to include any imaginable intellectual deficiency, disorder or glandular disturbance. Numerous physical factors were incorporated in the explanations as well, from the quality of soil, food, temperature and electrical storms—a vast elaboration from the brief comments on climate of earlier work. Again the assumption was that economic conditions were not causal factors. Theory of evolution provided the broad theoretical base for the school and one sub-school used atavism to account for the supposed continued growth of crime in the face of the refinement of the moral instinct. Evolution theory provided the stimulation to theorizing in law and sanctions as well—societies succeeding in eliciting co-operative behaviour among their members surviving better than societies which did not.

In the twentieth century an important switch took place between the theories. After World War I economic variables lost favour in conflict explanations to become respectable enough for consensus theory, at least in modified form. Ironically, this reliance on economic factors came when they began to lose their effectiveness. Or, consensus theorists rejected economic causes when the best evidence indicates they worked, to accept them when they were no longer applicable. But conflict theorists came to realize their obsolescence, at least for industrial societies, to turn instead to the role of official agencies in eliciting and shaping criminal behaviour. In consensus theory expansion and differentiation continued, in individual pathologies, various levels of social problems, and total societal problems as well. Biological theories, especially those stressing overt physical differences, lost ground, to assume rather a fringe status. They were replaced by much less esoteric theories of intellectual and physical deficiencies. Explanations at the level of societal structure remained important with theories of alienation joining anomie. Parsons's formulation of consensus theory brought together *all* levels of causation. Deficiences at any level could be causes of deviance, as well as disjunctions between any elements of the system. In both conflict and consensus theory increased attention was paid to the processes by which criminal behaviour was acquired and transmitted. In both as well there was considerable elaboration and precision in explanations of law, but with little change in substance.

CHOICE OF VARIABLES

A vast number of particular variables appeared in the course of the
review, many of them, like alcoholism and poor education, in both
theory types at the same time. Certain variables, notably economic
conditions, were involved in a very important change of camps. It
was not the substance of the variables themselves that differentiated
the two orientations, but how they were used and, more particularly,
how they were related to power. In this respect the differences
between the two theories were consistent. In conflict theory, poverty,
unemployment, alcoholism and poor home life were treated as the
results of other inequalities, intermediate in the causal chain leading
to criminal behaviour. When used in consensus theory, some further
explanation for them might or might not be offered, but in either
case, they were fundamental factors influencing criminal behaviour.
Differences in inherited wealth, or education, that might account
for later poverty or prosperity amounted to very much the same
thing. These were treated themselves as reflecting differences in
innate qualities, hard work and general merit. Power either played a
very subsidiary role, or none at all.

MATERIAL CONDITIONS VERSUS IDEAS IN EXPLANATION

Initially conflict theorists were undeniably materialistic. They emphasized absolute want and miserable living conditions as the fore-
most causes of crime, showing how they affected individual attitudes
and beliefs. Misery and want had a 'demoralizing' effect. In some
cases hypothesized causes were simple, external forces, but this was
rare. For most theorists material conditions had their effect through
ideas, 'reason' and 'understanding'.

Among consensus theorists of the same period there were some
who opposed *all* material conditions as potential causes of crime, no
matter how indirect their effect might be. Others treated material
conditions as part of the explanation, typically reflecting underlying
moral worth. Material conditions could then be an intermediate
factor, as ideas were in conflict explanations.

Gradually material conditions began to be accepted by consensus
theorists, certainly as reflecting more than moral worth, but still not
in the same way as in conflict theory. This is clear when one examines
how material conditions were used in Italian school explanations.
The moral component was still the predominant factor. Physical
factors, such as organic brain disease, served to explain *what went*

wrong, or what prevented the moral instinct from working. In the normal course of events people were effectively guided by the moral instinct, so that criminal behaviour represented something amiss. It, indeed, took something of the order of epilepsy to overcome it. In the case of atavism, again the moral instinct was accorded full powers. Now the explanation was that criminals were acting in accordance with the moral instinct of an earlier period of evolution. Material conditions, in other words, were used only to explain *defects* in the system. In conflict theory, they were an integral part of the explanations. Certain consensus theorists were still not prepared to accept *any* substantial role for material conditions. This 'spiritualist' school was a minority in the nineteenth century, but still a vociferous minority.

The debate always involved something of a crusade against godless materialism and, with Marx, this rather intensified. What is important with his formulation, however, was that it made explicit what was only implicit in the eighteenth-century conceptualization. This makes possible a much more precise comparison with consensus theory. Fundamentally, Marx related an infrastructure of relations of production to a superstructure of cultural elements. The critical level for purposes of causation was the social. Physical factors, including climate, soil, the flow of rivers, and anything else the Italian school might like to add, could have a part in the explanation, but in the distant past. These conditions determined the nature of the society's economy, what it produced and how. Productive relations then affected all others. Marx did not exclude the possibility of these physical factors having direct effects, but clearly he saw social matters as more important. Engels and the other major Marxist writers consistently showed this same orientation.

The commitment Marxist and other conflict writers had to social level causes can be seen in the attacks made on theorists who deviated. Ferri was one notable offender, and he was treated with contempt by Marxist writers. Kropotkin was ignored rather than attacked, but certainly he met with no favour. After the revolution in Russia, biological theories were actually banned. The ban has since been lifted, but there is still strong resistance to non-social elements among the purer theorists. In the west, there are contemporary writers who urge complete rejection of all physical factors as causes, whether environmental conditions or individual physical make-up.

With Parsons's development of the social system the full extent of the contrasts between the two approaches can be seen, as can the similarities. Shyness about admitting the material world was now an aberration of the past. Both the physical environment and the human biological system were themselves systems in the scheme, interacting with the social and cultural. The hierarchical structure of the elements was the same as in dialectical materialism. In both, ideas were placed at the top, as 'culture' in Parsons, as 'superstructure' in Marx. The political level was intermediate in both, and the economic beneath it. The order of the social system components has been described as beginning with those 'rich in information' to those 'rich in energy'.[1] Parsons allowed that all elements affected all others, as did Marx, somewhat differently, in his dialectical formulation. Nevertheless, for each, there was one primordial direction of influence, from bottom up for Marx, and from top down for Parsons. Again, the contrast is not between elements of the theories, but how they are treated.

The different choice of elements makes sense also in terms of the goals associated with the various approaches. Radical conflict theorists have believed that social and economic conditions could be changed with revolution, that crime would eventually disappear. Reform-orientated theorists have had milder aspirations, but have still hoped to reduce crime through the elimination of poverty, improvement of working conditions, education and so forth. Theories of crime based on congenital defects and immutable factors like climate are inconsistent with both these hopes. Within the consensus orientation, as well, there have been varying orientations to change. Theorists who were relatively reform-minded have preferred social level explanations, more in line with conflict theory.

EMPIRICAL WORK IN THE TWO TRADITIONS

The great bulk of the empirical literature has been associated with consensus theory. Consensus supporters have themselves done great quantities of work, and most research has been interpreted as supporting some or other consensus explanation. Conflict theorists have much more relied on criticism and re-interpretation of results than on conducting their own studies. The pattern is so marked that some critics have inferred a disdain on the part of conflict theorists for empirical work. The reason for the differing performance in research lies both in differences between the theories' propositions,

1. Rocher, *Introduction à la Sociologie Générale.*

and institutional opportunities proponents have had for doing research.

Firstly, for conflict theorists, behaviour has rarely had the fascination it holds for consensus theorists. Criminal behaviour could be accounted for in social and economic inequalities and these were crucial to study. For consensus theorists, on the other hand, behaviour was real and important. Behaviour ultimately shaped law and enforcement and, accordingly, whatever affected behaviour helped to explain law and sanctions. Consensus proponents had more to gain from empirical work than conflict.

All of this becomes even more evident when the careers of conflict and consensus adherents are compared, especially relative portions of them devoted to research work. For conflict theorists, work on criminal behaviour was peripheral to their main life's interests. They explored some aspect of behaviour, but, having said their piece, they moved on. None of the conflict theorists were professionals. Ducpétiaux, after one short, empirical paper, turned to studies of poverty and prison conditions, working as a civil servant to better conditions for prisoners. Flora Tristan began organizing her *Union ouvrière*. Jane Addams theorized to solve problems of practical importance to her work. Owen wrote on many other subjects besides law and crime, and was a leading organizer of the co-operative movement. Marx's and Engels's other works, academic and organizational, need hardly be commented on. Kropotkin's *curriculum vitae* is perhaps the least humdrum of them all, and of this, law and social control form only a small part. Bonger, who became a law professor after his first study, is the exception that proves the rule. After he became a professional he moved to a consensus position.

Consensus advocates, on the other hand, were largely full-time academics and practitioners, mainly doctors and judges. Among the more notable academics were Durkheim, Tarde, Ferri (also a politician), Ferguson, Pound, Sorokin, the Chicago school sociologists, and in more recent years, Parsons, Merton, Cloward and Ohlin, Eysenck, Cohen, and the Gluecks. Judges include Montesquieu, Colquhoun and Garofalo, All the early psychiatric theorists were doctors, many of them, like Lombroso, Thomson, Lauvergne and Goring, practising in prisons.[1] The studies on intelligence and crime were conducted largely by psychologists, who, along with social workers, did many of the studies on disturbed family relations as well.

1. Kropotkin also practised in prison—escaping.

Altogether the vast majority of consensus theory advocates had extensive institutional ties with their subject matter. There have been few exceptions: Adam Smith was a civil servant, Herbert Spencer an engineer, Quetelet a statistician and Darwin a biologist.

The vast empirical studies conducted were very much part of the daily work of the various contributors, done in the course of earning their livelihood. Moreover, they could not have been done any other way. Lombroso's original documentation of the born criminal thesis, for example, required measurements of up to 5,000 individuals, as did Goring's refutation decades later, with 3,000 subjects. Studies of any size requiring access to prisoners, confidential records, school children and so forth require at least the approval, if not the active support, of government departments. Government authorities can veto projects in view of their political implications, and often do. Even today, and even in liberal countries like Canada and the United Kingdom, governments refuse permission for research not sufficiently supportive of the *status quo*, and suppress unexpectedly non-conforming results. It is not that conflict adherents have had any principled objection to empirical work, but that they have not had the opportunity to do most of the kinds of work necessary.

The review of the literature ends with a number of unresolved issues: questions within both traditions and the fundamental dispute between them. Most important, for our purposes, is the contemporary debate between social and economic problems in consensus theory and the needs and resources for control in conflict. This will be the main focus in the empirical testing to follow. Questions as to *which* problems and *what sorts* of means will be explored in the context of problems or needs and resources at all. The issue of rising crime and size of the forces of order will be considered as particular issues within this larger perspective.

The focus will be on the macro level, since this is where the contentious issues are. I will not be investigating what types of people are more likely to commit acts believed to be criminal, for certain factors have been well established as having some effect—notably age, sex, education, marital status and ethnicity and, more debatably, social class. Nor do I wish to pursue the issue of what types of people are more likely to be charged, convicted or otherwise punished for offences, for these, the answers are only too well known: the poor, especially the unemployed, young, males, and persons of low ethnic status. I do not wish to add another study to the literature showing just that, and it seems unlikely that any other results could appear. The focus instead will be at the *societal* level, the ability of social and economic problems to explain levels of official crime and social control across whole societies, in comparison with indicators of the need, and social and economic resources available to the holders of power for control purposes.

PART II

Testing General Theories

Chapter 5

THEORY TESTING
WITH THE NATION-STATE

The concern of these next three chapters is the empirical testing of propositions drawn from conflict and consensus theory. The objective was to conduct a reasonable number of tests on what seemed to be the more important theoretical issues susceptible to empirical investigation under current conditions. The tests were designed as much as possible to permit comparison of results from the two theories, in that findings favourable to one theory would be disconfirming of the other. The intention was to show not only in what way each theory was supported and contradicted, but to relate the success and failure of each to the other. On the basis of these conclusions convergence between the theories will be considered, and the appropriateness of using *either* as a framework for analysis or a set of assumptions. These next three chapters as well explore the factual basis for the belief in crime as a serious and growing problem, requiring strengthening of the forces of order for its solution.

The main guiding principle to the whole enterprise was diversity in testing. Given the generality of the theories, the testing had to be broad. It was important not to base conclusions on small and perhaps atypical samples of atypical periods. Data can always be criticized for being inadequate, and results favourable to a theory a figment of the peculiarities of the data. The contention becomes less appropriate, however, when the range of indicators is broad, the time period long, the sources of data and methods of analysis varied. The empirical tests were constructed so as to embrace a good range of indicators, drawing on a number of distinctive data sources and covering the more important points with several different methods of analysis.

The choice of the level of the units of analysis was crucial. Perhaps the chief complaint with the existing empirical literature concerned inadequacies in units chosen. Typically the nature of the data collected permitted only the assessment of certain consensus-type hypotheses—relative to other consensus-type hypotheses. Insofar as variation in the power structure, legal and enforcement systems is restricted the possibility of the effects of these appearing is limited. In the extreme case, of data pertaining to only one sector of society, the possibility of the effect of conflict propositions appearing is completely excluded, the typical case in the empirical literature. It was important to choose units such that the elements of *both* conflict and consensus theory varied adequately. For conflict theory this meant units for which the power structure, legal and enforcement systems varied, and for this the nation–state is clearly the best choice. Social and economic conditions also vary substantially by country, making the nation–state level appropriate also for consensus theory, although other levels, higher and lower, would be acceptable too. An important consideration, the nation–state level is the one with the most available data. Data on sanctions are reported extensively by country, as are social, economic and political data. The nation–state level, in sum, was the best choice from the point of view of theoretical and practical considerations, and most of the analysis was based on it.

The hypotheses deal with the level and nature of *sanctions* imposed, as indicated by official rates of court convictions, police reports of offences and sentences. The place of sanctions in the two theories— what determines them and what their results are—differs sharply between the two theories and the causal chains vary as well within the two broad theory types. Desirably one would investigate the various stages of the various causal chains proposed, but this was not possible. Rather the better part of the causal processes theorized has to be treated as part of the 'black box', and the testing limited to the end results. What was actually tested was simply the relationship between the nature of the power structure and social and economic conditions, on the one hand, and sanctions, on the other. We are able to assess the relative success of the two theories in their predictions for sanctions, then, but without being able to say whether either theory had any effect in the *way* predicted.

In consensus theory sanctions are theorized to arise in response to criminal behaviour and, hence, to vary in nature and level with such behaviour. Criminal behaviour, in the theory, was determined by problems of some kind and, if the empirical evidence of past studies is a guide, by social and economic problems. The nature and level of sanctions actually occurring should then ultimately reflect the nature and extent of social and economic problems posed. More concretely, societies with extensive social and economic problems should have higher rates of official crime than societies with lesser problems. There may be some lag between the appearance of new problems, resulting increases in criminal behaviour and, in turn, in sanctions. Similarly, there may be a lag between the disappearance of problems, the consequent reduction of criminal behaviour, and sanctions meted out. In general, however, and in the long run, consensus theory holds that there will be an important, positive correlation between problems and sanctions.

In conflict theory, by contrast, the nature and level of sanctions occurring is held to be determined ultimately by the holders of power, in accordance with their needs and the resources at their command. In earlier versions the causal chain went through real criminal behaviour, so that sanctions, at least in part, reflected real social and economic problems. These social and economic problems were held to be in large measure the product of bad laws and inequalities, and thus were ultimately the responsibility of the holders of power. In later versions the role of real criminal behaviour was minimized. The crucial factors were the needs of, and resources available to, the holders of power, and the extent to which real behaviour played a role was not important.

The causal chains linking sanctions with the other components were radically different between the two theories, so that it is unfortunate that the empirical testing does not permit judgement as to the stage either theory was right or wrong. Only the overall results are known—the correspondence between power and sanctions on the one hand, and between social and economic conditions and sanctions on the other. Strong and consistent results favourable to a theory can reasonably be treated as supportive of that theory's causal chain.

Positive results suggest that the process hypothesized was right at least somewhere along the line—although not necessarily everywhere. Results contrary to a theory similarly indicate that the theory was wrong, again not necessarily at every stage.

EMPIRICAL TESTING

The first project of empirical testing involved a comparison of official crime statistics across a range of societies. The objective was to test the major versions of both theories as they developed from the eighteenth century on. It may seem pedantic to begin the testing with the earliest versions, but there are reasons for doing this, apart from an obsession with chronological order and a desire for completeness. The eighteenth-century explanations never entirely disappeared, but surface from time to time even in contemporary works. Other later versions involve only modest revisions, so that these initial tests serve also as approximate tests of the later.

DATA

The data for the dependent variables were drawn from two sources—the International Criminal Police Organization, for the bulk of the indicators, and the United Nations, for one indicator only, on juvenile court convictions.[1] The Interpol data were all obtained from the regular publications of that organization, based on reports submitted by member governments. The statistics used were of numbers of offenders; Interpol also publishes data on numbers of offences, but these are less adequate as indicators of sanctions, and less complete as well. There was one indicator for theft offenders (major and minor larceny in Interpol terminology), one for property offenders (including both theft offences, fraud and counterfeiting), and the total number of offenders. The total number of juvenile offenders was the fourth indicator, the age limit for juvenile depending on the age limit in the society concerned. The last of the Interpol indicators was the number of murderers and, if an indicator of sanctions at all, a very distant one. It was included rather for the testing of problem-oriented theories, so that the patterns of results found could be compared with those for property offences. Since these have typically been found to differ enormously, it seemed important to explore both types of offence and compare the results.

The objective throughout was to include as many countries as possible in the analysis. Countries reporting only partial sets of data were included for those portions of the analysis for which data were available. Altogether forty countries were used at some stage or another, covering 38 per cent of the world's population. European countries were over-represented in the study with fifteen countries, compared with eleven Asian, seven African, three Oceanic, two North American, and two South American. No Communist countries report data to Interpol. The rates were taken from the early 1960s

1. See Technical Note pp. 293–6 for the exact data sources.

and consist of the averages for the years 1961–6 where possible, or for whatever four- or five-year period was available from between 1960 and 1966, if the full series was not. All figures were deflated by population aged 10–40, the population most at risk for criminal behaviour and sanctioning. The averaged rates were then normalized and standardized.[1] The actual rates of total offenders are shown in Table 5:1, for each country, ranked from highest to lowest.

Table 5:1 *Total Rate of Offenders per Country*

Guyana	14,582	Cyprus	996
Japan	7,469	Philippines	993
Australia	7,284	Italy	988
Austria	6,465	United Kingdom	966
Aden	5,621	Ceylon	658
Israel	5,025	Norway	637
Thailand	4,519	Portugal	603
Finland	4,439	Morocco	593
Federal Republic		Ghana	585
of Germany	4,032	Malawi	549
Fiji	3,816	Formosa	399
Libya	3,707	Pakistan	364
Luxembourg	2,808	Denmark	340
Canada	2,692	Peru	260
France	2,303	Spain	174
Burma	2,120	Madagascar	151
Jamaica	1,953	Nigeria	134
Tunisia	1,751	India	117
Netherlands	1,569	New Zealand	n.d.
Hong Kong	1,274	Ireland	n.d.
Sweden	1,027		

Rates of total reported offenders per 100,000 population aged ten–forty, averaged for the years 1961–6.

In view of the premium placed on diversity in testing some trouble was taken to find another distinctive data source for the tests, for which United Nations juvenile court data were eventually settled on. This meant an extension of the testing to a slightly earlier time period (early post-war), and to a different level of sanctioning, now court convictions instead of police reports. It also meant a substantially different set of countries, for only half the countries

1. Edwards, *Statistical Methods for the Behavioral Sciences.*

were also part of the Interpol set.[1] The main drawback with the new data set was its quality, so suspect that it was only not to rely on only one data source that it was used at all. Briefly, the data were drawn from three United Nations publications, none of which was devoted to serious, ongoing data publication. Further, none was intended to be comparable with the others. The method of reporting was not described in detail in any of them, and a request for clarification went unanswered. The data on which the published figures were based were 'unfortunately not available'.

Thirty-one countries, including a quarter of the world's population,

Table 5:2 *Juvenile Court Convictions per Country*

Hong Kong	2,328·6	Canada	155·9
United States	769·9	Italy	153·3
Bermuda	690·5	Mauritius	152·0
British Honduras	440·0	France	146·3
Finland	432·5	Democratic Republic	
Barbados	386·6	of Germany	145·1
Austria	381·6	Greece	125·3
United Kingdom	349·1	Sweden	111·9
Jordan	311·2	Formosa	77·3
Japan	242·2	Belgium	74·5
Federal Republic		Singapore	69·7
of Germany	236·5	Fiji	61·8
Guyana	197·6	Yugoslavia	44·6
Turkey	189·1	Zanzibar	42·3
South Africa	186·9	Uganda	12·1
United Arab		Madagascar	10·0
Republic	160·3	Iraq	4·2

Rates per 100,000 population <20, averaged over the years 1946–56.

were included in some part of the analysis or other. Europe was again over-represented, with eleven countries, including Yugoslavia and East Germany. Otherwise, there were seven African countries, six Asian, five North American and one each from South America and Oceania. The rates were averaged from whatever years were available from the early 1950s, in most cases only two or three years.[2] No rates were based on only one year. The rates were all deflated by

1. Strictly speaking, it is 'countries and non-self-governing territories which report data separately' for not all the units were, at the time the data were collected, independent countries.
2. In the case of Morocco the years 1946 and 1956 were used.

population under twenty, and normalized and standardized in the same way as for the Interpol set. The range of the raw rates was immense, from over 2,000 per 100,000 population in the case of Hong Kong[1] and over 700 for the United States, to only ten and four per 100,000 respectively for Madagascar and Iraq.

Use of the United Nations data also meant the addition of another indicator of sanctions of juveniles, an important consideration in my view. The value of the data from the point of view of conflict theory lies in the greater extent of discretion typically permitted officials in dealing with juvenile delinquency. In most societies far more behaviour is unlawful for children than adults—failure to attend school, use of tobacco and alcohol and often, at least for girls, love-making. 'Incorrigibility' offences may be so broadly defined that virtually all children qualify at some time or another, if not every day. As a result, the number of children who go to court reflects subjective judgements to a great extent, and latitude in discretion is a virtue of the system. In short, since the authorities have much more power to determine the level of sanctions in the case of children than adults, data on juveniles should be even better as an indicator on sanctions than data on adults.

For consensus theory, as well, there were several good reasons for preferring data on children. Throughout the history of both theories, the special vulnerability of children, to whatever problems were considered to cause criminality, was stressed. Many have argued criminality in children to be more serious than in adults, and this has become the progressive view in corrections. If it is correct, an increase in social problems should affect children more than adults, meaning a more rapid increase in real crime among children than adults. Insofar as the view is *accepted*, the rates of official crime should also be affected. An increase in real crime among children would be responded to more vigorously and quickly than an increase among adults. As a result, the rate of official crime should be a closer approximation of real crime for children than adults, and better reflect the real problems conducive to crime.

The United Nations data all pertain to the early 1950s, or a period ten years earlier than the Interpol set, and a difference involving both advantages and disadvantages. A clear advantage, the difference in period meant a real extension of the tests, so that hypotheses

1. The high rate for Hong Kong includes a substantial number of trivial infractions, such as hawking without a pedlar's licence.

supported by tests from both periods could be accorded greater weight than hypotheses supported from only one or the other. On the other hand, much less data on the explanatory variables were available for the early 1950s. This meant that, wherever data for the earlier years could not be obtained, data from the Interpol period had to be substituted. Hence weaker relationships have to be expected in the tests involving the juvenile court data, simply on account of inadequacies in the explanatory variable indicators. Again, the deficiencies are such as to make us err in a conservative direction. Fewer significant results can be expected from the juvenile court analysis than the Interpol, so that those that do appear will deserve correspondingly stronger acceptance. On the other hand, the juvenile court tests provide less valid grounds for dismissing hypotheses, and relationships just missing the level required for statistical significance should be treated as possibly significant.

HYPOTHESES FROM CONFLICT THEORY

The earliest form of conflict theory to appear was 'economic determinism', with poverty, inequality, and unemployment the three fundamental causes of crime. Five indicators were used to represent these problems. Gross National Product per capita was the main poverty indicator, with the higher the GNP, the lower the poverty, and hence the lower the crime-sanction rates were hypothesized to be. For inequality, two indices were used, the Lorenz index of inter-sectoral inequality, as a proxy for disparities in income, and the Gini index of inequalities in land ownership. The greater the inequality, of course, the greater the real suffering for the poor, and the greater the sense of injustice. The greater the inequality, then, the higher the official crime rate was hypothesized to be. The proportion of the working age population unemployed was the main, and more direct, indicator of unemployment, at the same time also serving as an indicator of poverty and misery more generally. Again, the greater the unemployment, and the lower the proportion of the population gainfully employed, the higher the crime rate was hypothesized to be

Consensus theory was less well developed in this same period, but nevertheless a few concrete hypotheses could be tested. The dominant view was that poverty was *not* a factor and, accordingly, the hypothesis must be of a zero relationship. The two major causes of crime theorized were 'idleness' and 'ignorance', for each of which there were two indicators. The indicators of 'idleness' were the same unemployment and labour force participation rates already specified. What caused 'idleness', of course, differed between the theories, but that it had a deleterious effect on morality was held by both—hence the same indicators apply. The illiteracy rate and the proportion of the school-age population enrolled in school were the indicators of 'ignorance'—the higher the illiteracy rate, and the lower the enrolment, the higher official crime rates were hypothesized to be.

Both theories were considerably elaborated in the nineteenth century. The same variables appearing in the eighteenth-century versions remained, but numerous other causes were added. In the case of conflict theory the emphasis was still on economic variables, but the social consequences of poverty were given prominence as well. Lack of education was treated as an important cause of crime, hence the two indicators already appearing for consensus theory must now be added to the conflict list, the illiteracy rate and the proportion of school-age children enrolled in schools. The pressures of large families, especially given inadequacies in the means to care for them, was stressed by certain theorists. The indicator used for this was the ratio of children to women in the population. Urbanization became a factor in nineteenth-century conflict theory, for its problems of rapid industrialization. Economic fluctuations had more drastic consequences for urban dwellers than rural, hence the rate of crime must be hypothesized to be greater in urban areas. The actual indicator used was the percentage of the population living in cities size 20,000 or greater.[1]

Idleness and ignorance, along with related social problems remained important in certain nineteenth-century versions of consensus theory. Consequently, the schooling, employment and family-size indicators already discussed remain in the nineteenth-century consensus tests. A measure of population increase was added, as a further indicator of both pressures on families and, eventually, on society more broadly. Rapid population increase means an increased burden on all kinds of institutions, including those supposed to prevent and control criminality, like schools and churches.

1. Both *urbanism* (the proportion of the population living in cities) and *urbanization* (the rate of movement to cities) have been cited as causal factors. Urbanization has usually been treated as the more important, as reflecting the problems of dislocation as well as those of city life itself. It was not possible, however, to obtain data on urbanization for enough countries, hence only urbanism has been used.

Problems of heterogeneity in the population and lack of legitimacy of central authorities became important with the emergence of anomie theory. There were three indicators of heterogeneity—religious, linguistic and racial—for all of which the notion was that heterogeneity both causes problems and, through miscommunication, differential perception and disagreement on values and modes of behaviour, makes more difficult their orderly solution. Heterogeneity might be the result of conquest, or migration made necessary by conquest, famine, or any number of other problems. Hence, heterogeneity also serves, if somewhat indirectly, as a proxy for problems of societal breakdown, along the lines of the anomie 'moral crisis' argument. Extent of urbanism was also an indicator of problems in consensus theory, although for different reasons. Now it is part of the anomie argument, representing the breakdown of traditional influences in the village, extended family and religion.

There were several measures dealing with legitimacy.[1] One dichotomized variable rated societies as to whether or not they were conducted in accordance with recognized constitutional norms. Two other indicators concerned stability of the government and the executive respectively. Crime rates were hypothesized to be disproportionately high in societies with unstable governments and executives, and where there was substantial violation of the constitution. The proportion of the population voting in national elections provided another measure of legitimacy—high proportions suggesting broad acceptance of the system on the part of citizens. A related index, comprising extent of voting and other measures of adequacy of representation, was treated in the same way.

In the twentieth century, especially after World War I, conflict theorists began to de-emphasize economic variables in favour of variables of the desire and resources available for formal social control. Criminal behaviour became less and less of a 'real'phenomenon, to be increasingly something defined and labelled as such. The criminal law was written by, and its enforcement directed by, the holders of political and economic power, variously defined. The interests of this power segment—their 'need' for formal control measures—became important criteria determining the official crime rate. The resources available to it, social and economic, were the

1. Legitimacy must be understood in terms of the criteria commonly employed in American political science; the sources used for indicators were Banks and Textor, and Russett and Alker.

other criteria to be considered. The first task was to select indicators of the 'need' for formal control measures, viewed as increasing as traditional, informal measures became less viable. Next a range of indicators was chosen, of existing social machinery for control, experience of formal control in other institutional spheres, and attitudes likely to be accepting of formal control measures. Where possible indicators were selected that represented both the need for control and resources available for it.

The particular indicators selected for the need for formal control were extent of urbanism and paid labour force participation. With a high level of urbanism informal means of control, through the extended family and the village, for example, can be assumed no longer to be viable. Similarly, the higher the proportion of the population in the paid labour force, the less recourse is practicable to informal means of control. Insofar as the authorities seek a disciplined and dutiful population—necessary for a high level of productivity—they will have to resort to formal means. Urbanism and experience in paid employment both also imply greater familiarity with formal bureaucracies, and probably greater acceptance of control measures. Two indicators on the mass media, newspaper circulation and radios per population, were included for similar reasons. Extensive use of mass media suggests the breakdown of informal means of communication and, in its place, greater familiarity with impersonal means of control. The two inequality indicators remain in the twentieth-century consensus tests, for the greater the inequality the greater the real problems for those 'less equal'. The greater these problems are the greater the resentment should be and, in turn, the greater the crime. Whether inequality causes crime or not, the theory holds that with sizeable inequalities, the holders of power must resort to extensive means of repression to maintain their privileges.

The development of bureaucratic machinery for formal control was a major part of twentieth-century conflict theory, for which several indicators were used. Firstly, simple economic resources available for formal control were considered. Formal control measures are expensive, and many countries cannot afford a high rate of sanctions. Per capita GNP was used as the indicator, now the greater the GNP the higher the official crime rate was hypothesized to be. Another indicator was a simple dichotomized attribute on the existence, or not, of an efficient, universalistic bureaucracy.

Next, several indicators on the school system were used—enrolment in schools, as discussed earlier, and enrolment in higher education. As for GNP, the hypothesis was the opposite to earlier versions —now the greater the enrolment, the higher the rate of official crime-sanctions. The rationale for the hypothesis lies in the similarity between education and law enforcement institutions, so that experience in one is applicable to the other. The parallel between schools and prisons is no longer only a school children's joke, but a subject for scholarly work. Guidance counsellors can run a prison classification system, a principal can become a warden and the same firm of architects will do both buildings—and make them look remarkably alike.

The most direct indicator of the means of formal control was the size of the police force. The greater the number of police per population the higher the official sanctions rate was hypothesized to be. Authorities perceiving the need for a high level of formal control can be presumed to consider large numbers of police officers necessary. If resources are available for a large police force, they can be expected to engage, train, supply and otherwise maintain a large force. On the other hand, where either the need is lacking, or not perceived to exist, or financial resources are meagre, or experience of managing large bureaucracies deficient, numbers can be expected to be small.

An index of comprehensiveness in data collection was devised as the last indicator of the means of formal control. The greater the extensiveness of data collection, the higher the rates of sanctions were hypothesized to be. Extensive data collection indicates a good bureaucratic basis for a formal control system. Further, statistics are so obviously needed for the planning of any bureaucracy that extensive data collection can be assumed to indicate the perceived need for such measures. From the point of view of consensus theory, extent of data collection should be negatively related to official crime rates, for data collection is a step in the process of solving problems. It seemed better not to suggest this as a hypothesis, however, for there are even greater difficulties in sorting out cause and effect in this situation than in the case of other variables. A strong, positive relationship could mean only that the societies most proficient at the collection of social data generally, were the most proficient also at the collection of police and court data. For this reason the data collection index was used as well as a control variable. That is, after using it in sets of explanatory variables, it was tested with a range of other sets, both conflict and consensus. This meant that particular conflict and consensus variables could be examined as to their relationship with the dependent variables, controlling for efficiency of the data collection system.

All the social problem variables of nineteenth-century consensus theory were carried over into the twentieth, and a number more were added. Economic problems, including absolute poverty, became acceptable as causes of crime, hence all the indicators of social and economic problems of earlier conflict theory now became a part of consensus. In contrast with twentieth-century conflict theory, the greater the per capita GNP, the *lower* the crime rates were hypothesized to be. Similarly, the greater the participation in the paid labour force, the lower the crime rate should be, again a hypothesis opposite to that of twentieth-century conflict theory. Inequality, large families, rapid population increases, illiteracy, low school enrolment, urbanism, heterogeneity and unconstitutional, unrepresentative and unstable governments all remained as causes of crime and, hence, of official crime rates.[1]

For certain variables, like unemployment, inequality and urbanism, the same relationships were hypothesized for both theories, hence the testing on these points permits only the possibility of joint support or disconfirmation, with no basis for a choice between the theories. For certain important variables, however—extent of schooling, GNP and labour force participation—precisely the opposite relationship was hypothesized between the two theories and, accordingly, results supporting one theory will, at the same time, discredit the other. For several further variables predictions could be made for only one of the theories. For example, several of the problem variables, unemployment and heterogeneity, were used only in tests of consensus theory in the twentieth-century version, since results in

1. The choice of particular indicators is especially difficult when testing theories which arouse as much partisan feeling as these. In the attempt to be fair to consensus theory I consulted Talcott Parsons on the appropriateness of selection, and would like to acknowledge his kind assistance on this task. Interestingly, Professor Parsons did not think it necessary to include level of urbanism in the consensus tests, on the grounds that complexity did not itself necessarily cause strain or make more difficult the resolution of problems. The variable was included nonetheless. As it happened, the *exclusion* of urbanism would have meant even greater disconfirmation of consensus theory than actually occurred. Apart from this point, our views on the choice of indicators, as reasonable proxies for the phenomena in question, concurred.

either direction would be compatible with contemporary conflict theory. The police rate indicator, on the other hand, could be used only for testing conflict theory, for both positive and negative relationships have been suggested by consensus theorists, and there was no obvious way to decide which hypothesis should be used.

The indicators were arranged into a number of different two-variable and three-variable sets. Thus, for each version, of each theory, a number of tests was made, a range of different representations of the concepts investigated. Many of the tests could be treated at the same time as tests of related versions or, with a change in sign, of competing explanations—so the number of tests for any version was in fact greater than that initially specified for it. Each of the four Interpol variables and the one United Nations indicator was regressed in turn on each of these sets. The various combinations were next all tested with the data collection index, in effect using the index as a control variable.

The analysis involves, firstly, consideration of relationships between particular independent variables and the dependent (correct signs and statistical significance). Next, where relationships appeared as predicted, the level of explanation achieved is examined.

AN OVERVIEW OF RESULTS

The results altogether were strongly supportive of twentieth-century conflict explanations. Social problem explanations of all kinds were almost routinely disconfirmed, which means disconfirmation of consensus theory very generally, and disconfirmation of the early versions of conflict.

Most of the social problem indicators, notably poverty (negative GNP), illiteracy, large family size and rapid population increase proved not to be related to the crime indicators as hypothesized. In some cases, notably for poverty and school enrolment, the relationship was clearly in the opposite direction, GNP and enrolment being *positively* related to the crime-sanction indicators. The indicators of heterogeneity and illegitimacy, for anomie theory, were consistently shown not to be related to official crime rates. Apart from urbanism, the only social problem indicator to receive reasonable support was unemployment, a major early conflict indicator, and still a variable consistent with the basic thesis of that approach.

The variables most successful at explaining rates of official crime and sanctions were the indicators of the need for formal control, and economic and social resources for it. That is, urbanism, GNP, and the social machinery for control in the school system, police force, mass media and so forth, were what best explained rates of official crime. The societies with the highest rates of official crime were those which were highly urbanized, rich, had many schools, a modern and efficient central bureaucracy and police force, and extensive reliance on impersonal mass media for communication.

The pattern of results varied across the different crime-sanction indicators. The differences between murder and all the other indicators were especially marked, as expected, and the results on murder are reported separately. Briefly, murder was the only indicator for which social problem variables were at all successful. A number of them were related as predicted by consensus theory. The levels of explanation achieved were, however, considerably lower than those for the regular sanctions indicators.

Level of explanation was highest for the Interpol juvenile offence indicator and next for total property and theft. Explained variance was consistently lower for the indicator of total offenders, and no reasons for this were apparent. For none of the sets was the explained variance on total offenders as high as 40 per cent while on the other variables there were a number of sets explaining over 50 per cent of the variance, and a few even, for juvenile offences, over 60 per cent. The levels of explanation were lower for the juvenile court indicator than for Interpol juvenile offences, as expected; however, the juvenile court indicator was often more successful than the other Interpol indicators, and certainly more than the total crime score.

EIGHTEENTH-CENTURY TESTS

The earliest versions of the two theories were disconfirmed in all of the ways used to examine the data. The data reported in Table 5:3, on four of the combinations examined, show this clearly. From the point of view of individual variables the predictions were either unsubstantiated, or the opposite results appeared. The rate of participation in the paid labour force was not related in any significant way to any of the crime-sanction indicators. Contrary to the conflict prediction, official crime rates varied *with* GNP, or negatively with poverty. Similarly contradictory findings appear with the index on intersectoral inequality, the opposite direction of relationship occur-

Table 5:3 *Eighteenth-Century Conflict Theory*

	direction predicted	Interpol juvenile	Interpol theft	Interpol property	Interpol total	United Nations juvenile court
unemployment	+	·361*	−·054	·023	·218	·284
GNP	−	·612	·677	·691	·397	·294
(R²)		(·536)	(·452)	(·482)	(·241)	(·243)
land inequality	+	−·163	·280	·331*	·122	−·000
GNP	−	·226	·608	·590	·343	·525
(R²)		(·082)	(·419)	(·425)	(·122)	(·276)
intersectoral inequality	+	−·316	−·210	−·182	−·275	−·180
GNP	−	·461	·591	·596	·307	·374
(R²)		(·401)	(·508)	(·489)	(·249)	(·228)
labour force participation	−	·080	·124	·131	·307	·011
GNP	−	·614	·669	·676	·108	·325
		(·372)	(·427)	(·437)	(·092)	(·101)

Note: In the first column the direction of the relationship predicted is noted for each independent variable. Next are reported the betas, with an * for those statistically significant at the ·05 level (one-tail test) in the direction predicted by conflict theory. Relationships statistically significant in the *opposite* direction to prediction are underlined. The proportion of variance explained by the whole set of explanatory variables is indicated in parentheses below.

Table 5:4 *Eighteenth-Century Consensus Theory*

	direction predicted	Interpol				United Nations juvenile court
		juvenile	theft	property	total	
GNP	0	·137	·198	·120	−·067	−·108
illiteracy	+	−·546	−·416	−·523	−·427	·357
(R²)		(·439)	(·344)	(·388)	(·142)	(·197)
school enrolment	−	·640	·531	·563	·565	·473
GNP	0	·089	·102	·082	−·131	·026
(R²)		(·504)	(·378)	(·397)	(·220)	(·244)
unemployment	+	·105	−·203	−·138	·116	·387*
illiteracy	+	−·689	−·704	−·742	−·477	−·353
(R²)		(·548)	(·441)	(·501)	(·284)	(·298)
labour force participation	+	·101	−·010	·045	·020	·162
illiteracy	+	−·633	−·574	−·607	−·345	−·334
(R²)		(·476)	(·324)	(·392)	(·126)	(·089)

Note: The *'s denote betas statistically significant at the ·05 level (one-tail test) in the direction predicted by consensus theory. Relationships statistically significant in the *opposite* direction are underlined. The total amount of variance explained is indicated in the parentheses.

ring. In the case of the land inequality index, the results were mixed. Inequality in land ownership was significantly related, as predicted, to the number of property offenders. On one further indicator, theft offenders, the results were again as predicted, but barely missing the level required for statistical significance. The unemployment rate was significantly related as predicted to the juvenile offender indicator although not to the others.

The findings on consensus theory of the period were similarly dismal. All but one of the predicted findings failed to materialize and, in the case of school enrolment, the opposite results appeared. That is, crime rates were disproportionately high in societies with greater enrolment of school children. One isolated finding mildly supportive of the consensus position appeared in the findings on GNP. The pattern found was of a positive relationship between GNP and the crime rates, already noted as disconfirming of the conflict position. Insofar as the consensus hypothesis is understood simply to be the opposite to the conflict, these results support it. The question of *levels* of explanation is not relevant at this point, for either theory, since the variables failed the more elementary tests on signs. The amounts of variance are all reported, nonetheless, for a number of them are useful in the testing of later conflict theory.

NINETEENTH-CENTURY TESTS

Where the theories of the nineteenth century overlap with those of the eighteenth, the same disconfirmation holds. The basic poverty and inequality indicators have already been found not to have the predicted relationships. Of the new indicators tested, all but two failed to behave as predicted. One of the exceptions, urbanism, was, however, an important one. An element in both conflict and consensus theory, urbanism was positively, consistently and strongly related to the crime-sanctions indicators. Unemployment was related as predicted on one indicator, and the combination of urbanism and unemployment succeeded in explaining roughly half of the variance on several indicators. This was, however, the only combination of nineteenth-century indicators to explain a reasonable proportion of variance. Unemployment and urbanism being used in both conflict and consensus theory of this period, however, this finding does not help in the competitive evaluation of the theories.

Table 5:5 *Nineteenth-Century Conflict Theory*

	direction predicted	Interpol				United Nations
		juvenile	theft	property	total	juvenile court
unemployment	+	·358*	-·039	·039	·233	·395*
urbanism	+	·459*	·461*	·504*	·308	·428
GNP	-	·253	·306	·286	·149	-·067
(R²)		(·617)	(·528)	(·573)	(·276)	(·391)
intersectoral inequality	+	-·206	-·088	-·049	-·222	·192
GNP	-	·196	·309	·289	·205	·047
urbanism	+	·440*	·455*	·495*	·171	·746*
(R²)		(·495)	(·589)	(·585)	(·260)	(·437)
school enrolment	-	·515	·445	·465	·548	·272
urbanism	+	·276	·232	·276	-·040	·505*
GNP	-	-·032	-·024	-·067	-·113	-·128
(R²)		(·509)	(·375)	(·403)	(·193)	(·387)
school enrolment	-	·628	·710	·705	·464	·339
unemployment	+	·165	-·184	-·104	·107	·276
(R²)		(·500)	(·458)	(·463)	(·268)	(·269)
family size	+	-·283	·019	-·061	-·119	·071
urbanism	+	·501*	·318	·361	·136	·533*
GNP	-	·028	·282	·207	·115	·049
(R²)		(·476)	(·304)	(·325)	(·101)	(·275)

See note in Table 5:3.

Table 5:6 *Nineteenth-Century Consensus Theory*

	direction predicted	Interpol				United Nations
		juvenile	theft	property	total	juvenile court
linguistic heterogeneity	+	−·119	·064	−·105	−·193	·090
GNP	−	·447	·258	·224	·157	·004
urbanism	+	·185	·296	·324	·066	·622*
R²		(·438)	(·307)	(·331)	(·121)	(·358)
racial heterogeneity	+	·100	·119	·135	·202	·314*
GNP	−	·194	·239	·209	·133	·078
urbanism	+	·517*	·365	·414*	·215	·525*
R²		(·437)	(·317)	(·340)	(·130)	(·460)
religious heterogeneity	+ +	−·050	·176	·142	·099	·009
urbanism		·482*	·341	·384	·197	·568*
GNP	−	·211	·223	·201	·119	·038
R²		(·431)	(·335)	(·344)	(·104)	(·352)
constitutional status	+ +	−·259	·010	·006	·077	·190
urbanism	+ +	·532*	·527*	·547*	·310	·773*
R²		(·460)	(·273)	(·297)	(·082)	(·546)
unemployment	+ +	·363*	−·018	·059	·250	·375*
urbanism	+ +	·657*	·704*	·731*	·424*	·388
R²		(·593)	(·495)	(·544)	(·268)	(·389)
urbanism	+	·475*	·318	·360	·134	·572*
GNP	−	·224	·271	·245	·190	·046
R²		(·428)	(·304)	(·323)	(·092)	(·363)

See note in Table 5:4

Most of the other new variables were not related as predicted to the dependent variables, as shown in Table 5:6. Crime rates were not higher in societies with rapid population increase or large family size, the predictions of both theories. Nor was there any tendency for them to be higher in societies with relatively heterogeneous populations, in terms of religion, language or race. In the case of the juvenile court data, racial heterogeneity did have the predicted effect, but this was the only exception. The problems of agreement on values and legitimacy in anomie theory received no support in testing. Of three indicators of stability of government two failed to have the predicted effect. Crime rates were not higher in societies with unstable governments or unconstitutional regimes. They were, however, in societies with less stable executives, one of the few findings supportive of consensus theory. The findings were again contrary to consensus theory on two related political indicators, the political representation index and proportion voting in national elections. In both cases high crime-sanction rates were associated with high levels of voting and relatively extensive representation.

TWENTIETH-CENTURY CONFLICT TESTS

Results favourable to conflict theory appeared in a good range of tests. As evident in Table 5:7, individual indicators were related as predicted to the dependent variables in the vast majority of cases. The exceptions that did appear were trivial, very seldom involving a reversal in the direction predicted. Rather, in most cases where the predicted relationship did not appear, the relationship was effectively zero. The indicators for social machinery for control were clearly very successful as predictive variables. This was notably the case for school enrolment, an indicator of effective development of control measures in a related sphere. The data collection index, used in a large number of tests, was significantly related to the crime indicators in most of them. The modernity of bureaucracy indicator had the predicted effect in terms of direction of relationship, but, in the multivariate tests, not to a statistically significant degree. As a single variable, it was significantly related to the dependent variables.

The two political representation indicators also produced the predicted results. The average proportion voting in national elections was significantly related to the crime-rate indicators in most of its tests, as was the measure of political representation. GNP, as an

Table 5:7 *Twentieth-Century Conflict Tests*

	direction predicted	Interpol				United Nations
		juvenile	theft	property	total	juvenile court
police force	+	·102	·075	·169	·269	−·202
data index	+	·524*	·360	·352	·140	·025
urbanism	+	·240	·259	·250	·166	·612*
R²		(·557)	(·357)	(·386)	(·198)	(·362)
police force	+	·088	·056	·148	·253	−·227
GNP	+	·236	·119	·092	−·022	−·364
urbanism	+	·415	·430	·438	·292	·429
R²		(·429)	(·300)	(·330)	(·190)	(·247)
proportion voting	+	·374*	·202	·268	·283	−·187
urbanism	+	·367*	·287	·295*	·115	·690*
data index	+	·211	·226	·198	·050	·247
R²		(·609)	(·364)	(·409)	(·151)	(·598)
proportion voting	+	·421*	·240	·302*	·258	−·145
urbanism	+	·368*	·248	·265	·010	·482*
GNP		·118	·200	·169	·191	−·237
R²		(·587)	(·351)	(·399)	(·163)	(·429)

political representation	+	·375	·293	·364	·302	·502*
urbanism	+	·532*	·479*	·501*	·389	·258
data index	+	-·098	-·060	-·129	-·210	-·010
R²		(·532)	(·419)	(·460)	(·192)	(·467)
modern bureaucracy	-	-·139	-·191	-·311	-·132	·186
urbanism	+	·436*	·277	·256	·164	·769*
data index	+	·206	·184	·108	·030	·186
R²		(·465)	(·334)	(·372)	(·088)	(·556)
higher education	+	·268	-·003	·028	·198	·142
GNP	+	·205	·256	·229	·162	·028
urbanism	+	·319	·338	·360	-·054	·551*
R²		(·470)	(·309)	(·328)	(·126)	(·423)
radios	+	·643*	·221	·378	·400	-·201
urbanism	+	·343*	·274	·285	-·057	·529*
GNP	+	-·221	-·109	-·032	-·106	·139
R²		(·543)	(·314)	(·353)	(·125)	(·401)
newspapers	+	·129	·169	·185	-·207	-·115
urbanism	+	·396	·269	·303	·065	·636*
data	+	·236	·211	·177	·079	·214
R²		(·455)	(·344)	(·364)	(·106)	(·399)

See note in Table 5:3.

indicator of basic resources available for control, was less important by comparison. It was earlier shown to be positively associated with the dependent variables in sets of explanations with measures of inequality. When treated in a group with the more direct elements related to formal control, however, it declined in importance.

The police force indicator, the closest indicator of the *means* of formal control, was related as predicted to the crime-sanction variables, but only weakly. In the tests reported in Table 5:7, none of the relationships was statistically significant. Examined as a single variable, however, police force size was significantly related to the crime-sanction indicators. The fact that the relationship was not strong is of some interest. A very strong association between police force size and recorded crime rates could indicate spuriousness due to the role of the police in recording and reporting the data. Especially if the effect of other variables were weak (not the case in this analysis) one might suspect that a high association reflected simply this police-data recording function.

Of the two mass media indicators one, radio ownership, was strongly and consistently related to the crime indicators. In the case of newspaper circulation, the relationships were in the direction predicted but, in the multiple regressions, not to a statistically significant degree. As single variables, both were related in the same direction, and both to a statistically significant degree.

TWENTIETH-CENTURY CONSENSUS TESTS

The tests of twentieth-century consensus theory produced overwhelmingly negative results. Most of the indicators of social and economic problems simply were not related as predicted to the crime-sanction variables. There were only two exceptions, urbanism and unemployment, already discussed in the section on nineteenth-century theory, and neither indicating strong support for consensus theory. The only aspect of twentieth-century consensus theory to be supported, then, was that which was drawn from early conflict theory. In the case of urbanism the results were strong and consistent, but the relationship found was at the same time predicted by conflict theory, both in the nineteenth- and twentieth-century versions. In the case of unemployment, there was no prediction for the twentieth-century version, but the results were as predicted by earlier versions, and still consistent with the contemporary view. The com-

Table 5:8 *Twentieth-Century Consensus Theory*

	direction predicted	Interpol				United Nations
		juvenile	theft	property	total	juvenile court
constitutional status	+	-·234	·038	·031	·098	·230
urbanism	+	·429*	·329	·369	·162	·636*
GNP	-	·159	·278	·251	·208	·080
R²		(·472)	(·305)	(·324)	(·100)	(·408)
representative institutions	+	-·266	·027	·025	·041	·066
urbanism	+	·405*	·327	·369	·148	·576*
GNP	-	·096	·280	·253	·203	·067
R²		(·465)	(·305)	(·323)	(·093)	(·367)
government stability	+	·189	·105	·158	·315	-·046
urbanism	+	·471*	·373	·415*	·093	·566*
GNP	-	·299	·280	·285	·390	·038
R²		(·437)	(·319)	(·348)	(·146)	(·365)
proportion voting	-	·374	·202	·268	·283	-·145
urbanism	+	·367*	·287	·295*	·115	·482*
GNP	-	·211	·226	·198	·050	·237
R²		(·609)	(·364)	(·409)	(·151)	(·429)
executive stability	-	-·251	-·112	-·182	-·431*	-·038
GNP	-	-·027	-·009	-·033	-·052	-·065
urbanism	+	·732*	·637*	·686*	·499*	·622*
R²		(·533)	(·382)	(·424)	(·328)	(·329)

See note in Table 5:4.

Table 5:9 *Tests with the Data Index*

	direction predicted	Interpol				United Nations
		juvenile	theft	property	total	juvenile court
unemployment	+	·329*	−·044	·034	·232	·042
urbanism	−	·423*	·424*	·471*	·204	·392*
data		·360*	·393	·366*	·306	·042
R²		(·665)	(·570)	(·609)	(·312)	(·390)
urbanism	+	·498*	·364*	·398*	·226	·696*
data		·272	·274	·255	·088	·094
R²		(·458)	(·323)	(·340)	(·082)	(·521)
executive stability	+	−·245	−·098	−·179	−·482	−·076
urbanism	+	·694*	·571*	·643*	−·654*	·540
data		·026	·079	·021	−·265	·183
R²		(·533)	(·386)	(·424)	(·359)	(·357)
family size	+	−·221	·051	−·029	−·156	·251
urbanism	+	·471*	·372*	·393*	·201	·750*
data		·149	·299	·240	·007	·224
R²		(·488)	(·324)	(·341)	(·097)	(·513)
population increase	+	·035	·138	·116	·146	·285
urbanism	+	·499*	·372*	·405*	·241	·711*
data		·292	·351	·320	·164	·216
R²		(·459)	(·335)	(·349)	(·096)	(·542)

	(1)	(2)	(3)	(4)	(5)		
intersectoral inequality	·198	−233	−040	−076	−169	+	+
urbanism	·778	·227	·561*	·520*	·424*		
data	·030	·128	·225	·247	·277		
R²	(·437)	(·249)	(·574)	(·578)	(·523)		
racial heterogeneity	·256	·217	·157	·144	·124	+	+
urbanism	·666*	·272	·430*	·394*	·527*		
data	·127	·080	·253	·272	·268		
R²	(·585)	(·127)	(·364)	(·343)	(·473)		
linguistic heterogeneity	·074	−052	−135	−098	−157	+	+
urbanism	·728*	·217	·330*	·315	·425*		
data	·081	−081	·258	·276	·272		
R²	(·518)	(·045)	(·354)	(·330)	(·478)		
government stability	−053	·206	·099	·049	·132	+	+
urbanism	·685*	·256	·448*	·392*	·500*		
data	−095	·136	·248	·267	·293		
R²	(·524)	(·106)	(·357)	(·334)	(·458)		
constitutional status	−187	−082	·022	·028	−241	+	+
urbanism	·754*	·259	·407*	·375*	·413*		
data	·087	−093	·257	·276	·252		
R²	(·553)	(·087)	(·341)	(·323)	(·507)		
GNP	−137	−022	·064	·082	·004	−	+
urbanism	·634*	·133	·369*	·327	·496*		
data	·236	·208	·222	·230	·269		
R²	(·396)	(·093)	(·341)	(·324)	(·458)		

bination of urbanism and unemployment was the only set for which all the variables were related as predicted by consensus theory. In addition, in many of the instances in which the predicted relationships did not appear, the opposite did, to a statistically significant degree. Examination of the results reported in Table 5:7 further supports this conclusion.

THE EFFECT OF DATA COLLECTION MACHINERY

All the explanatory variables were included at some stage in regressions with the data collection index, to insure that relationships found were not spurious ones, due to differing proclivities for, and efficiency at, data collection. It was necessary to establish this both for positive findings, of significant relationships, and for negative, or 'non-findings'. The analysis, in fact, furnished the necessary assurances in both cases. Briefly, variables found to be significantly related to the crime-sanctions indicators remained so when the data index was included, and variables not related significantly to the dependent variables similarly remained insignificantly related. The extent of relationship declined in some cases but, on the whole, not to a great degree. Nor did addition of the data index result in changes in sign for any of the explanatory variables. The relevant data for these tests are reported in Tables 5:7 and 5:9.

Urbanism, the social problem indicator to be most strongly related to the crime-sanction rates, and the only one to be related consistently, clearly remained so. When just the two indicators were examined together, urbanism proved to be the stronger one, although the data index also explained a significant amount of the variance. In other combinations urbanism remained significantly related to the dependent variables, while the data index did not. Unemployment was the next most important problem indicator, significantly explaining rates of juvenile crime, although not the other categories. It remained a significant variable with the data index, in the case of juvenile crime, but did not improve its ability to explain variance of the others. The executive stability indicator, which had also been found to be significantly related to two of the crime-sanction indicators, remained significantly related to these two and, again, did not change on the two for which the relationships were weak. The numerous problem indicators which had not explained significant amounts of the variance earlier still failed to: family size, population

increase, racial and linguistic heterogeneity, inequality and government instability and unconstitutional status.

The same pattern held for the conflict social control indicators.
Those that already explained significant amounts of variance continued to: GNP, school enrolment, population voting, political
representation and radio ownership. Those that had weak relationships before similarly continued to with the data index, namely:
police force size, newspaper circulation and bureaucratic status.

The fact of considerable amounts of missing data provided a built-
in check of reliability of the data. The different regressions inevitably involved different sets of countries, for certain countries would
drop out on account of missing data on one variable, and others
would on others. The variables which were included in a large number of regressions, notably urbanism and GNP, were then tested with
varying combinations of countries. The range of missing data was, in
fact, substantial. For the land inequality indicator there were data
for only twenty-two countries, in the Interpol set, and for the police
rate only twenty-eight. Complete data were available for only a
small minority of the explanatory indicators, and even urbanism
and higher education data were unavailable for three countries. On
the total crime indicator two countries had to be excluded, and six
had to be on the juvenile crime. Slightly more data were unavailable
in the juvenile court data set, and the range of combinations of
countries tested was, then, slightly greater.

RESULTS PREDICTED BY NEITHER THEORY

One final exploration of the data was made, with rather instructive
results. This involved a simple ordering of the sets of explanatory
indicators on the basis of amount of variance explained, irrespective
of sign. The analysis then consisted of examining these sets, in relation to what version of what theory was supported. What is most
useful about the exercise is that results not supportive of any version
of either theory (that is, with one or more wrong signs) stand out.
This information then can be used to consider where the two
theories should be combined. The ordering, for the Interpol sets
only, is shown in Table 5:10, where all sets explaining at least 55 per
cent of the variance are reported. There seemed little point in including the few juvenile court sets to qualify, for the bulk of the variance
explained was due to just one variable, urbanism.

Table 5:10 *Amount of Variance Explained*

variance explained %	dependent variables	independent variables	all signs correct for:
66·5	juvenile	unemployment, urbanism, data	—
63·5	juvenile	constitutional status, urbanism	—
61·7	juvenile	unemployment, urbanism, GNP	—
60·9	property	unemployment, urbanism, data	—
60·9	juvenile	% voting, urbanism, data	20th c. conflict
59·3	juvenile	unemployment, urbanism	19th c. consensus /conflict 20th c. consensus
58·9	theft	inequality, GNP, urbanism	—
58·7	juvenile	% voting, urbanism, GNP	20th c. conflict
58·4	property	inequality, GNP, urbanism	—
58·2	juvenile	% voting, urbanism	20th c. conflict
57·8	theft	inequality, data, urbanism	—
57·4	property	inequality, data, urbanism	—
57·3	property	unemployment, urbanism, GNP	—
57·0	theft	unemployment, urbanism, data	—
55·7	juvenile	police, data, urbanism	20th c. conflict
55·2	juvenile	police representation, urbanism, GNP	20th c. conflict

The results show that a number of the most successful sets, in terms of amount of variance explained, were combinations not predicted from either theory. The majority, including the top two sets, depart somewhat from the predictions derived from the theories. The set explaining the highest proportion of variance, 66·5 per cent, was comprised of unemployment, urbanism and the data index; the higher the unemployment, the greater the urbanism and the greater the extent of data collection, the higher the rate of reported juvenile crime was. From the point of view of contemporary conflict theory, two of the variables were related as predicted (urbanism and the data index) but unemployment was not part of this prediction. Similarly, for consensus theory two variables were related as predicted, urbanism and unemployment, but the data index was not part of the prediction.

In the next best set, the results were the higher the unemployment, urbanism and GNP, the higher the juvenile crime rate. Again, two variables were related as predicted by twentieth-century conflict theory, urbanism and GNP, but unemployment appeared, for which there was no prediction. From the point of view of consensus theory, there were also two correct predictions, but GNP was related in exactly the opposite direction.

That twentieth-century conflict theory provided the best explanation of the crime-sanction rates is clearly shown in the table. All but one of the predictions consistent with prediction supported this version, the exception being the unemployment and urbanism combination already discussed. Consensus theory predictors, apart from that, simply did not appear among the sets explaining substantial amounts of variance, either above the 55 per cent cut-off used for this table or, for that matter, above 45 per cent, which was also examined.

THE EXPLANATION OF MURDER RATES

The findings on murder rates were sharply different from those on all other indicators. For certain variables, like urbanism, GNP and the data index, the findings were exactly the opposite, with murder rates rising as GNP, urbanism and data collection declined. The social control variables of contemporary conflict theory had either the opposite effect, as in the above examples, or no effect at all, the result for most of the variables tested, including police rate, the voting indicators and school enrolment. The indicators that did succeed in explaining significant amounts of variance were the indicators of social problems, notably economic deprivation (negative GNP), inequality, population increase, linguistic heterogeneity, and government instability. The levels of explanation, however, were lower throughout than those for theft and total property offenders, and considerably lower than those found for the juvenile rates. The actual results are reported in the next two tables, in a somewhat condensed fashion. Table 5:12 contains the results, effectively non-findings, for contemporary conflict theory, while all the other results are combined together in Table 5:11.

Table 5:11 *Explanation of Murder—Consensus Theory*

	direction predicted	
intersectoral inequality	+	·347*
data index		−·605
urbanism	+	·289
R^2		(·422)
population increase	+	·479*
urbanism	+	−·126
data index		−·065
R^2		(·341)
executive stability	−	−·271
data index		−·637
urbanism	+	(·392)
R^2		
population increase	+	·428*
GNP	−	−·251
R^2		(·364)
government stability	+	·366*
urbanism	+	−·017
GNP	−	−·287
R^2		(·352)
land inequality	+	·073
urbanism	+	·212
data index		−·703
		(·397)
linguistic heterogeneity	+	·295*
data index		−·341
urbanism	+	−·009
R^2		(·260)
racial heterogeneity	+	·089
GNP	−	−·567*
urbanism	+	·100
R^2		(·256)

	direction predicted	
religious heterogeneity	+	·032
urbanism	+	·026
GNP	−	−·512*
R^2		(·240)
family size	+	·005
urbanism	+	·065
GNP	−	−·542*
R^2		(·249)
school enrolment	−	−·061
data index		−·305
urbanism	+	−·184
R^2		(·242)
unemployment	+	·067
urbanism	+	·002
GNP	−	−·321
R^2		(·102)
labour force participation	−	−·000
urbanism	+	−·121
data index		−·231
R^2		(·099)

The findings on the effect of economic deprivation and inequality, at the top of Table 5:11, indicate clear support for the early versions of conflict theory, and later consensus theory. Murder rates were higher in poorer countries than better off, a finding consistent with the bulk of earlier studies. The rates were higher, similarly, in societies undergoing rapid population increase, than in societies with moderate or low rates of increase, a finding entirely in keeping with the economic deprivation explanation. Again, consistent with other studies, rates were higher in less urbanized societies. Thus, while the murder rate was associated with miserable living conditions, it was *rural* misery that counted rather than urban, and in this respect the findings depart from the standard social problem explanations. Murder rates were higher in societies that were heterogeneous with respect to language, although neither religious nor racial heterogeneity had any effect. The rates were higher in societies with unstable governments and executives, another finding at contrast with the results on property offences. The legitimacy indicators, however, on voting participation, political representation and the constitutionality of the regime had no effect. Unemployment was *not* a

Table 5:12 *Explanation of Murder—Conflict Theory*

	direction predicted	
police force	+	·078
data index	+	− ·382
urbanism	+	− ·118
R^2		(·216)
police force	+	·057
GNP	+	− ·454
urbanism	+	− ·030
R^2		(·223)
bureaucracy	−	·243
urbanism	+	− ·045
data index	+	− ·217
		(·212)
political representation	+	− ·081
urbanism	+	·136
GNP	+	− ·678
R^2		(·395)
newspaper circulation	+	− ·312
urbanism	+	− ·071
data index	+	− ·173
R^2		(·267)
radios	+	·078
urbanism	+	·049
GNP	+	− ·602
R^2		(·250)
proportion voting	+	·136
urbanism	+	·044
GNP	+	− ·581
R^2		(·235)

factor in explaining the murder rate, again contrary to the social problem argument, and another departure from the findings on property offences. Neither were several other of the social problem indicators: family size, illiteracy, low school enrolment and low participation in the paid labour force.

The results were strongly and consistently contrary to the predictions of twentieth-century conflict theory. This had already been well established in the case of economic resources for formal control, in the negative relationship of GNP with murder. The results were similar on social machinery for control. The data index was negatively associated with murder—or the murder rate was higher in societies collecting relatively little social data. In the case of indicators of the means of formal control, the results were simply of no effect. This included the nature of the central bureaucracy, the size of the police force and extent of school enrolment, newspaper circulation and radio ownership.

CONCLUSIONS: A MODIFIED CONFLICT THEORY

The theory best to survive empirical testing was contemporary conflict theory. The indicators of the need for formal control on the part of the authorities, and economic and social resources available were the most successful in explaining rates of official crime in both data sets studied. Specifically, the indicators of urbanism, GNP, police force size, extent of the school system, data collection apparatus, political representation and mass media managed to explain substantial amounts of variance, in numerous different combinations. The indicators of social problems were successful in explaining significant amounts of the murder rate, but not, with rare exception, of rates of ordinary crime-sanctions. The most important exception, in both data sets, was unemployment. The combinations of unemployment and urbanism with either GNP or the data collection index were the combinations that achieved the highest levels of explanation, in the case of Interpol juvenile offences explaining over 60 per cent of the variance. A revised conflict explanation would include the level of unemployment in a society as one of the factors affecting the *need* for formal control measures.

The analysis was throughout disconfirming of social problem explanations. A large number, covering a good range of types of problems was considered, and the large bulk of these failed to be significantly related to ordinary crime-sanctions indicators. These 'non-findings' include such fundamental problems as poverty, rapid population increase, large family size and illiteracy. Indicators of heterogeneity in the population, thought both to cause problems and make their solution more cumbersome, completely failed to have the predicted effect in the main data set. Racial heterogeneity did have the predicted effect in the juvenile court data, an isolated exception. The numerous indicators of legitimacy, including proportion of the population voting, representativeness of the political system, its constitutionality and stability of the government and executive all failed in their tests. Official crime rates, far from declining with increased measures intended to solve problems, were either unaffected, or increased.

The actual point at which the consensus explanations failed could not be determined in the analysis. The theory specifies that social and economic problems exert pressures towards deviance, including real crime. Increases in crime pose problems to which some response is necessary. Adjustments are made in the social control system, in time manifested in increasing rates of official crime. The data do not serve to isolate at what stage this process broke down. Nevertheless, it is abundantly clear that the end-result predicted did not. Rates of official sanctions were not related to their supposed causes in social and economic problems.

CRIME AS A SERIOUS AND GROWING PROBLEM

My conclusions differ profoundly from those given in the main United Nations data source.[1] Several issues are in dispute, notably the relationship between recorded crime and social problems on the one hand, and economic resources and social machinery for control on the other. Next there is the contention that crime is a serious and growing problem, calling for ever more stringent measures of control.

The notion that ordinary crime poses a serious problem to society was propounded in several ways. Firstly, it was argued that the 'actual' rates were probably two to five times as great as the recorded. Estimates were cited, for the United States, that about 12 per cent of the population, and as much as 20 per cent of the male population, would become delinquent at some time during adolescence. Next, the problem of delinquency was said to be much more extensive than was indicated by these rates.

> Even assuming that as much as 20 per cent of juveniles [the girls have now been forgotten] at the vulnerable age are delinquent, this percentage will still not constitute in itself an appropriate assessment of juvenile delinquency as a social problem, since especially from the preventive point of view, juvenile delinquency affects all juveniles and to a great extent adults, if account is taken of the

1. *New Forms of Delinquency.*

fact that a great percentage of adult offenders started their careers as criminals between 14 and 21 years of age. (p. 38)

Juvenile delinquency is a social problem affecting all juveniles, then, at least so far as preventive measures are concerned. Should one ask why preventive measures are required for all juveniles, the answer is that it is a grave problem and it is a grave problem, of course, because it affects so many people!

Delinquency, the argument continues, is not only a serious problem, but a growing one.

> If the present trend, already marked in certain countries towards an increase in delinquency among juveniles under 14 years of age, continues, juvenile delinquency as a social problem promises to become more serious in every respect.

And, while every juvenile and a great number of adults are already affected by this problem, somehow now an even 'greater number of juveniles and adults will be affected'. There is no respite for the honest. All types of delinquency are becoming more serious: offences against property and against the person, sex, morality, drug and liquor (p. 37). Violence was 'becoming more and more a feature of juvenile delinquency'. The number of homicides and bodily injuries 'seemed to be taking an upward trend in some countries', and the same applied to burglary and breaking and entering (p. 34).

> Another manifestation of violence, although often hidden, is typified by the delinquent activities of certain gangs who, by offering protection, or without offering it, obtain various advantages, services or goods, including food. . . . Violence seems to have increased through the growing number of acts of serious damaging or vandalism, committed in revenge, or for the fun of it, as an expression of a more or less rebellious attitude.

Only two qualifications to this rather dismal summary were made, and both of them tentatively. There was, firstly, the suggestion that minor forms of damage committed by children, and even by some very young juveniles 'should not always be labelled as delinquency'. Secondly, it was noted that excessive publicity given to juvenile delinquency might sometimes result in an exaggerated view of its gravity (p. 39). Otherwise the situation was grim. Delinquency was spreading both to lower age groups and across all social milieux, even, it would seem, to the children of respectable citizens. It was no longer confined, alas, to the offspring of those groups 'in need of assistance and protection' (p. 38)—and we know who they are!

None of the above points was documented with actual data, and in many cases the data which were reported, elsewhere in the publication, were stated in a rather misleading way. For the thirty-two countries for which some data were reported, increases of a substantial nature were described for twenty-six. This included many increases over 50 per cent, and some even exceeding 200 and 300 per cent. For three countries increases and decreases were described, and for two others the rates were said to be decreasing or constant. There was only one country for which an unambiguous decrease was allowed—Italy, and the report accorded these data was one of the briefest in the study: three lines. Some of the increases reported involved only the raw figures, that is, without taking into account population growth. The 329 per cent increase given for the United States, for example, was of this type and, since the period ran from 1918 to 1960, the effect of population growth would have been substantial. For a number of other countries only the increases were given, without raw data, so the reader had no possibility of correcting for population.

Often the increases reported were so trivial that the slightest improvement in reporting procedures could account for them, a point nowhere made in the discussion.

My own data from United Nations sources, most from the same publication, present quite a different picture. Average annual rates of increase were computed for the thirty-one countries in the study, in all cases proportional to population under twenty. For ten of the countries actual decreases appeared: France, Italy, Iraq, Jordan, Turkey, Guyana, British Honduras, Fiji, Hong Kong and Singapore. In some cases the decreases were trivial, but so also were some of the increases. And, in view of the known improvements in reporting practices over the period, it is the *increases* that should be suspect.

Nor, from the lesson in Chapter 3, should this be any surprise. Reported there were a number of instances of declining rates, for Britain and France in the nineteenth century. Here a few more examples can be added, now all American, mainly this century, but all examining fairly long-term trends. Willbach found an absolute decrease in crime, personal and property, in New York City between 1916 and 1936, despite an increase in population. In the case of

Chicago there were increases between 1919 and 1927, but then decreases to 1939, again despite growing population. Powell found decreases in all forms of crime in Buffalo between 1946 and 1964. Warner's data for Boston show a general decrease from the late nineteenth century to the end of his series in 1932.[1] Ferdinand's study of Boston over 1849–1951 shows declining rates of arrests, consistently in the case of murder, manslaughter and assault, and generally declining, but with periodic reversals, in the case of robbery, burglary and larceny.

Discussion of causes in the United Nations study was confined to the practical objective of finding a solution to the problems involved. None of the traditional consensus hypotheses of family problems, lack of education and so forth were favoured. Consistent with this, the usual social welfare solution to the 'crime problem', more schools, better treatment, was opposed. It was noted that delinquency rates continued to increase even in industrialized, well-organized societies like Sweden and the United States, but this line of reasoning was not pursued. Had it been, it would have been found that economic growth and bureaucracy, far from helping to reduce delinquency, have been associated with its increase. There was scepticism, then, of the reformist consensus approach, but the authors were not willing to entertain the conflict alternative. What they would prefer by way of programme was not clear. More studies and better statistics were recommended, and indeed were considered 'axiomatic' for the finding of a solution. Apart from that, some preference for comprehensive preventive programmes was suggested. This is at least implicit in the criticism of existing programmes as being too narrowly based—dealing only with particular groups, when delinquency was a 'general phenomenon' affecting *all* juveniles. This is the familiar tactic of 'if something does not work, try more of it and harder', and one that we shall see again shortly, in the next chapter.

1. Biderman, in an article on bias in American crime data questions that there has been any general trend to greater criminality at all in the United States. He argues instead that increases in index crimes reflect *progress*. Material prosperity has meant more bicycles and cars to steal, and steal from—both important items in the crime index. *Social* progress is reflected in greater responsiveness to black demands for police services. Bell, in *The End of Ideology*, has also challenged the whole rising crime myth.

Chapter 6

ENGLAND AND WALES
AS A TEST CASE

Law and order has long been one of the more popular public issues in Britain. It is now a comfortable, familiar issue with a remarkable facility for unity. The 'rising crime rate' is less disputed than the monarchy and, indeed, the whole set of beliefs about the threat of crime seems to be a matter above partisan debate. From the highest public officials of the land to the lowest of the evening press, it is staunchly believed that official crime rates represent real and growing threats to civilized society. Further, there is just as much consensus over the solution to the 'problem' as its nature: more police. Increases in the police force have been a major recommendation in discussions of crime, not only from the police themselves, but from judges, Home Office officials, academics, voluntary groups and political parties. Crime, according to a Labour Party statement, is 'one of the gravest social problems of our time', while the Conservatives urge, *'The effective strength of the police forces must be increased.'*

The Conservative Party and Labour Party have traditionally taken sharply different lines on issues of crime and criminal justice, but now only the vestiges of these differences remain. Labour has historically been 'softer' on crime, stressing preventive and treatment measures over the more frankly punitive. The Conservatives have consistently been less 'sentimental' about criminals, and the die-hard supporters of capital punishment have, for the most part, been Conservative. Yet, the 'bring back flogging' wing has increasingly become a matter of embarrassment to the party leadership. Both parties have mellowed in their positions. Still, certain differences remain, and both the differences and similarities are germane to our inquiry. As sources on these points the publications of the two parties' policy discussion groups were used: *Crime in the Sixties* for the Conservatives, and *Crime—a challenge to us all* for Labour.

The Conservatives, consistent with age-old consensus theory, revealed themselves as openly and explicitly opposed to 'economic determinism'. The idea that poverty was a cause of crime was a 'socialist error' (p. 25). Instead, prosperity was suspect; wherever there was an increase in material prosperity, there was a 'marked increase' in crime (p. 13). 'Inadequacies' in penalties were stressed as other 'probable' causes, and there were explicit recommendations for tougher penalties for adults, and only slightly more veiled hints in the case of children. Among other probable causes was the disproportionate number of Commonwealth citizens and people from other countries, 'notably West Indians and Irishmen' (p. 8). Listed as a 'possible' cause was declining respect for the law and police, which was itself blamed on political extremists, for deliberately breaking the law (p. 27). No doubt was expressed as to the 'fact' of rising crime. 'Some people go so far as to suggest that one cannot even be sure that there has been a significant increase in crime at all.' But, 'we do not accept this view' (p. 17). Examples of crime increases were given, ranging from 50·7 to 122 per cent.

The Labour Party statement was much more sympathetic in tone. The stress was on prevention, through increased family services, and community treatment was favoured over incarceration. There was an explicit recommendation against capital punishment, while the Conservatives had to admit being divided on the issue. Nevertheless, the Labour statement concurred with the view that the poor were more criminal than the better off. They were more vulnerable to temptation, on account of poorer living conditions, and were more likely to be caught. Still, psychological problems were to blame, rather than economic. Criminals did not come from 'stable and closely knit working class families, however poor their circumstances' (p. 5). The problem was said to lie rather in the 'inferiority complex' the poor had, in an 'acquisitive society' with 'get rich quick ethics'. It is telling that the document recognized the greater liability of the poor and working class to being caught, but without making any recommendations towards ending this inequity. Further, the recommendations that were made were such as to insure unequal treatment continued if not increased.

The recommendations of both policy groups were centred on increases in the police force and the various correctional agencies.

The Conservatives went into more detail than Labour. The police force was to be increased by 10,000 men, and substantial increases in salaries were called for to effect the necessary recruitment. 'Police housing must be given priority in areas where there is an acute shortage of police, or where crime is rife' (p. 7). The probation service needed 400 additional officers and a campaign was to be launched to obtain 1,400 more prison officers. The institutional building programme should be 'speeded up'. Statutory 'after-care' was recommended, with provisions for returning offenders to prison to finish their sentences if they misbehaved.

The tone of the Labour recommendations was characteristically milder, but the content was effectively the same: more of everything. This included a 'strengthening' of the police 'to forestall delinquency', 'more comprehensive after-care', a 'substantial strengthening' of the probation service, and an emphasis on early treatment (pp. 2–21). There was no more questioning of the effectiveness of these various measures than in the Conservative report, and no more attention paid to the issues of human costs or civil rights.

The conventional wisdom on crime and punishment has been little challenged. There are no contemporary equivalents to John Howard and Elizabeth Fry, and no organizations comparable to those that fought to abolish hanging and make prisons more humane. Serious questioning on the part of academics has been rare. Wilkins is perhaps the best example to date, for challenging both aspects of the belief in rising crime and, with extensive documentation, the effectiveness of correctional treatment.[1] A number of young dissidents have recently emerged, associated with the National Deviancy Conference, but so far they have not engaged on a refutation, or even a serious questioning, of the relevant 'facts'.

TESTING THE CONVENTIONAL WISDOM

Testing of the conventional wisdom was confined to three elements: the view that crime is a real and growing problem, reflected in high and rising official crime rates, and to which an essential response is a substantial increase in the forces of order. The testing was itself approached in two ways. Firstly, prominence was given to the role

1. *Social Deviance* and *Evaluation of Penal Measures*. For a critical view with nineteenth-century data see Gatrell and Hadden, discussed pp. 60–1 above.

of the police in the ongoing tests of conflict and consensus theory. These tests were confined to the contemporary versions of the theories, and the role of the police and other labelling agencies is a central part of contemporary conflict theory. Secondly, the academic arguments for the law and order view were examined through two major studies. One was the massive *Crime in England and Wales*, a work reaching essentially the opposite conclusions to mine with similar methods and data sources. I attached particular importance to that study, for it was conducted by researchers of good reputation, under the sponsorship of a prestigious institution, the Institute of Criminology at Cambridge University. The project as well had a quasi-official status. It was ultimately the product of a Home Office initiative, and the Home Office participated actively in it throughout. The other project examined was a much smaller and lesser known work, conducted by the Home Office Scientific Adviser's Branch. Again there was the problem of resolving diametrically opposed conclusions, reached this time with *identical* data; indeed I am indebted to the Scientific Adviser's Branch for the data.

What makes England and Wales good examples for testing purposes is the welfare state. The same conditions that should reduce the crime rate from the point of view of consensus theory—the expansion of welfare services—increase it from the point of view of conflict—by expanding the machinery that can be used for formal control purposes. Clearly opposite predictions follow from the two theories, a situation ideal for comparative testing.

Choice of the actual indicators was guided by the need to cover the *ranges* of concerns of the two theories with a small number of variables.

Indicators were accordingly chosen that could be used in the tests for both theories, with a reversal of sign. There was only one variable, unemployment, that was used only for consensus tests and only the two policing variables were confined to the conflict. The other indicators—GNP, welfare state expenditure, school enrolment and school expenditure—were used in both sets of tests. The different *meanings* they have in the two theories is important and, accordingly, this is explained rather fully below. Exact references for data sources are listed in the Technical Note (pp. 296–8). The discussion of data problems in the preceding chapter may be treated as applying here too.

For conflict theory, the indicator of the basic economic resources available for formal control purposes was per capita GNP, as in the preceding analysis.[1] At the same time, GNP represented resources for problem solving in consensus theory or, negatively, poverty. From the point of view of conflict theory, then, the higher the GNP, the higher the crime rate was hypothesized to be, since the greater the means were which ultimately could be devoted to control measures. In consensus theory, by contrast, the hypothesis was of a negative relationship—increases in GNP meant increases in the goods and services people enjoyed, a reduction in poverty, and a lessening of pressures towards crime.

The next concern was with resources more directly available for control purposes, for which per capita social security expenditure was the indicator. Again increases in expenditure signified, in conflict theory, expansion of the means available for control. The hypothesis, then, was similarly of a positive relationship. In consensus theory, on the other hand, increases signified growing social concern and the allocation of resources for concrete problem solving. The greater the social security expenditure, the lower crime rates should be. The indicator signified, as well, *experience* of control, which meant not only increased numbers of trained officials, but increased experience of bureaucracy on the part of the general public. Familiarity may sometimes breed contempt, but it may also breed a certain habituation. Experience of bureaucratic control measures in one area of life may mean greater acceptance of them in others.

The school system being the closest institutional sphere to crime control, two indicators were devoted to it: school enrolment, relative to school-age population, and public expenditure on education per pupil. Enrolment, in conflict theory, indicated extent of control achieved in a parallel institution, and experience of control at the early, impressionable ages. Increases in enrolment mean expansion of the school bureaucracy, more teachers, administrators, and custodians—more people experienced in relevant bureaucratic methods. The greater the enrolment the higher the official sanction rate was hypothesized to be.

In consensus theory, by contrast, enrolment means success in the provision of an essential service. The expansion of formal schooling means the expansion of the more skilled sectors of the paid labour force, and eventually higher productivity. At the individual level,

1. GNP, and the other expenditure indicators, were all deflated for changes in the value of the pound.

children who go further in education have better job prospects than those who leave early, and generally know this. Staying on in school, then, is associated both with a more secure future, and a more optimistic view of it. Insofar as formal education also means enlightenment, the expansion of the school system means also the growth of the civilizing forces of society. At the very least, expanded enrolments mean 'kids off the streets', hence less opportunity for misbehaviour.

School expenditure was intended to tap a slightly different dimension. In the case of consensus theory, it indicates concern for *quality* of education provided, as opposed to mere numbers exposed to some amount. Increases in expenditure mean not only better intentions, but realization—the allocation of more resources to educational goals. In conflict theory, expenditure also signifies concern, but now the concern of the authorities for measures of control. Expenditure, after all, is something determined by government authorities, in a way GNP, or even enrolment, is not. Governments can decide to raise or lower expenditure in accordance with their priorities. Actual increases and decreases may reasonably be thought to reflect government decisions to exert more or less control over the population.

The final indicator for conflict theory was the police rate (number of full-time officers per total population), as the closest proxy for the *desire* for level of formal control on the part of the authorities. The size of the police force is very much within the power of the central authorities to decide. Within reason, a decision to expand the police force can be effected, so long as the necessary budget is made available. The hypothesis is the greater police force size, the higher official crime rates. Expenditure on the police is even more a matter of policy decision, and this indicator, too, was used in parts of the analysis.

The final indicator for consensus theory was the rate of unemployment, a variable which produced some interesting results in the cross-national study. In a society as industrialized as Britain the unemployment rate is an especially important measure of problems. Regular, paid work is an expectation of virtually all able-bodied persons, certainly the case for the years before the hippy boom around 1970. Increases in unemployment, in short, can be assumed to represent increased strain and suffering of various sorts. Unemployed persons need not go hungry in Britain, but unemployment usually means some material hardship, anxiety, and even shame.

CRIME INDICATORS

Most of the problems of using official crime statistics concern their portrayal of 'real crime', and are problems avoided in this study. In the case of conflict theory the avoidance is complete. Official sanctions are real sanctions, so that an increase in official sanctions, for whatever reason, signifies an increase in real sanctions. An increase may mean only that people are being punished for acts previously not worth the trouble, but the fact remains they are being punished, and the recorded rate reflects just that.

The matter is more complicated in the case of consensus theory, but still not unmanageable. Official rates are *theorized* to reflect real crime and, in turn, real social and economic problems. The connection between official and real rates is beyond our competence to investigate, but rather the tests concern initial problems and eventual official rates. As Quetelet pointed out, it is not necessary that official rates be identical with real, but only that the ratios between them reasonably be thought to remain constant. Undoubtedly there has been some change in this ratio over the years, but not so much as to preclude analysis.[1] Clearly studies are better done over relatively short periods of time, and over periods known to be relatively free from reporting changes. For this reason most of the analysis was kept to a twenty-year period, beginning in 1948—or after adjustment to peace-time conditions had been made. Further, in considering the 'rising crime' question additional safeguards were introduced.

The choice of indicators for testing conflict theory entailed an embarrassment of riches. The official statistics abound with data on sanctions, so that it was only a question of settling which ones should be used. The concern was to cover a good *range*—from the level of police reports, through convictions to incarceration. Care was taken to include the most general indicators—total indictable and non-indictable convictions, and total indictable reports—and basic groups of offences by type: violence, theft, breaking and entering, fraud and receiving, and sex offences. Two indicators dealing

1. England was one of the first countries to institute a centralized statistical office, and English crime statistics are among the best in the world. Reliability is relatively good for the police, courts and prisons have long been centrally administered, and centralized reporting has been compulsory for many years. See Walker, Wilkins, Lodge, McClintock, McClintock and Avison, Mays, and Jones.

specifically with children were used, the total number found guilty of indictable and non-indictable offences respectively. Level of incarceration was represented by the average daily population in prisons and borstals. All the crime data were deflated by population at risk, the age group 10–40.

The same criteria for selecting indicators applied in the case of the consensus tests: a good range of types of indicator, and indicators relatively free of definitional shifts. The range in terms of types of crime was particularly important, and it was largely with these in mind that sex crimes, violence, and the different theft categories were included. The prison population variable is undoubtedly remote as an official crime indicator, however, it was decided to include all the indicators for each theory's tests. (In hindsight, this did not seem to be such a good idea, however, that was the plan.) Given that different patterns of results appear between murder and property offences, two indicators of murder were included. One was the estimated number of murderers (convicted murderers and suspects), and the other the estimated number of murder victims. Again, these indicators were relevant far more for consensus theory than for conflict, but were included in both analyses.

THE EMPIRICAL TESTS

The first stage of testing concerned the nature of the relationships between particular explanatory variables and the crime-sanction indicators. Two sets of multiple regressions were computed, one each for conflict and consensus indicators, in each case for all thirteen crime-sanction indicators. Both sets of explanatory variables included five indicators. For conflict theory these were police rate, per capita GNP, social security, school expenditure and school enrolment, all with positive relationships hypothesized. For consensus theory the indicators were unemployment (with a positive relationship hypothesized), and the latter four variables, now with negative relationships hypothesized. The basic results[1] are reported in Tables 6:1 and 6:2 with a summary comparing results in Table 6:3.

The results indicate moderately better support for conflict theory than consensus. On each of the comparisons made, correct signs and

1. The equations (the regression coefficients and constants) are reported at the end of the chapter (pp. 219–20), along with the Durbin-Watson statistics on autocorrelation.

Table 6:1 *Results of Tests of Conflict Theory*

	Police rate	School expenditure	School enrolment	GNP	Social security
General indicators					
Indictable convictions	/	///	/		
Summary convictions	///	///	///	/	
Indictable police reports		///	/	/	
Prison population	///	/			
Particular offences					
Juvenile indictable convictions	/	///	///		
Juvenile summary convictions	/	///	///	/	
Breaking and entering	/	///	//		
Violence	/	///	///	///	
Sex	///	/	/		
Fraud/receiving	/	///			/
Larceny	/	///	/		
Murder suspects			/		/
Murder victims				/	/

/   correct sign
// correct sign and statistical significance at the ·10 level (one-tail test).
/// correct sign and statistical significance at the ·05 level (one-tail test).

Table 6:2 *Results of Tests of Consensus Theory*

	Unemployment	GNP	Social security	School expenditure	School enrolment
General indicators					
Indictable convictions	/	/	/		
Summary convictions	///		/		
Indictable police reports	/		/		/
Prison population	///				
Particular offences					
Juvenile indictable convictions	///	/	///		
Juvenile summary convictions	///		///		
Breaking and entering	///		///		
Violence	/		/!		
Sex	//		/		
Fraud/receiving	/	/			/
Larceny	/	/	/		
Murder suspects		/			
Murder victims				///	//

/   correct sign
// correct sign and statistical significance at the ·10 level (one-tail test).
/// correct sign and statistical significance at the ·05 level (one-tail test).

statistical significance, conflict theory did better. The only consensus variable to have a good number of correct and significant associations was unemployment—or precisely the same result as in the tests in the preceding chapter. Among the conflict indicators, by contrast, there were three successful variables—school expenditure and enrolment and police force size. An important point, the *range* of crime indicators for which significant associations were found was more than adequate. The only indicators for which no significant relationships were found were the two murder indicators, the least relevant indicators for conflict theory testing. The most important, general, indicators were all related to a reasonable number of conflict indicators.

The most 'successful' variable was clearly school expenditure, indicating commitment to comprehensiveness and quality of control in an important institutional sphere. Next was school enrolment, with a similar meaning. Police force strength, the most direct proxy for the means of formal control, fell third. GNP per capita, the indicator of the *economic* resources available for control, was clearly less important. Instead, it was the indicators of the *social machinery* for control that were the most influential in determining actual levels of control achieved. Successful development of the welfare state evidently did not lead to a reduction in social problems and an eventual reduction of official crime rates. Rather the expansion of the welfare state meant also the expansion of the 'infrastructure' for formal control measures—and it seems that the infrastructure was indeed put to use.

There was one apparent exception to the pattern in the results of total social security expenditure. Social security expenditure was negatively related to most of the indicators in the multiple regressions, that is, when regressed along with more direct indicators of social control machinery. Treated as a single variable, however, it was *positively* correlated to all the crime indicators, and significantly with most. In other words, when its effect as a single variable was considered it proved to behave as the other indicators of the means of control—the higher the expenditure the higher the crime rates.

From the consensus tests only one variable was clearly successful, unemployment, a result similar to the cross-national comparison. Social security expenditure was the next best, falling slightly behind the third best conflict variable. But, as just noted, the correct social security results hold only for the multi-variate case. When considered as a single variable, the higher the social security expenditure, the *higher* the official crime rate.

The next stage to consider was *levels* of explanation, and here conflict theory performed considerably better than consensus. The object now was to ascertain which theory's variables did better at explaining variance, either as single variables or sets, correctly related to the range of crime-sanction indicators. Practically speaking,

Table 6:3 Comparison of Test Results

	Signs Correct		Significant ·10 level		Significant ·05 level	
	conflict	consensus	conflict	consensus	conflict	consensus
Indictable convictions	3	3	1	0	1	0
Summary convictions	4	3	3	1	3	1
Indictable police reports	3	3	1	0	1	0
Prison population	2	1	1	1	1	1
Juvenile indictable convictions	3	3	2	2	2	2
Juvenile summary convictions	4	2	2	2	2	2
Breaking and entering	3	2	2	1	2	1
Violence	4	3	3	3	3	3
Sex	4	1	1	1	0	0
Fraud/receiving	3	3	1	1	1	1
Larceny	3	3	1	1	1	1
Murder suspects	2	2	0	0	0	0
Murder victims	3	2	0	0	0	1

this involved directing the computer to examine all five explanatory variables for each theory, in turn, and to select first the variable contributing most to the explanation of the dependent variable. Each of the other variables was then added to the regression in order of its ability to increase the proportion of variance explained. The results were then inspected step by step. The intention was to select best *sets* of variables, best set defined as that obtaining the highest $\bar{R}^2$ for the dependent variable in question, with all signs correct and statistical significance at the 10 per cent level or better.[1] In fact it was not possible to construct any best set for consensus theory, for in no case did any set of consensus variables meet the required criteria. In the case of conflict theory there was no best set for murder victims, and for all but two of the others the set consisted of only one variable.

To make the comparison a compromise had to be made now to use unemployment as the best single consensus variable, and the conflict best sets (including single member sets). These results are reported in Table 6:4, and further show the superiority of conflict variables. The conflict indicators consistently achieved a higher level of explanation than the consensus, by a wide margin. For seven of the conflict indicators the level of explanation achieved bettered 90 per cent, and in four cases 95 per cent. Most importantly, the proportion of explained variance was high for the general indicators— 95 per cent for indictable convictions, 96 per cent for summary convictions, and 98 per cent for indictable police reports. By comparison, the *highest* level attained by unemployment, the best consensus indicator, was only 26 per cent.

This analysis can also be viewed as a means of separating the stronger from the weaker variables, and thereby explaining why the earlier support for certain consensus predictions did not hold up. The consensus indicators that were related in the direction predicted, even when statistically significant, were never the strongest variables in the equation. Rather, there was always at least one conflict

1. The statistic used for explained variance in this chapter is $\bar{R}^2$, or the proportion of variance explained adjusted for loss of degrees of freedom (thus taking into account increases in R^2 through the introduction of further independent variables). In the last chapter the unadjusted R^2 was used, since the computer programme used for that analysis did not provide the adjusted figures, but was otherwise a more convenient programme to use.

Table 6:4 *Levels of Explanation*

	Empirical best set*	Consensus (unemployment)	Conflict best set	Variables in conflict best set
Indictable convictions	·954	·236	·948	School expenditure
Summary convictions	·990	·236	·956	Police, GNP
Indictable police reports	·983	·177	·983	School expenditure
Prison population	·907	·177	·887	Police
Juvenile indictable convictions	·836	·248	·657	School expenditure
Juvenile summary convictions	·927	·149	·796	GNP
Break and enter	·946	·264	·910	School expenditure
Violence	·994	·165	·993	GNP, school expenditure
Sex	·628	·060	·581	School expenditure
Fraud/receiving	·969	·253	·959	School expenditure
Larceny	·936	·209	·934	School expenditure
Murder suspects	·198	·015	·198	Social security
Murder victims	·174	·027	—	—

* The highest R̄² found, with any combination of variables, with any sign.

indicator also correctly related in terms of its theory, and having greater ability to explain the dependent variable.

One further comparison was made between the level of explanation attained by the conflict best sets and 'best empirical sets'. These empirical sets were simply the variables achieving the highest $\bar{R}^2$, with any combination of indicators from the conflict and consensus five-variable runs, with any sign. This indiscriminate approach clearly did not improve the level of explanation for most dependent variables. Only in the case of the two juvenile indicators was there more than a trivial improvement. In other words, a 'fishing expedition' did not improve the results very much, but rather we did about as well as we could simply by using the predictions of conflict theory.

LABOUR OR CONSERVATIVE GOVERNMENTS

The next step was to examine the effect of party in power on official crime. As discussed earlier, the differences between the two parties had more to do with style than content, so that it was impossible to derive specific hypotheses as to which would be the more conducive to high crime rates. Labour has historically been 'softer' on criminals than the Conservatives, but its greater confidence in the power of the state to rehabilitate might offset any tendency to leniency. The cynic might indeed predict *higher* rates with Labour for all the 'hang 'em and flog 'em' talk of the Conservatives.

A new set of multiple regressions was computed, using party in power as the first variable, and then adding social security expenditure and police force size. This meant that we could first ascertain the effect of party alone, and then in conjunction with the means of formal control known to be related to party. The results confirmed the cynic's supposition, at least at the first stage. As a single variable party was significantly related to all but one of the crime indicators, sex offences, where it had no significant effect. Otherwise there were higher official crime rates with Labour in office than the Conservatives. With social security expenditure and police force size added (and even just with social security expenditure) the effect of party dropped to nil. (Again sex offences were an exception, now with rates significantly higher under Conservative governments.) The effect of party, then, was one made through the apparatus for social control. That considered, there was no tendency to higher rates with

Labour. Rather, the rates tended to be slightly higher with Conservative governments, but not significantly so.

As a final step in exploring the relationship between party in
power and officially-recorded crime a number of graphs were constructed. The story begins in the chart opposite where party in power
is noted, along with graphs of total government consumption
expenditure, expenditure on social security and on the police, all
proportionate to total population. In the second chart the graph of
police expenditure is repeated, now with the police rate and the rate
of indictable convictions. Several points stand out unmistakably, all
supportive of modern conflict theory. Firstly, there was a very close
relationship between social security expenditure and expenditure on
the police. Increases in the social welfare budget meant increases in
the measures taken for formal control, as well as increases in the
provision of other goods and 'services'. Secondly, increases in police
expenditure were translated into increases in the police force and the
rate of indictable convictions, the point of the second chart. Moreover, and the third point, the sharp and sustained rise in indictable
convictions was *preceded* by increases in police expenditure and
police force size. Increases in the police budget may not properly be
blamed on 'rising crime', for they began before the official crime rate
began to rise.

Once these few obvious points have been made, the interpretation
becomes more susceptible to that of 'finding what one is looking for'.
The reader duly warned, I proceed. In the early post-war period,
1948–51, Labour was in power, government expenditure of all kinds
increased, and with it the size of the police force. The crime rate fell
between 1948 and 1949, contrary to the economic trends, but from
1949 began to rise. The Conservatives came into power late in 1951,
but evidently too late to stop the large increase in expenditure
already budgeted. The Conservatives, did, however, keep total
consumption expenditure to the same level for the next few years,
that is, between 1952 and 1954. Social security expenditure declined
slightly between 1952 and 1953—its only decline in the post-war
period—but then began to rise again. Police expenditure continued
to increase with the new government, although at a lower rate than
later. Police force size rose sharply between 1951 and 1952. It fell then
after 1952, continuing to decline until 1955. Indictable convictions,
consistent with these trends, fell between 1952 and 1954.

Government consumption expenditure continued to decrease after

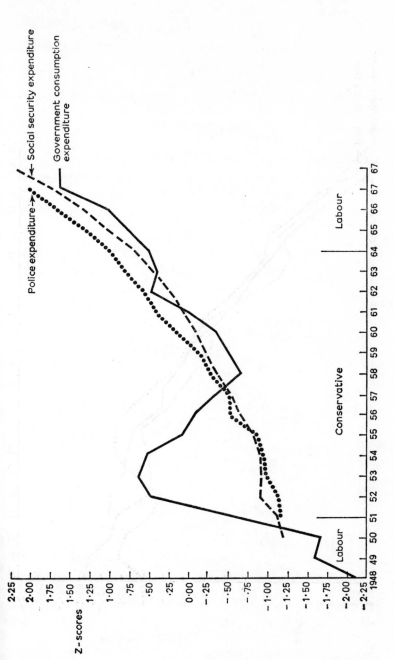

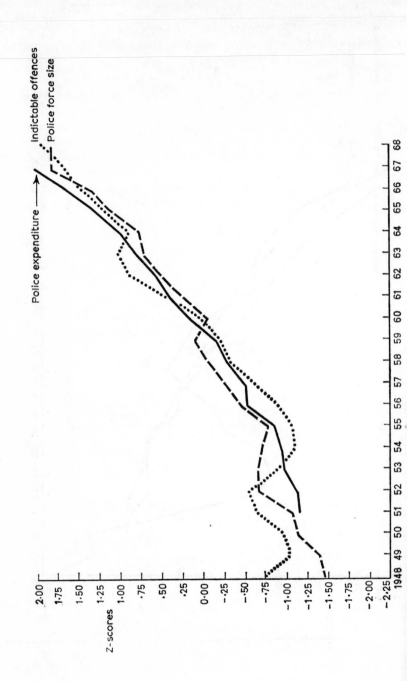

1954 under the Conservative Government, until 1958, when a long period of increases began, with only one, brief, break. Yet it was not until 1965 that expenditure reached the level it had in 1952. Social security expenditure increased throughout the 1954–8 period, although not at as steep a rate as later. Police expenditure continued to rise, but police force size was still falling, although this, too, changed to an increase in 1955. The pattern becomes more complicated after 1954, the changes in direction occurring at slightly different times for the different variables. The conviction rate, which had been falling between 1952 and 1954, began to rise again in 1954, at first slowly, and then, after 1956, more rapidly. The rise was consistent with increases in social security expenditure and police expenditure, but it preceded by a year the rise in police numbers and, by several years, the rise in total government expenditure.

In 1958, government consumption expenditure began to rise markedly, continuing to rise while the Conservatives were in power, until 1964. Social security expenditure also rose throughout this period, especially in the last few years before the 1964 election. Police expenditure rose consistently throughout the period as well. There was one brief decline in the police rate, between 1959 and 1960, but otherwise it was increasing. Indictable convictions rose at a steep rate between 1958 and 1962, but dropped between 1962 and 1963, then to increase again. The decline in the police rate was not accompanied by a drop in convictions, although the increase slackened. Similarly, for the decline in convictions, there was no parallel decline in police numbers, but the rise in police numbers was weaker that year.

After Labour came back into power in 1964, government consumption expenditure, already rising sharply, continued to rise until the end of the series, and at a steeper rate. Social security expenditure, police expenditure and the police rate all rose sharply and consistently throughout this period. Indictable convictions showed the same trend, consistent with the conflict interpretation of the expenditure-control variables.

'RISING CRIME' AND THE POLICE

The most important difference to resolve between this study and *Crime in England and Wales* concerns the relationship between police force size and the crime rate. My findings on that point were unequivocal—the greater the number of police per population, the higher the rate of recorded crime. McClintock and Avison came to the opposite conclusion, indeed urging an *increase* in the size of the police force as a means of reducing the crime rate (pp. 118, 251).

The research on which *Crime in England and Wales* was based arose out of a conference, initiated by the Home Office, to engage academics in the search for practical solutions to what it conceived to be the problems of crime and delinquency. Government officials contributed extensively to the collection, organization and interpretation of the data. The authors made no claim to speak for any government agency, and took full responsibility for the results in the usual academic way. Nevertheless, the project had a quasi-official status, and the aim of providing information of practical use was given prominence throughout.

The study was at the same time an academic one. The authors recorded their unhappiness with crime data not suitable for academic purposes. They were critical of existing theories of crime in the literature, on grounds of inadequate empirical verification. They were modest in their own theoretical aspirations, defining their role as a pre-theoretical one. The material they gathered would serve in the search for explanations 'of a higher order of scientific validity' by indicating some of the factors that should be taken into account in such explanation (p. 17). Notwithstanding this disclaimer, the authors did entertain causal explanations throughout the book, always in the consensus tradition. They cited, for example, as causes of crime: social unrest, growing leisure in 'all social classes', emergence of the 'affluent society' and leniency in punishment (pp. 20, 27). The main task of the book, however, was a descriptive one, and on this the authors were ambitious. According to the then director of the Cambridge Institute of Criminology, who introduced the book: 'No survey on such a scale and of such exactness has ever before been undertaken in this country nor, I believe, anywhere else' (p. ix). The study had associated with it the names of several of the most distinguished scholars of crime in Britain. Not a trivial point, the study was, in style, quantitative. Masses of tables, charts and statistics were provided by way of documentation. An eminent statistician and several professional mathematicians were cited as advisers and consultants.

Despite all of these scholarly attributes there are, in my opinion, several grave methodological defects in the study. Indeed, these would seem sufficient to cast doubt on the very *direction* of the findings (the rising crime rate, the need for increased police), not to speak of the weight attached to them. There was, firstly, an overwhelming reliance on one type of crime indicator, police-reported crime, a type highly susceptible to changes in reporting practices. Compounding the difficulty, most of the analysis involved only the period 1955–65, a rather short time span and, worse, a period of unusually rapid increase in the rate of recorded crime. Further, some assertions were based on comparisons of only two points in time, 1955 and 1965, a very dubious practice indeed. Whatever the extent of documentation, the problem remains. The bulk of the analysis was based on data which bear the two basic defects mentioned, and the multiplication of tables and charts does nothing to alter this fact.

The first statement to dispute is the claim, for the period 1955–65 that, while there was a sharp rise in the size of the police force, it was not sufficient to account for the increase in the crime rate. Figures were cited showing that the police handled double the load per person in 1965 than in 1955 (13·4 reported offences per police officer to 6·7). Further, it was stated that tne increase in the police force had been insufficient to cope with the rising crime rate (pp. 118–19). The link between police force size and crime rate was seen as a vicious circle. Insufficient numbers of police meant an excessive work load and, as a result, many cases remained unsolved. The low detection rate, in turn, encouraged crime, for many people learned that 'crime really does pay' (p. 120).

There are two questions to be sorted out, one dealing with extent of explanation (R^2 in regression analysis) and the other the nature of relationship (b), especially whether or not the ratio of crimes per police has increased. So far in this chapter only the former has been of concern, and one could well ask if this has not served to obscure a 'real' crime rate increase. In the McClintock and Avison study the only data reported concerned the *nature* of relationship question, but inferences were also made to *amount*. Clearly what must be done is to compare the answers to both these questions from both studies.

The issue as to amount of explanation is an empirical question, and one that can be dealt with simply. The amount of variance explained by police force size is high any way it is computed. Police rate explained 86 per cent of the variance of indictable convictions and 88 per cent of indictable reports for the 1948–68 period. For the period of the McClintock and Avison study, 1955–65, it explained 91 per cent of the variance for indictable convictions and 96 per cent of indictable reports. Their conclusion, that police force size did not account for the increase in the crime rate, is simply incorrect in the ordinary statistical sense.

We disagree on the *nature* of the crime/police relationship, as well, but the difficulties here are of a different order. There are data demonstrating increases in crime/police ratios for both the 1955–65 and 1948–68 periods. My point is that these increases are exaggerated, much of the supposed 'real' increase being due to inadequacies in indicators. The numerator McClintock and Avison used, indictable offence reports, is one which overestimates increases over time, and the denominator, police force size, underestimates increases in effective police force strength. The problem of police report indicators has already been discussed, so there remains only the issue of police numbers.

The police size indicator used in both our studies was the commonly used rate of regular, uniformed police officers and full-time auxiliaries per population. Part-time staff and civilian employees were excluded, the exclusion of the latter accounting for a good part of the problem. The exclusion of part-time staff would be important for a period including war years, but not of concern at the moment. The distortion in the police rate occurs in that civilian employees, few in number throughout most of the century, have increasingly been added to the force in recent years. The change was especially strong in the 1960s, hence comparisons of these years with earlier are somewhat misleading. Civilian employees were outnumbered by regulars 18:1 in 1948, but only 5:1 in 1967. In addition, a Traffic Warden Corps has been in operation since 1961, adding further to the growth of the civilian staff.[1] Both types of new civilian employees have the same effect, freeing regular, uniformed staff from duties they previously performed. Exclusion of these civilian employees means that rates for the later years will be underestimates of effective police force strength.[2]

This is all to suggest that there is no single, correct way to compute police force size, any more than there is any one, authentic 'crime rate'. I accordingly made a number of computations, using

1. Report of H.M. Inspector of Constabulary, 1967, p. 15.
2. The fact of these changes was acknowledged in the study (p. 252), but no account was taken of it in the statistics used.

a new indicator (civilian employees as well as uniformed), and both court convictions and police reports. The changes were computed both for the years of my study, 1948–68, and the McClintock and Avison, 1955–65. These various ratios are reported in Table 6:5, where it is clear that quite different results occur when different methods are used. The increases were much greater for the ten-year period of the McClintock and Avison study than for my twenty-year period, any way the ratios were computed. Even with the old police indicator and indictable reports, the increase for my period was 63 per cent, substantially lower than the 104 per cent for theirs. When convictions were used instead of police reports, the increases dropped further, from 61 per cent for the 1955–65 period, to 32 per cent for mine. The lowest increase of the series appeared when the new police indicator was used, with convictions, for the 1948–68 period— only 15 per cent. This is not to suggest that this is the *only* ratio that is valid. The point is that different methods of computation produce different results, and McClintock and Avison's 'better than doubling' conclusion was an extreme one. Quite reasonable, alternative methods would indicate much more moderate conclusions. When a series between 1900 and 1968 is examined, it will again be seen that the results are much more modest.

Table 6:5 *Ratio of Crimes to Police Force Size*

	McDonald			McClintock and Avison		
	1948	1968*	% Change	1955	1965	% Change
Court convictions/ Old Police rate	2·14	2·82	31·5	1·61	2·58	60·2
Police Reports/ Old Police rate	8·66	14·12	63·0	6·57	13·41	104·0
Court convictions/ New Police rate	2·03	2·32	14·7	1·50	2·30	53·8
Police Reports/ New Police Rate	8·19	11·58	41·3	6·11	11·85	94·2

* 1967 for uniformed and civilian police numbers.

Data on police *expenditure* provide perhaps an even better indication of real police strength than mere *numbers* of police, however defined. The expenditure variable may be the most realistic indicator of effective police strength for it reflects, as well as numbers, the extent and quality of facilities, training and organization. This is an especially relevant point for the period under consideration, for massive changes in all these respects occurred within it. A royal commission on the police, reporting in 1962, made a number of recommendations towards increased efficiency, many of which were subsequently implemented. When expenditure was used as the denominator it is clear that the increases were much more modest still. For the years of the McClintock and Avison study, the increase in convictions was only 15 per cent, and 46 per cent for police reports. For the years of my study, the data actually indicate *decreases* in the rates.

There is a rather fundamental principle at stake on this point, namely the propriety of basing any serious inferences on comparisons over only two points in time. Certainly it is wrong to do this when there is any reasonable alternative, which happens to be the case. One simple solution is to examine the linear regression slopes of the ratios over time, a positive slope indicating an increase in the ratio, a negative slope a decrease, and a zero slope no change. Regression slopes were accordingly computed for the 1948–68 period, for all thirteen of the crime rates, relative both to the new police figures and police expenditure. Again, the results were of much more modest increases and some decreases. Where the numbers of crimes were related to numbers of police, there were increases for eight of the ratios, decreases on two, and no change on two.[1] When related to police expenditure there was an increase on three ratios, decreases on six, and no significant change on four.[2] The argument is not that the results indicate conclusively a decline in the crime rate relative to effective policing. Rather, the question of changes in rates is a complicated one, properly approached carefully, from several perspectives. Clearly there are increases relative to some indicators, but not to all, and indeed decreases with respect to other indicators, so that conclusions should be expressed with the appropriate qualification.

CRIME RATES 1900–68

The time series analysis was extended to the 1900–68 period for further consideration of two points. Firstly, the tests of the more

1. Ratios of crime/police decreasing significantly were murder suspects and murder victims; there was no change in sex offences and juvenile indictable offences.
2. Indicators increasing significantly were indictable police reports, violence and breaking and entering. Total indictable and summary convictions, fraud and juvenile summary convictions showed no change.

successful, conflict theory were continued, for results accruing from this greater period would naturally add considerably to the credibility of the conclusions. It was not possible, however, to extend the consensus tests at all, simply for lack of data. Even for the tests on conflict theory the analysis was limited to only three independent variables—police force size, expenditure on police and party in power (dichotomized between Labour and non-Labour). There were only two indicators of rates of sanctions, total indictable convictions and total summary convictions. Next, there was some further analysis of the position taken in the McClintock and Avison study, again in a much briefer fashion than for the post-war period.

Table 6:6 *Conflict Tests*, 1900–68

	$\bar{R}^2$	
	indictable convictions	summary convictions
as single variables:		
police force size/population	·800*	·260*
police expenditure/population	·805*	·214*
party in power	·223*	·016
all together	·857	·215

*T values statistically significant at the ·001 level (one-tail test).

Note: In the multiple regressions party in power was not statistically significant, nor was police force size in the case of summary conviction. The other relationships were significant at the ·001 level.

The results, with these limitations in mind, were supportive of conflict theory. As shown in Table 6:6, police expenditure explained as much as 80 per cent of the variance of indictable convictions, and 21 per cent of summary, while police force size explained 80 per cent and 26 per cent of the same two indicators respectively. The relationships were not as strong as those found for the 1948–68 period, but still adequate, and considerably better than adequate in the case of indictable convictions. Party in power had a somewhat stronger effect on indictable convictions than in the shorter period, accounting for 22 per cent of the variance, and only 2 per cent of the variance for non-indictable offences.

Again, Labour governments were associated with higher crime rates in the single variable case. When party was considered with the police variables, however, it had no significant effect. Considering the three variables together the total proportion of variance explained was 86 per cent in the case of indictable convictions, and 21 per cent for summary, in neither case much of an improvement on the level of explanation obtained with police expenditure or police force size alone.

These relationships can be further examined in the next two charts. There the indictable conviction rate is graphed, firstly with party in power and the police rate, and then with police expenditure. Again the close relationship between the conviction rate and both expenditure and police force size is obvious. The only marked exception occurs in World War I, when police expenditure declined while the official crime rate rose. The rises in *all* rates under Labour is also clear in the graphs.

There was a contradiction as well on one other point. McClintock and Avison stated, without citing any data to this effect, that police force strength was more closely related to summary offences than indictable (p. 287). The argument is a reasonable one—greater availability in police numbers should mean additional time available for enforcement of less serious offences. This indeed was found in my study of post-war crime rates in Canada. In the English case, however, no such relationship appeared; the relationships for both police variables were greater between indictable convictions than summary.

The last question to be investigated in this section was that of increases in crime rates—the extent to which there have been increases over the period, relative to what factors. I examined the two crime rate indicators in turn relative to police force size and expenditure, as in the earlier analysis, and with roughly similar results. Indictable convictions increased relative to police force size, consistent with statements in the McClintock and Avison study. When the crime rates were examined relative to police expenditure, however, the slope was now effectively zero–negative, but not to a statistically significant degree. For summary convictions the slope was nil in the case of police force size (negative, but not significant), and significantly negative for police expenditure. The answer to the question as to whether or not crime rates have been rising relative to policing then is conditional; it depends on how you look at it. The four answers I obtained include one significant increase, one significant decrease, and two draws.

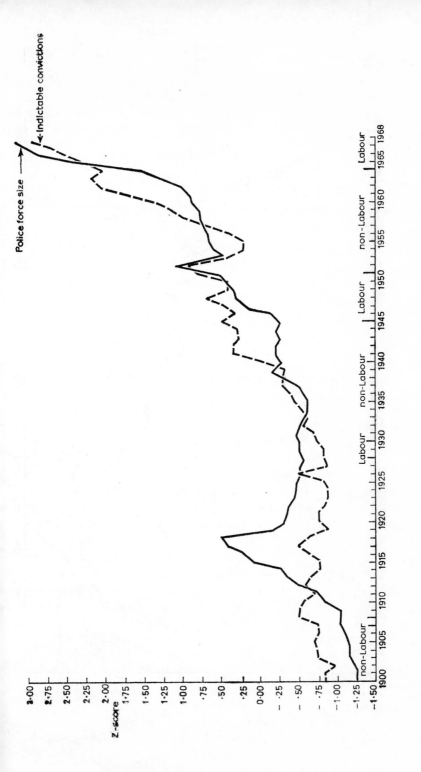

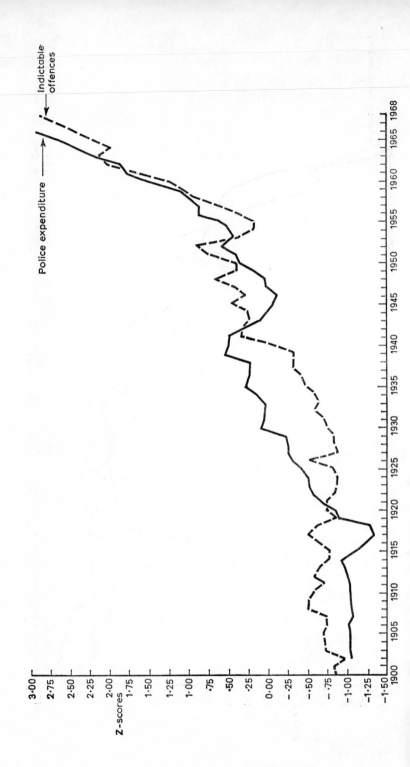

CRIME RATES BY BOROUGH

Criticism of this next, short, and comparatively unknown work, *Police Regression Analysis* is perhaps even more important than the criticism of the substantial and prestigious *Crime in England and Wales*. One reason is that McClintock and Avison relied on arguments from it in making their case for more police. Another reason lies in the impressively complicated research techniques used. Whether or not difficulty adds to the credibility of the argument is a moot point. Suffice it to say, I took its conclusions and supporting analysis seriously enough to take some trouble to challenge them. The study was not directed to hypothesis testing in terms of theory for its own sake, but was concerned rather with an understanding of crime for more effective policing. It was, then, unlike the McClintock and Avison study, directed to causal explanation, although with this qualification.

The approach taken to crime explanation was solidly consensus throughout. All the explanatory variables were of the social problem type, for the most part reflecting absolute needs and problems, such as unemployment and overcrowding, rather than problems of system adjustment. A few classical Victorian variables were given prominence in the analysis: alcohol outlets per population, and betting shops *per working-class* population! Not the least of the charms of this study is just this juxtaposition of sophisticated quantification with the familiar old variables of moral degradation. No variables comparable to our conflict indicators were used as such, although it was possible to construct variables on police strength and expenditure per population out of the raw data provided. Rather, the police variables were also treated as problems—population per officer, for example, as an indicator of work-load.

The findings on crime rates were sharply at odds with those from my time series. The results are not precisely comparable, given differences in the nature of data between time series and cross-sectional analysis, but the brunt of the conclusions differ unmistakably. My task, accordingly, is to show *how* the results of the *Police Regression Analysis* were reached, and what is wrong with them. Next, I shall try to show how reasonable, alternative methods produce quite different results.

Three factors were cited to account for the variation in reported crime—crime failure rate (the ratio of offences not satisfactorily cleared up over the total recorded), population density, and the distribution of the social classes (p. 9). There is no dispute with the finding on population density, and the dispute with respect to the crime failure rate is a matter of interpretation. I do take issue with the findings on social class distribution and, more importantly, the findings on the effect of policing. A crucial point, the study claimed that police variables, apart from what was indirectly reflected in the crime failure rate, did not have any impact on the crime rate.

These conclusions were based on three distinctive pieces of analysis, to each of which certain objections can be raised. Firstly, there was a 'trial and error' construction of non-linear and rather complicated equations to explain *the* crime rate. No equation was reported for the main crime variable used, indictable offence reports. There were only two crime rate indicators used at all throughout the study— indictable offences and a selection of property offences. Next there was a bivariate correlational analysis of each of a set of thirty-three variables, reported crime, socio-economic problems and policing, with each other. Certain variables, very limited both in number and type, were then selected from this matrix for inclusion in the multiple regression analysis. The basis for selection, apart from statistical independence, was not stated.

For indictable offences only two multiple regressions were reported, in each of which only two variables were found to have contributed significantly to the variation—the crime failure rate and population density. The social class variable (proportion of working class) was not significantly related to indictable offences in either equation. The same results occurred when the bivariate case was considered—no significant relationships.[1]

The conclusion of social class being one of the three factors explaining 'the' crime rate would appear to be based on the results from the regressions on the other crime indicator. When the content of this indicator is examined the reason for the relationship becomes all too clear. The indicator was comprised of offences known to be more characteristic of working-class persons than middle-class: shop-breaking, house-breaking and miscellaneous entering offences. Property offences more typical of middle-class people, like embezzle-

---

1. Indictable offences per population were correlated at ·01 with the fraction of the population in classes I and II (upper and upper middle class), −·19 with class III (lower middle and upper working class), and ·11 with classes IV and V (middle and lower working class).

ment and fraud, were entirely excluded. The finding of a social class distribution affecting *the* crime rate, then, was a tautology; offences more characteristic of working-class people appeared disproportionately in working-class areas. A point not made anywhere in the analysis, but noted by Carr-Hill and Stern in their re-analysis of the same data: *there were more police per capita in working-class areas than middle.*

The basis for the conclusion of police variables as such not affecting the crime rate had to be, in part, surmised, for it was not made explicit. Certainly the bivariate correlation results did not support such an interpretation. The police strength variable (population per officer) was correlated at $-\cdot28$ with indictable offences per population, and at $-\cdot14$ with the selected property offence variable. The proportion of the police force in the criminal investigation department was correlated at $\cdot51$ and $\cdot25$ with the same two indicators respectively. What the author probably meant was, that since the *direction* of the findings was opposed to what he predicted, there was no relationship. What he predicted was a high work-load per officer and, by extension, a low proportion dealing with criminal cases, to result in a high crime rate. What appeared was precisely the reverse, or, the greater the number of police per population, and the greater the proportion devoted to criminal cases, the higher the rate of recorded crime.

The conclusion of no association between the police variables and the crime rate was no better supported in the multiple regression analysis. Population per officer was simply not used in either of the regressions of indictable offences. It was used in only one of the selected property offences, with effectively no relationship appearing. Again the results were in the direction opposite to that expected by the author, but not to a statistically significant degree. None of the other police indicators was used in the crime rate regressions published and, accordingly, how their failure to have affected the crime rate can have been determined remains unclear. There is, however, no need to speculate on this matter, for the relationships can be readily computed and examined.

The results for the bivariate case can be disposed of simply. Both the number of police and expenditure on police per population were significantly related to indictable offences, as single variables explaining 8·5 and 11·5 per cent of the variance respectively. Next the same multiple regressions reported in the original study of indictable offences were recomputed, now adding each of the police variables in turn. For both the equations modest increases in level of explanation were obtained. With police force size added the proportion explained rose from 25 per cent to 34 per cent in the case of the first equation, and from 36 to 42 per cent in the case of the second. With police expenditure the explained variance rose to 32 and 39 per cent respectively for the two equations. Computations were made for several other combinations of problem variables with the police indicators as well, but in none of them was the level of explained variance improved.[1]

In the case of the property offence equations, the addition of the police variables to the original equations did not improve the level of explanation. The proportions initially obtained were 31 per cent for two of the equations, and 32 per cent for the third. Yet several other combinations of variables did improve the level of explanation, among them some incorporating police indicators. The most successful equation, explaining 44 per cent of the variance is reported in Table 6:7, along with the best equation from the original study.

Table 6:7 *Levels of Explanation for Property Offences*

Best *Police Regression Analysis* equation	b		R^2
population density	·126	3·59*	
% working class	5·478	1·73*	
failure rate†	3·983	2·38*	·322
betting licenses/working-class pop.	·446	1·32	
retail licenses/ratable value of shops	·0026	1·22	
Best McDonald equation			
vehicle licenses/pop.	−·0237	−4·87*	
failure rate†	3·914	2·56*	·438
population density	·085	2·64*	
expenditure per officer	1·955	1·28	

* statistically significant at the ·05 level (one-tail test).
† re selected property offences.

1. Analysis by Carr–Hill and Stern similarly failed to turn up any indication of police force size acting to reduce crime. This included both a reanalysis of the same data as in the *Police Regression Analysis*, and an extension to later years. Those authors were interested in rather different questions from mine, but as well were moved to question policy recommendations of increases in the police force.

Altogether it is clear that, if a high level of explanation is desired, police force strength and expenditure are required. Finally, the police variables, in all the equations tested, were related to the crime variables in the direction I hypothesized, that is, the greater the size and expenditure on the police per population, the higher was the crime rate.

The final point is the recommendation, couched in suitably academic terms, for an increase in the police force. The argument made was necessarily circuitous, and unsatisfactory on several levels. Firstly it was stated that the key to the reduction of the crime rate lay in the crime failure rate (p. 9) on which point my objections are modest. I concede that the approach through the crime failure rate is plausible although hardly the most obvious one suggested by the data. (One could equally well argue for a reduction in the police force, or in betting licences, or an *increase* in the number of alcohol licences.) The next stage, however, is serious, for the author recommended an all-round increase in the police force as the chief means of reducing the crime failure rate and, in turn, the crime rate. The data reported immediately above, of course, indicate precisely the opposite; the higher the police rate the greater the crime rate. The indirect argument, however appealing it may be on some intuitive level, is simply wrong according to the normal rules of argument.[1] Speculative, indirect arguments have their place, but hardly when data on the point at issue are available suggesting precisely the opposite.

CONCLUSIONS

The drawing of conclusions from the time series analysis was relatively simple. A large number of tests of both theories was conducted, and a reasonably consistent set of results appeared across them, favourable to conflict theory. Conflict theory was well supported in absolute terms, and it was clearly better supported than consensus. High levels of explained variance were achieved for a good range of crime-sanction indicators, including the more general ones, and those known to be least vulnerable to distortion through changes in report-

1. The argument is unsound statistically as well. In multiple regression it cannot be assumed, for example, that if variables A and B are positively related in one equation, and B and C are in another, that A and C will be in a third.

ing procedures. As in the preceding chapter, the only non-trivial support for consensus theory occurred with the variable of unemployment, support which does not at the same time imply disconfirmation of conflict theory.

The variables that best accounted for variation in crime-sanction indicators were the indicators of the social machinery for formal control and experience of control in other institutional spheres. School expenditure and enrolment and police force size were the most important variables of this type. Next came the indicator of economic resources available for social control, GNP. The variables of the welfare state, the economic base and social machinery for problem solving, turned out not to have the effect predicted by consensus theory. Prosperity, far from reducing crime, was associated with crime increases. The expansion of the school system, for whatever other enlightening effects it might have, did not result in any reduction in official crime.

There was some further corroboration of these results in a brief secondary analysis of data from another study, *Police Regression Analysis*. While the support found for conflict theory was modest it is nonetheless of interest, for it was derived from a different dimension of analysis, a cross-sectional study now instead of time series. The analysis indicated a certain amount of support for consensus theory as well as conflict. Several problem indicators, notably population density, were found to be positively related to the crime indicators. The set of variables to explain the highest proportion of variation was a combination of social problem *and* social control indicators.

IS THE 'CRIME RATE' RISING?

The question of crime rate increases was approached by examining rates for different indicators, relative to different denominators. The results, for crime rates relative to population, were consistent increases throughout, some of them substantial. One could still quarrel with the increases in the McClintock and Avison study, which were based on one type of indicator only, police reports of offences. My results, examining crime rates relative to police indicators, were rather different. Most of the crime rates relative to police force strength were of modest increases, but there were exceptions in the case of police expenditure. McClintock and Avison, by contrast, found a 'more than doubling' of the crime rate per police officer and for a shorter period. In my judgement this is a misleading statistic, being based on two relatively unreliable statistics—a numerator which is an underestimate, and a denominator which is an overestimate. As well, the particular years chosen for the comparison exaggerate the differences. Data on rates between the twenty-year period of my study consistently yielded lower estimates for the various comparisons, as did similar data for the 1900–68 period.

The approach that I would recommend in analysing crime rate changes over time is laborious, involving consideration of a number of different crime indicators, relative to a number of different denominators. There are many ways of depicting even a simple concept like 'total crime', and a credible analysis would have to deal with a reasonable range of them. The crime indicators should include general indicators, including those known to be relatively unsusceptible to changes in reporting practices. In case of conflicting results those based on the more general, and less susceptible, should be given the greater weight. The denominators should include population and, where there have been important demographic changes in the period in question, these should be taken account of. Changes in the age-distribution should be carefully considered. Property offences should probably be examined relative to property at risk, as well as population. Probably all crime data should be examined relative to the means taken to deal with it, in terms of policing and recording practices. Desirably, effective police strength would be considered, as well as numbers. Except under very particular circumstances, crime increases should not be computed simply between two particular years, however selected. Rather, comparisons should be based on averages of different periods, or summary statistics, like linear or logarithmic slopes. This recommended approach necessarily entails more work than the usual, and involves a risk of complicated patterns of findings to make sense of—two decided disadvantages. On the other hand it is more in keeping with notions of crime rates that people in fact use. Conceptually, such an approach implies a rejection of a simple notion, *the* crime rate, in favour of a more complicated notion of crime as a many-faceted phenomenon.

THE EFFECT OF POLICING

The relationship between police force size and rates of recorded crime was considered at length, largely in the context of criticizing two other studies. The differences in conclusion could not have been greater, for in both these other studies a negative relationship between police force size and crime was asserted. Indeed, these authors were sufficiently convinced of that to recommend an increase in police force size as a means of reducing crime. The argument in both cases was firmly grounded in consensus theory. Rates of recorded crime were treated as indicators of real crime, and real crime was viewed as the product of various social problems. The persistence of social problems implied that there had not been adequate attempts at problem-solving. An inordinately high crime rate, in short, indicated *insufficient* societal response, for which at least one remedy was obvious—an increase in the forces of order. My findings would suggest just the opposite if they are to be used for policy recommendations at all. The results were unequivocally of a positive relationship between police force size and recorded crime— the greater the number of police per population the higher the crime rate. Moreover, these results were based on an extensive analysis, of both cross-sectional data and longitudinal, the latter not only for the post-war period, but the entire 1900–68 period as well. A number of different multiple regressions were examined in both cases, as well as the simple bivariate case.

THE NOTION OF 'REAL' CRIME

The question of crime rates and crime increases is complicated enough when the relevant data are taken at face value, as measures of numbers of recorded offences or offenders. When inferences are to be drawn to some other concept, such as 'real' crime, or real damage or suffering caused to victims, society itself, or 'the law', the problems multiply. I share the view that rates of recorded crime do not sustain inference to concepts at any higher level. If any fundamental notion of immorality is to be entertained rates of recorded crime would be even more inappropriate. Social class biases in crime definitions and social class selection in the administration of the criminal law are enough to make such indicators suspect. It is not that these other levels are too esoteric to be measured at all, but that quite different kinds of indicators would be required. Some work has already been done along these lines, by way of studies of victimization, and no doubt other indices of fear and suffering better capturing the spirit of crime could be developed.

The process by which recorded crime comes to be seen as real crime is an intriguing one. It is by no means natural or inevitable, but can be either promoted or discouraged. The McClintock and Avison study clearly encourages readers to take a 'crime rate as objective danger' view, through a variety of subtle and not so subtle means. A few examples illustrate this point. Firstly, note how the discussion shifts, almost imperceptibly, between simple *recorded* crime and some notion of *real* crime.

> While the annual increase in recorded crime in England and Wales is not a recent phenomenon, it has been seen that the upward trend in crime has, in fact, accelerated in the last decade. (p. 250)

The initial fact refers only to *recorded crime* but, we are told, 'crime has, in fact, accelerated'. Recorded crime not only becomes crime 'in fact', but many things more colourful, like 'lawlessness' (p. 272), so that an increase in the recorded rate becomes the 'spread of lawlessness'. Some aspects of the 'problem', however, are more serious than others:

> Perhaps the largest problem that gives concern is the annual increased and actual volume of 'unsolved' crime (p. 119).

The unsolved crime rate is further dramatized with a medical term, 'immunity', the immunity rate suggesting the extent to which offenders are 'immune' from detection. The indicator of unsolved crime has, as well, a deeper meaning:

> The volume of unsolved crime is a measure of how far the police have not been able to achieve their ultimate target of detecting all those who have violated the criminal law (p. 120).

Insofar as trivial violations are included, it must be remembered, 'all those who have violated the criminal law' includes most of us at some time or other, including most police. Such a fact is ignored in the discussion, and the general public is treated as sharing with the authors their awe of the 'rising crime rate' and rising 'immunity' to detection.

> Not only is there much public concern over the increase in crime, but there is also considerable disquiet as to the apparent growth in the immunity of offenders from detection (p. 127).

That so many responsible individuals consider crime such a serious problem might be expected to have some effect on the reader. No *data* on public views of crime are cited, though the point is made in several places.

> Parliament, the central administration, and indeed society are naturally primarily concerned with the extent to which the police fall short of catching all the actual perpetrators of crime (p. 94).

The 'naturalness' of this concern is stressed time and again.

> The size of the unsolved crime problem naturally leads to concern in Parliament and among the general public as to the extent to which law and order are being properly maintained (p. 120).

The recommendations for increases in the police force are made in the same tenor, and the book ends on the same note, fittingly with a chapter on 'The Challenge of Crime to the English Penal System'. That the title may be a play on the American Government's *The Challenge of Crime in a Free Society* has occurred; given the general lack of wit in the book, however, this is unlikely.

Altogether the reader can be forgiven for getting caught up in the hushed tones of the discussion. One is accustomed to using the tone of a discussion as a cue to its substance, and normally this is a reasonable practice. The problem in this case is that the tone lends itself to incorrect inferences, notably to a blurring of the distinction between the indicator and the reality it is supposed to represent. One forgets that what is 'really' being discussed is simply a rate of recorded crime.

The recorded crime rate becomes 'lawlessness', and as it increases the public grows more anxious, Parliament sits later into the night, and the police begin to sink under the burden. The only problem 'fully' demonstrated, of course, is the recorded crime problem, and for this any number of solutions are possible: reduction of the police force, increased emphasis on non-criminal work, greater attention to more serious crime and time-consuming investigations of white collar offences.

The extent to which crime itself is a real problem in contemporary Britain is the last of the three law and order issues to be discussed. Here we must consider crime in relation to other social problems, comparing the unfortunate consequences of crime to the harm caused by these other problems. My remarks are confined to property offences, which constitute the vast majority of offences for which people are sentenced. Obviously offences of violence are of greater concern, but the point holds for the great bulk of the 'crime problem'.[1]

Crimes against property mean that people are out of pocket by certain amounts of money. The sentimental value of property lost by crime of course cannot be estimated, but the simple economic value can. The estimate, for England and Wales for 1965, is that £26 million of money and goods were lost in larcenies and breaking and entering offences, roughly half a pound per person per year. When this is compared with the losses people suffer in other ways the sum seems trivial. Anyone losing so much as one day's work loses far more than the average loss due to crime in a year. Inflation reduces everybody's buying power, and causes real deprivation to those on low incomes. Again, especially for recent years, the losses have been considerably greater than those from crime. A family with a £3,000 total income may, for example, enjoy wage increases of 10 per cent, but lose 15 per cent in buying power for the year, for a net loss of £150, or again much more the average loss due to crime. Women incur major losses in income through being paid at lower rates than men, and being largely restricted to jobs with low rates of pay. Women manual workers in Britain earned on average £10 per week less than men[2] in 1964, or in any one week losing twenty times more than the average loss per year on account of property crimes.

While I take issue with the view of recorded crime as a major social problem, there are legitimate concerns about the meaning of the rates, and especially increases in them. Hence, after discussing what they do not represent, I will discuss what they do. Certainly rates of recorded crime represent the application of social control measures, the compilation of dossiers, invasion of privacy and certain real hardships. Increases in recorded rates then indicate increased interference in individuals' everyday lives, and an increase in real suffering at the extreme, through loss of job, damage to reputation and so forth. An increase in the size of the police force, staffs of the courts, prisons and other correctional agencies means an increase in the proportion of the population devoted to regulatory work. This

1. I would like to have considered *subjective* views of crime as well, but was unable to find any appropriate material. Surveys on crime in Britain, for example Durant, have *assumed* seriousness, inquiring only as to which offence is worse than which other, and not making any comparison between crime and other problems.
2. Sullerot, p. 126.

means necessarily a detraction from productive work or the provision of services, or both. Questions of crime, in short, should not be examined in isolation, and not without rather careful consideration of the costs of proposed solutions.

	Constant	Police	School Expenditure[a]	School Enrolment[b]	GNP[b]	Social Security[c]	Durbin–Watson Statistic
Indictable Convictions	−2,797·9	6·575 (0·64)	27·47 (3·02)	131·93 (1·26)	−120·37 (−0·92)	−1·66 (−1·14)	1·90
Summary Convictions	−17,267·8	68·0 (2·07)	76·21 (2·60)	641·85 (1·91)	85·98 (0·21)	29·88 (−1·59)	1·94
Indictable Police reports	−7,326·1	0·017 (0·00)	9·76 (2·76)	60·58 (0·15)	196·66 (0·39)	−6·33 (−0·28)	2·05
Juvenile Indictable		3·89 (0·80)	16·24 (3·74)	124·40 (2·49)	−45·58 (−0·73)	−7·57 (−2·72)	2·00
Juvenile Summary	−2,512·4	4·54 (1·06)	14·87 (3·90)	112·04 (2·56)	46·15 (0·84)	−8·64 (−3·52)	2·06
Prison population	−322·6	2·69 (1·93)	1·11 (0·90)	−1·29 (−·09)	−0·717 (−0·04)	−0·972 (−1·22)	1·20
Violence	−243·3	0·104 (0·28)	1·47 (4·49)	11·81 (3·15)	9·23 (1·97)	−0·251 (−1·20)	2·37
Larceny	−789·7	0·619 (0·10)	14·12 (2·57)	61·49 (0·97)	−100·86 (−1·28)	−1·34 (0·38)	1·89
Breaking and entering	−1,349·9	3·88 (1·20)	8·84 (3·09)	46·90 (1·42)	−13·76 (−0·34)	−3·91 (−2·13)	2·17
Fraud/receiving	−40·9	0·199 (0·26)	1·46 (2·16)	−0·621 (−0·08)	−14·48 (−1·50)	0·208 (0·48)	1·60
Sex	−94·0	−94·04 (0·19)	0·0509 (0·19)	3·76 (1·24)	4·18 (1·11)	−0·342 (−2·02)	1·44
Murder suspects	1,795·8	−7·77 (−0·71)	−1·38 (−0·14)	18·29 (0·16)	−57·16 (−0·41)	6·01 (0·96)	2·82
Murder victims	1,929·9	10·48 (0·96)	−2·23 (−2·29)	−227·76 (−2·04)	126·55 (0·91)	5·08 (0·81)	2·49

T values in parentheses.
[a] Move decimal point three places to the left.
[b] Move decimal point four places to the left.
[c] Move decimal point five places to the left.

Consensus Theory Equations

	Constant	Unemployment	GNP[a]	Social Security[c]	School Enrolment[a]	School Expenditure[b]	Durbin–Watson Statistic
Indictable Convictions	−2,005·06	4·999 (1·21)	−7·27 (−0·55)	−4·36 (−1·18)	11·77 (1·20)	258·61 (2·92)	1·95
Summary Convictions	−9,150·83	43·433 (4·30)	44·27 (1·36)	−5·39 (−0·59)	56·30 (2·35)	641·08 (2·96)	2·00
Indictable Police reports	−7,223·78	9·841 (0·60)	35·79 (0·68)	−7·41 (−0·50)	−2·07 (−0·05)	921·71 (2·61)	2·15
Juvenile Indictable	−1,640·27	3·459 (1·87)	−0·920 (−0·16)	−6·28 (−3·77)	11·18 (2·55)	150·16 (3·78)	2·04
Juvenile Summary	−1,961·39	3·831 (2·51)	8·52 (1·74)	−7·11 (−5·18)	9·91 (2·74)	135·57 (4·14)	2·08
Prison population	−6·45	1·193 (2·07)	0·475 (0·26)	0·0571 (0·11)	−0·00516 (−0·00)	9·19 (0·74)	1·10
Violence	−230·41	0·114 (0·76)	1·06 (2·17)	−0·219 (−1·61)	1·13 (3·15)	14·22 (4·38)	2·36
Larceny	−712·82	0·693 (0·27)	−9·27 (−1·11)	−1·15 (−0·49)	5·83 (0·95)	138·47 (2·49)	1·91
Breaking and entering	−882·84	2·88 (2·46)	1·31 (0·35)	−2·56 (−2·44)	3·91 (1·41)	79·34 (3·16)	2·21
Fraud/receiving	−15·86	0·259 (0·83)	−1·13 (−1·13)	0·265 (0·95)	−0·194 (−0·26)	13·50 (2·02)	1·66
Sex	−28·42	0·194 (1·49)	0·443 (1·06)	−0·121 (−1·03)	0·448 (1·45)	0·412 (0·15)	1·48
Murder suspects	866·34	−5·109 (−1·15)	−10·03 (−0·70)	3·22 (0·81)	2·85 (0·27)	0·851 (0·01)	2·89
Murder victims	3,097·46	−0·141 (−0·30)	4·87 (0·32)	9·76 (2·28)	−17·29 (−1·53)	−197·47 (−1·93)	2·77

T values in parentheses.
[a] Move decimal point three places to the left.

Chapter 7

LAW AND ORDER IN CANADA

Public views on crime—what threat it poses to society, what the law should be and how it should be enforced—for the first time become the main subject of inquiry. The attitudes and opinions so far discussed only peripherally now are the central concern of the study, and a very difficult part of the analysis this proved to be. Objective statistics on crime and social control continue to be relevant, but now in a different way. It is the *relationship* between crime and social control as revealed by objective data and subjective views of it that is now at issue.

It is here that we begin to explore the consensus hypothesis that the criminal law reflects the dominant values of a society, and the contradictory view from conflict theory of its reflecting the interests of the holders of power. Similarly, we consider the hypothesis of enforcement practices reflecting public views of the threat of crime, along with the conflict proposition of their reflecting the interests of the holders of power. Attitudes and perceptions of crime are hypothesized to differ as between the two approaches, to be supportive of the respective policy positions taken. The analysis was based on Canadian materials, and largely from a survey conducted expressly for this project.

The task undertaken proved to be much more difficult than anticipated, and the work more difficult in many ways than the other chapters. Statistics on mere numbers of offenders present their own difficulties to be sure, but the problems encountered in exploring people's ideas are all that much greater. The result is a much more cumbersome analysis, and a much higher incidence of ambiguous and contradictory results. The discussion as well turned out to be unbalanced. Certain important points were given relatively little space since they had already been discussed elsewhere, while others of no greater importance took much longer to report—the new material from the survey. Certain points I would like to have investigated proved not to be amenable to the survey type interview, so that only very rough and impressionistic material could be gathered on them. This included the issue of views on the seriousness of crime relative to other problems, a part of the testing of consensus theory.

Since the survey was the basis of so much of the data probably its basic outlines should be described without further delay. I did not attempt to cover a complete cross-section of the population, but only a range of distinct segments, and an important part of the hypothesis testing was based on differences in responses across these different segments. Six groups were included in the study, all from Ontario, and most from southern Ontario. Firstly, there was a civil liberties association, which served as a yardstick for the civil liberties position, and non-punitive attitudes and views generally. Next there were two workers' groups, hypothesized by conflict theory to be next most favourable to civil liberties views, and next in holding non-punitive views. In consensus theory, the workers were hypothesized to be the *most* punitive, and least accepting of civil liberties views. There was a group each of lawyers and businessmen, hypothesized to be the *most* punitive and least favourable to civil liberties in conflict theory, and the opposite by consensus. A teachers' group was hypothesized to be intermediate in both.

Access to power, as earlier, was the crucial consideration in the conflict approach—the better the access the more to gain by punitive measures and, hence, the more favourable people should be to such measures, and the more likely to have attitudes and perceptions regarding crime consistent with the position. In consensus theory, education, occupational prestige and security were the crucial variables. The higher the standing on these factors, the less punitive people should be, and the more favourable to civil liberties. The occupational groups were chosen so as to vary on all the components —the lawyers and businessmen both having the greatest access to power, education, occupational prestige and security, the teachers being intermediate on all these points and the workers with least access to power, the lowest average level of education, security and occupational prestige.

The groups referred to for convenience simply as the 'businessmen' and so forth were not random samples from their respective occupations, and do not represent these occupational groups in any statistical sense. Rather they represent only limited sectors of the broader groupings, but ones which seemed adequate. Specifically, the businessmen were all the available members of a businessmen's organization in an industrial city in southern Ontario. The lawyers were drawn randomly from the Bar Admission course at Osgoode Hall, from law graduates throughout the whole province. The teachers were drawn from among members of the profession taking summer courses at a provincial Ontario university, McMaster University. One of the workers' groups consisted entirely of textile workers, drawn randomly from among the employees of a textile plant in Brantford, Ontario. The other was a random sample of persons giving a manual occupation, from the voters' list in a predominantly working-class district in Hamilton. Details of the sampling procedure, the construction of the interview schedule, and the mechanics of the fieldwork are reported in the Technical Note (pp. 298–302).

The approach taken in the fieldwork was consistent with the general conceptualization of social control as a central sociological subject. The survey included questions on views of civil liberties very broadly defined, rights and responsibilities of government and citizens respectively, rights for particular groups, notably women, and a range of problems facing the country, as well as some basic questions on crime and punishment.

THE 'CONVENTIONAL WISDOM': RISING CRIME AND EASIER SENTENCES

It seems best to begin with the hypotheses to be disposed of quickly, those for which earlier findings can be cited,[1] then to go on to the more complicated survey analysis. This earlier work was, in a sense, a smaller version of the present book. At least it was with these Canadian data that I began to explore the factual basis of the conventional wisdom, and through them that my suspicions were aroused as to the validity of the consensus approach more generally. The results were of persuasive disconfirmation of the official position on the rising crime rate, the effects of police force size, easier sentences and, a point not discussed so far in this book, on declining disparities in sentencing. The theoretical implications of these findings were

1. 'Crime and Punishment in Canada: a statistical test of the "Conventional Wisdom" '.

described, but without 'conflict' or 'consensus' theory being named
as such.

The 'rising crime rate' turned out to apply only to trivial infractions. Neither total indictable convictions nor charges were found to
have increased significantly, in the 1950–66 period (p. 218). Summary
convictions were increasing significantly at the rate of 5·5 per cent
per year, and reported parking offences at the rate of 5·2 per cent,
with data now for only the 1955–66 period. Even so, this did not
necessarily indicate more perverse driving practices on the part of
the population, but rather an increase in the number of drivers and
motor vehicles on the road. The rate of registered motor vehicles
accounted for 97 per cent of the variance in traffic violations, and 62
per cent of the variance in reported parking offences.

An examination of offences of violence showed no general increase either. Of the five most serious offences, two were increasing
significantly (murder and attempted murder) and three decreasing
(manslaughter, shooting and wounding, and aggravated assault)
(p. 220). The increase found in murder, moreover, may well have
been more a function of changes in legislation than any growing
predilection for violence on the part of the population. With hanging the compulsory punishment for murder before 1961, it is possible
that some offenders were charged only with manslaughter (with a
penalty of life imprisonment) who would now be charged with
murder. This turned out to be a plausible explanation, for when the
rates of murder and manslaughter were collapsed into one rate,
there was no increase.

Police force size proved to be significantly related to all the indicators of the less serious offences—traffic offences and parking, total
summary convictions, Criminal Code summary convictions and the
number of children adjudged delinquent. It was related to only one
of the more serious indicators, breaking and entering convictions, a
finding in contrast with the pattern found elsewhere in this study.
Police force size was not related either to total indictable convictions
or charges, or the various particular indicators, either of offences of
violence or property.

There was no consistent trend towards *leniency* in sentencing.
The pattern for most sentences studied was of mild fluctuations
without any significant trend in either direction. The first test
involved examination of the proportions of offenders sentenced to
long terms of imprisonment (five years or more) for three serious

offences: manslaughter, rape and robbery. There were no significant decreases over the period, but rather non-significant increases. There were, on the other hand, slight trends of leniency, as indicated by the proportions sentenced to prison at all, for indictable offences, theft and Criminal Code summary convictions. Since convictions on theft and summary offences had increased in the period, however, the declining proportions do not necessarily signify declining numbers sentenced to prison. It could be that 'treatment in the community' was being increasingly used, but rather than replacing incarceration becoming the sentence for offenders who previously would not have been brought to court at all. To explore this possibility proportions incarcerated were examined relative to *population*, rather than convictions. This was to ascertain simply whether a higher or lower proportion of the population was being sent to prison irrespective of the numbers convicted. Prison sentences did continue to decline in the case of theft, but not so for Criminal Code summary offences, or total indictable. This suggests that the increased use of community treatment measures served rather to take up the slack in the face of increased numbers brought to court, rather than replacing prison sentences.[1]

Finally, the contention that disparities in sentencing were progressively being reduced was examined. Concerted efforts have been made in recent years to 'improve' sentencing, through the establishment of legal aid schemes and the professional training of magistrates. The data consisted of proportions sentenced to prison for any length of time and the proportions fined for six offences: theft, breaking and entering, false pretences, possession of stolen goods, assault causing bodily harm and assault of a peace officer. Differences among provinces only were considered, since data by court within provinces were not available. The differences in proportions imprisoned and fined respectively were then compared over several points of time, the whole 1950–66 period, and between two shorter periods,

1. The same misperception holds for parole. While commonly believed to be a measure of leniency its effect in reducing incarceration has been found to be minimal and declining. A study by Macnaughton–Smith showed that parole reduced 'man-days' in penitentiaries by only 6 per cent, or three weeks per year. The recent implementation of compulsory parole, for time previously remitted for good behaviour, means a prolongation of sentence. (And persons returned to prison while on parole re-do the time spent.) Yet, all the time the average length of sentence has increased—perhaps in reaction to the perceived leniency of parole?

1955–66, and 1961–66. The results showed somewhat more decreases in disparities in sentences than increases, but for the majority of comparisons there were no significant differences, even when a weak test, the 10 per cent level, was used. It is especially noteworthy that there were no more decreases in the most recent period, 1961–66, when attempts to reduce disparities were greatest (pp. 231–2).

CRIMINAL LAW: WHOSE INTERESTS, WHOSE VALUES?

A fundamental component of consensus theory is the view, in Sorokin's terms[1] that 'the gradation of punishments is a fairly good indicator of the comparative gravity of [the] ... prohibited action ... The greater the crime, the greater, usually, the punishment.' This view appears, in more or less the same words, across the full range of consensus theorists, yet seems never to have been seriously tested. One suspects it is a case of a proposition 'so obviously true it doesn't need to be tested', but there are any number of other good reasons for the lack of empirical work as well.

Efforts to formulate tests began several years before the project proper got underway, but were relatively unsuccessful. Basically, questions to the effect of what *ought* to be in the criminal law were not very meaningful. There is fairly broad agreement on the orderings of the seriousness of offences *within* the criminal law, a point well demonstrated in many studies. But to compare, as to their seriousness, actions forbidden by the criminal law with either civil matters, or simply immoral behaviour, is something people resisted. Criminal and non-criminal acts were viewed as two quite different sorts of things.[2]

What was forbidden by the criminal law must have been for good reason, as seriously harmful to the community. Respondents asked about other harmful actions, though, seldom wanted these added to the criminal law. Further, it was widely agreed that certain acts, formally against the law, were not harmful—liquor and certain

1. *Social and Cultural Dynamics*, p. 528.
2. This is not to say that people will not make comparisons when asked to. I tried a variety of forced-choice comparisons and ratings, and got responses. Rather, resistance appeared in ordinary language discussion of the subject. Most of the indices developed have been confined strictly to traditional blue-collar type offences.

other drug offences for example. Yet this did not alter people's view of the law as essentially embracing genuinely harmful acts. These inconsistencies troubled no one apparently, and the fact that the criminal law possesses such legitimacy has to be taken as at least prima facie support of consensus theory.

The data did show that ordinary crime was not taken to be much of a problem. Very few respondents (disproportionately teachers) mentioned crime spontaneously as a threat or a problem when asked what they felt the most serious threats or problems to the country were. Only 8·5 per cent agreed that crime was a problem of any seriousness when asked specifically that. There were no significant differences among the groups viewing crime as a problem. Within the sphere of crime, offences of violence were seen as considerably more serious than offences against property, the standard finding of surveys on crime.[1] These findings differed from others, though, in the *extent* of the gap between the two. This is an impression from eye-inspection of data, rather than the reporting of a statistic, but an impression held with some conviction. Few people viewed property offenders as serious criminals, and few saw them as deserving prison sentences. Another departure was the emphasis on *moral* criteria in making assessments of acts. Crimes involving innocent victims were treated very seriously. Children as victims of sex offenders were one obvious example, but crimes due to drunken driving were also treated very seriously, and property offences against the poor and aged.[2]

Whereas ordinary crime did not seem to be of much concern to most respondents, a number of other problems were. Unemployment headed the list, half the respondents mentioning it spontaneously as a serious problem or threat to the country. (The interviewing took place in 1972 when the unemployment rate was high.) American ownership of the Canadian economy, French–English relations (the threat of Quebec separatism), and inflation came next—all with more than a quarter of the respondents raising these matters.

1. Akman and Normandeau, Sellin and Wolfgang, Mäkelä, Rossi, Prévost Commission, Boydell and Grindstaff, Gibbons, Podgorecki, Segerstedt, and Léauté.
2. This is my interpretation also of the Prévost Commission findings, based on a Quebec survey. The gravity of the crime, circumstances and methods were stressed by more respondents than past conduct of the accused, family and social milieu or personality.

Numerous other problems were raised as well, largely in the area of injustices to particular groups and decline in quality of life.

On the purely objective level, Canadian criminal legislation is no more relevant to protecting crucial interests than was the case for Britain. It is a crime to steal $50 from a man's wallet, but not to deprive him of his means of livelihood. It is a crime for an employer to steal any amount from his bookkeeper's handbag, but not to pay her thousands of dollars less than his male 'accountants'. The losses people incur through ordinary crime are trivial in comparison with those suffered through inflation, unemployment, underemployment and discrimination.

Even in the case of death and injury one is at much greater risk to suffer through accidents than crime. Of the 157,272 deaths in Canada in 1971, 473 were attributed to homicide, compared with 5,690 motor vehicle accidents, 762 drownings, 1,774 falls, 2,559 suicides and 699 poisonings, to mention only a few examples.[1]

Much as unemployment, inflation. American ownership, pollution and so forth were mentioned as problems, and even serious threats to Canadian society, there was no serious suggestion that they should be dealt with under the criminal law. Some people stated that raising prices should be a 'crime' but this was meant only as a joke. Polluters ought to be dealt with more severely, but still not in the same way as the ordinary criminal. Many people were concerned about loss of jobs through plant shut-downs by multi-national corporations. But still, immoral and irresponsible as this was considered to be, individuals were not prepared to view it as criminal. This included, notably, workers employed at such plants, the people most liable to suffer in such instances.

The criminal law reflects social priorities to the extent of treating offences of violence more seriously than offences against property. The penalty for ordinary murder is life imprisonment, hanging for the murder of a police officer or prison official on duty. Flogging used to be a penalty for rape. Rape and armed robbery are punishable by life imprisonment. After these most serious offences of violence, however, the propositions of conflict theory fit the available facts much better.

Offences in Canadian criminal legislation concern largely the interests of the holders of economic and political power. There are long and detailed provisions for acts against private property, while

1. *Vital Statistics*, 1971–2, p. 6.

the harmful and immoral acts of owners and managers are largely dealt with outside the criminal law. Monopolies, price fixing, false advertising, the use of unsafe equipment and the like either fail to come under the criminal law at all, or the offences are so defined that most offenders escape through loopholes. Moreover the trend has been to take such offences *out* of the Criminal Code, on the grounds that they are better dealt with under special legislation.

It is a curious fact that no statistics are published on 'white collar' offences in Canada. Presumably, some offenders are charged and convicted, their offences reported in the 'other' category of the official statistics, but evidently not many. It is perhaps for this reason that there has been almost no study of white collar crime in the country. Little research has been done on the subject elsewhere, of course, but the lack is even greater for Canada than other bourgeois societies.[1]

Until 1972 it was a Criminal Code offence to beg in Canada—for which the typical sentence was a fine. It is an offence for women to solicit sex partners in public, but there is no equivalent offence for men. Until recently, there were liquor offences which applied to Indians but not to whites. Clearly these anomalies reflect differences in power—between rich and poor, men and women, and whites and Indians respectively.

Still, the Law Reform Commission of Canada, with a mandate to make recommendations of a most fundamental nature, has apparently not seen fit to raise these questions. It has discussed the problem of changing values, and even conflicting values in certain respects as, for example, in drug use and sex, but it has not questioned the consensus assumption itself that the criminal law is basically concerned with the protection of important social values.

ENFORCEMENT OF CRIMINAL LAW

The same pattern of results occurs in the case of enforcement practices as in the content of the law. The hypotheses were again of the interests of the holders of power versus shared basic values as the determining factor. Again the consensus proposition, that the application of sanctions reflects threats to the most basic values of the

1. It is perhaps telling that in one of the few publications on white collar crime in Canada, by Normandeau, the examples all come from other countries.

Table 7:1 *Sentences and Seriousness of Offence*

	No. of Prison Sentences	No. of Convictions	% Convicted sentenced to prison or jail
Offences against the person			
murder	27	27	100·0
manslaughter	67	70	95·7
rape	64	65	98·5
criminal negligence—death (motor manslaughter)	14	14	100·0
criminal negligence in operation of a motor vehicle	14	28	50·0
criminal negligence in operation of a motor vehicle (summary)	36	412	8·7
dangerous driving	26	94	26·6
dangerous driving (summary)	150	1,991	7·5
impaired driving (summary)	1,216	24,762	4·9
driving >80 mg. alcohol (summary)	284	24,734	1·1
assault causing bodily harm	664	1,879	35·3
offensive weapons (summary)	156	1,119	13·9
duty to provide necessaries (summary)	4	136	2·9
duty to safeguard dangerous places (summary)	4	14	28·6
Protection of Children	8	4,241	0·2
Deserted Wives & Children's Maintenance	66	9,626	0·7

Offences against property and others—lower- and working-class offences

armed robbery	42	48	87·5
breaking and entering	3,587	6,785	52·9
theft	4,305	20,238	21·3
damage under $50 (summary)	325	3,291	9·8
vagrancy (summary)	1,179	3,281	35·9
disorderly conduct/disturbance (summary)	1,167	12,530	9·3
drunkenness (summary)	7,438	69,284	10·7

Offences against property and others—middle- and upper-class offences

fraud and corruption	535	1,049	51·0
Income Tax	3	7,366	0·04
Weights and Measures	0	0	—
Weights and Measures (summary)	0	95	0·0
bankruptcy	0	0	—
Combines Investigation	0	1	0·0
Excise	0	1	0·0

Source: *Statistics of Criminal and Other Offences*, 1971, pp. 38, 40, 140, 141.

Data exclude Quebec and Alberta. Number of prison sentences computed from total number sentenced less numbers fined and sentence suspended. Offences are indictable unless otherwise noted.

society, was simply not borne out. As summarized by the Law Reform Commission[1] 'crimes brought to the courts under the Criminal Code in rank order of frequency are (1) thefts and possession of stolen property, (2) automobile offences including impaired driving, (3) being drunk or causing a disturbance, (4) assaults, and (5) break and enter'.

Further, as the Commission pointed out, 'Many of the thefts involved property values of less than $50 and even in break and enter, in general, the average value of property stolen is less than $150.00. In short, the bulk of the work of the courts in Criminal Code offences involves rather minor violations of property values or such problems as impaired driving or being drunk in public.'

This is clear in the listing of offences by seriousness, with sentences shown for each alongside, in Table 7:1. Data on average sentences were not available so we have had to rely on the number of prison or jail sentences for the offence, and the proportion of those convicted sentenced to incarceration as indicators of seriousness of punishment. The disparities begin in the section on offences against the person, where the great public concern over offences of violence falls off quickly after murder, manslaughter and rape. Criminal negligence in driving, and dangerous and drunken driving offences got relatively few prison sentences, both in absolute terms and proportionately. The concern for defenceless persons, especially children, is only weakly reflected in the four prison sentences for 'failure to provide necessaries' and eight for protection of children.

In the case of property offences and others even more glaring disparities appear, again with a quick falling off after armed robbery, breaking and entering, and theft. There were more than 7,000 sentences for drunkenness, over a thousand for disorderly conduct and over a thousand for vagrancy—all offences for which there is virtually no public demand for prison sentences. (And many of those sentenced to fines end up in gaol for non-payment.) For children, also, incarceration is frequently used for matters not considered worthy of serious punishment. More than a quarter of the 2,200 boys sent to training schools in 1972, and more than half of the 1,200 girls, were sentenced for non-criminal offences.[2]

1. Working Paper No. 3, p. 7.
2. Of the 2,234 boys incarcerated, 704 had not been found guilty of an offence, of the 1,195 girls, 491 had not been found guilty of an offence (*Training Schools*, 1972). It is often pointed out that children sent to

The better than 300 sentences for damage under $50 makes for an interesting comparison with the three for income tax violations. There were no imprisonments for frauds dealt with under Weights and Measures legislation, and none under the Combines Investigation Act and the Excise Act. There were no *convictions* even for bankruptcy.

To document the consensus position it would be necessary to show that the rankings of the citizenry were reflected in the measures taken by the state at the various stages of crime control: policing, prosecution, conviction and sentence. Substantial numbers of police would be deployed to apprehend the offenders deemed the most serious and prosecutors would strive to bring such cases to trial. Judges would award the stiffest sentences to the worst offenders and parole boards would be wary to release such persons early. Yet, apart from the seriousness accorded murder and the most heinous crimes of violence, this is patently not the case. Rather the priorities exhibited in actual practice reflect the interests of the owners of private property and the owners and managers of industrial and commercial enterprises.

This question can be pursued further with a recent American study, by Rossi and colleagues, in which quantified rankings were computed for a good range of white- and blue collar-offences, and a number of improper or controversial activities not necessarily defined as crimes. Blue-collar offences still dominate in this study, but such non-criminal matters as joining a demonstration, and commercial offences like fraudulent merchandising were included as well. Fairly strong agreement on rankings of seriousness appeared among the respondents, with only minimal differences by sex, race, education and social class. This the authors interpreted as disconfirmation of conflict theory for 'to the extent that empirical investigation shows great consensus the conflict model loses support' (p. 224).

On the other hand, the rankings of seriousness of offence bear little resemblance to actual practice, a point never admitted in the paper,

---

training schools under 'care and protection' legislation could have been sent there anyway for criminal offences, so that the high proportion on non-criminal matters may be misleading. What must be remembered, however, is that many even of the criminal offences concern trivial matters, such as thefts of no more than $1 worth of goods. I have personally seen a Children's Aid worker urge committal of a young boy for the theft of a cheap toy car, on the grounds that he was a recidivist.

and the crucial point.[1] This can be seen in Table 7:2, where the rankings of all the white-collar offences have been extracted with a selection of blue-collar for comparison. Clearly actual enforcement practices are much more severe for many lower-ranking blue-collar type offences than for many commercial crimes considered much more serious. The manufacture and sale of harmful drugs ranked twenty-fifth, in advance even of armed robbery of a payroll or a drugstore, and several of the murder examples (the killing of a spouse's lover, caught together, ranked only fifty-eighth). The manufacture and sale of defective cars was similarly viewed as a serious matter. Even overcharging interest on a loan, refusal to make repairs to rental property, and dishonest weighing of meat, were more serious than minor shoplifting and damage, for which the penalty is often enough a gaol term.

Being drunk in a public place was the lowest ranked of the 140 offences studied, not even as serious as refusing to answer the census taker. Yet drunk charges are a major source of clients for American courts and local gaols. Causing a disturbance, often a liquor-related offence, ranked 135th, and again is an offence for which imprisonment is often the penalty. Repeated truancy and running away from home ranked 136th and 137th respectively, and yet are frequently the offence for which children are incarcerated, especially girls.

Clearly, the clientele of American police stations, courts and prisons would be dramatically different if the priorities expressed in the Rossi survey were in fact the guide to practice. There would be fewer unemployed alcoholics in the gaols, and fewer working-class children in reform schools. Indeed there would be few children incarcerated at all.

There would be more car dealers, drug manufacturers and supermarket managers in prison or paying heavy fines. In place of the often unemployed petty vandal, there would be overly prosperous merchants, apartment owners and even butchers. There would be more drunks in public places, but fewer on the roads. Pornography would be out as an offence, while child beating would be in.

1. A study by Rose and Prell produced precisely this finding, in comparing public assessment of the seriousness of thirteen particular crimes, and the severity of sentence actually imposed. The results indicated no positive relation, but a slight negative one. Nor was there any close relationship between provisions for punishments in the law, and actual punishments. The authors accounted for the discrepancies in terms of culture lag.

Table 7:2 *Rankings on Seriousness of Offence: Rossi Study*

White collar offences	Blue collar offences	
		Average Rank
	1	Planned killing of a policeman
	9	Armed robbery of bank
	22	Impulsive killing of an acquaintance
25		Manufacturing/selling drugs known to be harmful to users
26		Knowingly selling contaminated food resulting in death
	32	Armed robbery of neighborhood druggist
51		Causing death of employee by neglecting to repair machinery
57		Causing death of tenant by neglecting to repair heating plant
63		Manufacturing/selling autos known to be dangerously defective
73		Public official accepting bribes for favours
79		Knowingly selling defective used cars as completely safe
	80	Burglary of appliance store stealing several TV sets
90		Knowingly selling worthless stocks as valuable investments
97		Lending money at illegal interest rates
103		Bribing public official to obtain favours
106		Under-reporting income on income tax return
107		Wilfully neglecting to file income tax returns
	115	Shoplifting pair of shoes from shoe store
116		Overcharging for credit in selling goods
	117	Shoplifting carton of cigarettes from supermarket
120		False claims of dependants on income tax return
121		Knowingly using inaccurate scales in weighing meat for sale
122		Refusal to make essential repairs to rental property
	125	Breaking plate glass window in shop
126		Fixing prices of consumer product, like gasoline
127		Fixing prices of machines sold to businesses
	129	Shoplifting book from bookstore
132		False advertising of headache remedy
	135	Disturbing the peace
	136	Repeated truancy
	137	Repeated running away from home
	138	Loitering in public places
	140	Being drunk in public places

One final example concerns the creation and processing of crime in labour disputes, within the framework of Ontario legislation. The law in Ontario grants most workers the right to strike, after various attempts at negotiation have been made. At the same time it grants employers the right to continue production, hire scab labour and, in brief, to do what they can to break the strike. Both sides have certain rights and obligations, then, but the forces of order are used almost exclusively for the protection of the rights of employers. An employer continuing production with scab labour may obtain extensive police services, to escort strike-breakers in and out of the plant, insure supplies arrive and the finished product goes off to market. Provocation of picketers occurs in many strikes, and assault charges, both of police and strikers, are a part of many strikes. Seldom, however, are strikers' charges of police successful, while strikers are convicted of assaults, obstruction of the police and trespass in large numbers.

As a concrete example, consider the Artistic Woodworking strike in Toronto in 1973. The 120 employees, largely foreign-born women, were on a legal strike for a first contract. By the end of the strike 108 individuals had been arrested (union members, organizers and a large number of supporters, including an alderman, minister, lawyers and students). About half of the persons charged were eventually acquitted, and some were still under appeal at the time of writing. None of the twelve charges individuals laid against the police resulted in conviction. The company had the services of up to 150 policemen for a good part of the four-month strike. Yet, while the Labour Relations Board found a prima facie case that the employer had failed to bargain in good faith, an offence under the act, the Attorney-General refused the union's request to prosecute. It would not be 'in the public interest'.

CONCEPTUALIZATIONS OF CRIME AND CRIMINALS

Conceptualizations of crime and criminals according to consensus theory should, in the long run at least, be fairly accurate. The system works through information being produced and disseminated on its own functioning, the adequacy of current measures to control crime, and the assessment of new problems. The production and dissemination of accurate information on the criminal justice system is an integral part of its operation, and the fact of reasonably widespread, accurate information a sign of its healthy functioning.

To ascertain the extent to which accurate information was held on the system respondents were asked their views on several questions of fact. Firstly we asked about trends in the crime rate, whether increasing, decreasing or staying the same. There was a question on trends in sentencing, whether getting longer, shorter or staying the same. There were questions on psychiatric treatment of offenders, whether or not in favour, and effectiveness. There were questions on the nature of the prison population, and specifically as to whether any race or ethnic group was over-represented or under-represented. These are all matters on which factual information is available, so that the perceptions of respondents can be compared with an objective report of the situation.

In conflict theory there is no comparable belief in information being accurate. Whether expressed as Michel's 'political formula', or the construction of official ideologies there has typically been a notion of the holders of power disseminating views on the operation of the system most conducive to their own ends. In this case accurate information does not serve the ends of the powerful on any of the mentioned points. Rather, recourse to repressive measures can be better defended if it is believed that crime is rising. Severe measures can be justified if it is thought that past trends have been of increasing leniency, so that an increase in severity would mean simply redressing an imbalance. The more that punitive measures are presented as treatment, the more important it is that people believe that it works. The just operation of the criminal justice system is one of the best defences of its use. Perceptions of its not dispensing justice equally to all citizens, irrespective of race and social class, are an argument against its expansion. From the two theories, then, quite different patterns of perceptions are predicted, although what constitutes 'high' and 'low' proportions of accurate information is open to debate.

The results displayed in Table 7:3 indicate a fairly impressive level of mis-information. Roughly 80 per cent of the respondents shared the rising crime myth, including even 67 per cent of the civil liberties members. As many as 64 per cent over-all, and up to 73 per cent of the businessmen, viewed a trend to greater leniency in sentencing. Only among the civil liberties members was there any extended awareness of race being a factor in sentencing to prison; close to half the respondents explicitly denied that any race or ethnic group was over- or under-represented in Canadian prisons. Those who were aware of the race factor were for the most part accurate in naming Indians as the most over-represented group.[1] There were also occasional mentions of southern Europeans, and under-representation of Chinese.

The proportions viewing psychiatric treatment as effective were also high, although often this was expressed with considerable

Table 7:3 *Information on Crime and Sanctions*

	Range	
% perceiving	Low	High
Crime rate increasing	67·2	86·9
Sentences becoming lenient	46·3	73·3
Sentences too short	15·0	84·1
Race not a factor regarding prison sentences	19·6	86·0
Psychiatric treatment effective	44·8	72·1
Prisoners violent	7·5	31·2

Note: The percentages reported are the low and high ends of the range, the civil liberties group in each case being at the low end; the businessmen were the high group on the second and third items and the Hamilton East group for the others.

qualification. More than half the respondents on balance gave a favourable view, up to 72 per cent of the Hamilton East respondents. The point on sentences being *too* lenient is not, strictly speaking, a matter of information, but the punishments meted out by Canadian courts are severe compared with western European and other industrial societies.[2]

1. The best information available indicates that the rate of indictable offences is the same among Indians and Métis as among whites, but Indians and Métis are four times more likely to go to provincial prisons and jails than whites, and at least twice as likely to go to federal penitentiaries. This means that in provinces with sizeable Indian populations, like Manitoba and Saskatchewan (with 12 per cent and 16 per cent respectively), more than half the admissions to provincial institutions are of Indians and Métis. (Data from Heumann, *The Native Offender in Canada*.)
2. Waller and Chan.

RESPONSES ACROSS THE SAMPLE GROUPS

The next stage of the testing was to examine responses on punitiveness and civil liberties across the different groups in the study. The groups varied in the access to power enjoyed by their members and hence, according to conflict theory, should vary also in attitudes on crime, sanctions and civil liberties. Conversely, according to consensus theory, the responses should vary by education, occupational status and security, for it is these factors that are held to be most influential in determining views on these questions. The two theoretical approaches lead to contrasting sets of hypotheses, and precisely the opposite predictions on most points.

THE RATIONALE FOR THE HYPOTHESES

According to conflict theory, it is the holders of power who have the most to gain by a high level of sanctions and a low level of civil liberties. The powerful have their rights anyway, as it were, by virtue of their power, and consequently it is they who have the most to lose by extending such rights to others. Moreover, by controlling the sanctioning system they face little risk of being sanctioned themselves. Those who are sanctioned lose in status and other privileges, in the process providing a good example to others not to trespass on the privileges of their 'betters'. Those without power, by contrast, have an interest in norms and sanctions being relatively lenient. It is they who suffer most by severe sanctions and, in the long run at least, people's perceptions must be reasonably consistent with objectively determined reality.

Similarly, it is those with the least power that have the most to gain by an extension of civil rights.[1] The working class has been the last social class to gain political and economic rights. Consequently, its members should be the most committed to the recognition of basic political and economic rights, as fundamental, inviolable rights. Proponents of the conflict argument have emphasized the traditional role of the working class in the struggle for rights of all kinds, the authorities of the day consistently opposing. This has included the right to vote, hold office, the abolition of hereditary privileges and the right for trade unions to organize.

1. The argument on civil liberties was drawn largely from Miller and Riessman's critique of the Lipset working-class authoritarianism thesis. The application to crime and sanctions involves a simple extension of the argument.

The working-class struggle for rights has been particularly devoted to economic rights—workmen's compensation, sickness and unemployment insurance and old age pensions—all measures essential for political rights to have any meaning. Again it has been the holders of political and economic power who have resisted. Working-class groups such as unions and labour parties have more often been supporters of peace movements than have comparable middle-class organizations. Further, despite the economic threats posed by immigration, it has more often been working-class groups that have opposed racist immigration policies than middle-class.

Living conditions are more productive of a democratic spirit among working-class persons than middle-class. Co-operation in the work place is more often the norm for the working-class person than the middle. Business and professional people often work alone, and often in clear competition with their fellows.

Patterns of lending and sharing are much more prevalent among working-class people than middle-class, through extended family and neighbourhood networks[1]. In times of financial need money is lent back and forth, as are food, babysitting services and practical assistance in times of sickness, childbirth or death in the family. Economic insecurity, far from producing hostility, fear and suspiciousness, then, develops a spirit of co-operation and mutual aid, qualities essential to the give and take processes of ordinary government.[2] Working-class people, it is further argued, learn to see through snobbishness better than middle-class. They are less impressed by empty rhetoric and generally maintain an attitude of scepticism regarding the qualities of those above them. They suffer the bad consequences of government more rapidly and more thoroughly than others, and learn, therefore, to be more cautious in their judgements.

The mainstream consensus approach is based on broad agreement on values, which should apply to criminal norms as well, since these deal with threats to the most important of these values. Identical views across all the sectors of a society is not expected, however, for people vary in the vantage point from which they make their observations, and in the knowledge with which they process them. Generally speaking, the greater the education, and the broader, more

1. This point has been documented for many societies, notably by Kropotkin in *Mutual Aid* and by Young and Willmott in *Family and Kinship in East London*.
2. Bax, 'La Nouvelle Éthique'.

comprehensive the view of society the person has, the less there will be to fear from deviance and, consequently, the less punitive will be the response to it. The argument is basically that of knowledge being a liberating force, or 'the truth shall set you free'.

Working-class people are said to consider less information in making their judgements. They have a less adequate time perspective, both in the sense of awareness of long series of events shaping things and less of a future orientation as well. Judgements have to be made on a very immediate basis. They have less material on motivation and mitigating circumstances with which to judge as well. They do not have the rich associations that middle-class people have as context for their interpretations.[1] Their framework is typically either inadequate, in the quantitative sense, or overly rigid. As a consequence, the judgements of working-class people are frequently of an 'all or nothing' nature. They too often choose the least complex interpretation of events. Harshness to criminals may reflect this black or white, good-evil dichotomy rather than, or in addition to, punitiveness *per se*.

Bernstein's language-code theory fits into this part of the argument as well, although rather peripherally in the case of Canada. The notion is that working-class people, on account of their failure to acquire an elaborated language code, lack the means for complicated reasoning. Working-class people then, whatever their motivation, will have less facility for considering the historical context of particular events. They are forced, in a sense, to rely on more immediate, black and white judgements.

The effect of recourse to physical punishments in child rearing has probably been exaggerated, but it is, nevertheless, part of the argument.[2] Working-class parents have been found to use physical punishments more than middle-class in many societies, middle-class parents relying more on threats to loss of love. Middle-class people may then acquire a greater abhorrence of physical punishments, or a general preference for non-physical means of control. Their greater opposition to corporal punishment and hanging as punishments for crime may simply be a reflection of this general orientation.

Educational differences intensify the pattern formed by early child-rearing practices. Firstly, working-class people typically

1. These arguments are a compilation of points from Lipset, Spinley, Hoggart, Bernstein, Adorno, and Bronfenbrenner.
2. Erlander.

receive much less formal education than middle-class. Any deficiencies established early in childhood, then, far from being rectified on entry into the school system, are increased. This occurs both with respect to the development of analytical skills and the fund of knowledge used in the processing of information about deviance. Secondly, the particular subjects that do most to dispel fear of deviant behaviour, by accounting for its origins and describing its bounds, are psychology and sociology. These are taught in the later years of schooling, when few children of working-class origin remain. Again, then, working-class people may be more fearful of deviant behaviour and, insofar as fear provokes a punitive response, they will be more punitive in their attitudes to criminals.

For similar reasons, membership in formal organisations is thought to intensify the differences between the classes. Middle-class people tend to belong to more organizations than working-class, which means that they are exposed to a greater range of people and experiences. Again, then, they have a broader, richer perspective within which to judge and interpret events, to find motivations that make otherwise incomprehensible acts comprehensible.

WORKING-CLASS AUTHORITARIANISM

In Lipset's working-class authoritarianism approach all the above arguments apply, with class interests added. The lower the status of the group the more there is to gain from policies of punitiveness, hence the greater the support for punitive measures, and the more perceptions of crime and sanctions will support this position. Those at the bottom rung of the social hierarchy have the most to fear by being identified with criminal and other unsavoury elements. It is they, consequently, who have the most to gain by separating off a criminal group, with which they can compare themselves favourably, and which can be seen by others to rank clearly below them. The more marginal the group, the greater the need for a margin.

The class interest argument applies across the board, as the mainstream approach, to ethnic and religious minorities, immigrants, women, lepers or, in general, any minority in the political sense. Working-class people are more threatened than middle-class by these groups and react accordingly. In response to the threats perceived they favour tougher measures of control, such as stricter immigration laws, and oppose measures intended to improve the circumstances of the groups in question, such as equal opportunities for women.[1]

Also important between the mainstream and the working-class authoritarianism approaches is the extent of differences expected in the responses of the various groups. In the case of the mainstream approach the argument was of broad agreement on basic values, hence on criminal norms, and the traditional civil liberties. Some variation across the occupational groups was expected, by virtue of variation in education, exposure to information, experience with deviance and so forth. Now, in the working-class authoritarianism approach, class interests play a positive role, the least advantaged class having some *incentive* to favour punitive sanctions, and oppose civil liberties and related measures. Hence stronger differences between the groups must be hypothesized. Further, while it is expected that some of the differences by occupational group may be the effect of education, it is important that there be significant differences apart from education.[2]

RESULTS

From the results of the first tests of the hypotheses it is clear that neither the conflict nor the consensus predictions appeared consistently. As predicted by consensus theory, and especially the argument of knowledge being a liberating force, the lawyers were, with rare exception, the least punitive group after the civil libertarians. The businessmen, however, were often more punitive than the teachers and workers, in line with conflict theory. Again consistent with consensus theory, formal education had a moderating effect. The proportions favouring lenient measures were greater among the

1. I have referred here only to 'working-class' and 'middle-class' groups, the major concern of the analysis. All the same points could be applied to other units, so long as they have some sort of class interest in common.
2. It was not possible to control for education in the proper sense, since education and occupation are so closely linked. None of the workers had a university degree, for example, while none of the lawyers were without one. For this reason also techniques of analysis of variance could not be used. There was sufficient overlap on the intermediate levels of education for certain comparisons to be made, as between high school graduates, and persons with some post-secondary training short of a degree. Wherever there were sufficient numbers for comparisons to be made they were. Further, within each group (except the lawyers) comparisons could be made between those with 'more' or 'less' formal education.

Table 7:4 *Crime and Sanctions: Views by Groups*

	Civil Liberties	Lawyers	Businessmen	Teachers	Hamilton East	Textile Workers
Perceives crime rate rising	67·2	74·8	86·6	80·2	86·9	84·7
Perceives sentences becoming lenient	46·3	58·3	73·2	70·2	70·5	59·6
Sentences *too* lenient	15·0	23·1	84·1	66·0	80·4	60·8
Considers treatment effective	44·8	50·6	53·3	55·6	72·1	63·5
Race not a factor in prison sentences	19·6	31·6	61·2	64·6	86·0	81·1
Favours psychiatric treatment	91·0	97·8	91·6	97·1	96·8	86·6
Favours compulsory treatment	41·8	59·4	53·3	63·2	67·3	61·6

better educated in each of the occupational groups tested, however, the differences were not great. Neither age, sex nor religion had any significant effect on responses.

The strongest differences concerned the view of sentencing as being *too* lenient, a result well reflecting the inconsistency of results. Only 15 per cent of the civil liberties members expressed this view, and 23 per cent of the lawyers, but up to 80 per cent of the Hamilton East group and 84 per cent of the businessmen. On the two questions on actual trends, the rising crime rate and perceived leniency in sentencing, there were no significant differences among the groups. Again there were no significant differences on the proportions favouring psychiatric treatment of convicted criminals. Apart from these three items, however, there were fairly strong differences across the groups.

As a test of consensus theory only, questions on capital and corporal punishment were asked, the results for which are shown in Table 7:5. No comparable hypotheses could be derived from conflict theory, for there is no reason to suppose that access to power would affect tastes for *particular* punishments, as opposed to overall *levels* of sanctions preferred. The results indicated fairly strong support for capital punishment, although our method of probing probably exaggerated the favourable response. (Persons who initially gave a 'no' answer were asked if they thought it might be suitable for *some* cases.) The proportions giving strongly favourable responses were a majority in none of the groups. Further, many of the respondents who gave a qualified approval had in mind either extremely rare use, or that capital punishment remain on the books for symbolic purposes only. For example, it was suggested that capital punishment be confined to cases of professional mass murderers caught in the act—an unlikely feat. It was only among the civil liberties members and the lawyers, however, that a clear majority was firmly opposed.

Support for corporal punishment was considerably more restrained in all groups. The proportions favouring it ran from 3 per cent among the civil liberties members to 20 per cent of the textile workers. The vast majority who expressed favourable views at all had in mind very rare use, such as for brutal sex assaults on young children. The 'qualified approval' category, then, meant extremely qualified approval in most cases. This was the finding also for Quebec respondents in the Prévost Commission survey, of considerably higher

Table 7:5 *Capital and Corporal Punishment: Views by Groups*

Capital Punishment	Civil Liberties	Lawyers	Businessmen	Teachers	Hamilton East	Textile Workers
Strongly favours	6·0	8·8	21·7	18·1	39·3	43·6
Favours	0·0	7·7	13·3	9·9	6·6	20·2
Qualified approval	13·4	22·0	46·7	39·8	36·1	22·1
Opposed	74·6	61·5	18·3	29·8	16·4	13·5
No opinion	6·0	0·0	0·0	2·3	1·6	1·0
Number of respondents	67	91	60	171	61	104
Corporal Punishment						
Strongly favours	1·5	2·2	8·4	2·4	3·0	8·6
Favours	1·5	3·3	3·3	6·4	0·0	11·6
Qualified approval	10·4	12·1	38·3	31·0	54·1	34·6
Opposed	85·1	80·2	41·7	59·1	42·6	43·3
No opinion	1·5	2·2	8·3	1·2	0·0	1·9

support for retention of the penalty on the books than use. The proportions betraying any enthusiasm for the punishment in either study were very low.[1]

TRADITIONAL POLITICAL AND ECONOMIC LIBERTIES

On the issue of traditional political and economic liberties the hypothesis from conflict theory was of greatest support on the part of the workers, least among the lawyers and businessmen, with the teachers intermediate. Predictions from consensus theory on political rights were the opposite. On economic rights working-class authoritarianism exponents have taken a different position—that workers should be more supportive than middle-class persons, for reasons of economic self-interest.[2] Hence no differences between the two theory approaches are predicted. Again, from the mainstream approach the prediction was of relatively minor differences, accountable to differences in education and exposure to information, while from working-class authoritarianism stronger differences were expected. The question as to what constituted stronger and weaker differences was left open. As it happened, this did not have to be resolved since the pattern of results appearing was contradictory to both theories in certain respects.

The results on political rights were mixed, somewhat more supportive of conflict theory than consensus, and clearly contrary to the predictions of working-class authoritarianism. The workers were significantly more favourable to freedom of speech and religion, as general principles, than the other groups. On right to a jury trial they were more favourable than the teachers, but less so than the businessmen and lawyers. On economic rights the workers were clearly the most favourable, as predicted by both theories. When it came to qualifications to freedom of expression, however, the workers proved to be the least libertarian, with the businessmen and lawyers the most, the prediction of consensus theory. This was examined relative to four particular instances where freedom of

1. It is interesting to note also the evolution of professional opinion on corporal punishment. In the Archambault Report in 1938 there was concern over undue severity in whipping; straps with holes in them were used in some prisons, which did not 'serve any useful purpose'. Hence the recommendation that only holeless straps be used.
2. Lipset.

expression might be problematic: the right for Communists to speak in a high school (regarding a general election), the right for a group of radicals to hold a public meeting advocating violence, the right to publish anti-semitic material, and the desirability of pornography laws in general.

The pattern becomes more complicated again when responses to political and economic issues are considered. Conflict theory was somewhat better supported than consensus, but again not consistently. There were ten political and five economic items for which statistically significant differences appeared and the workers took the view most favourable to liberties on seven and three respectively. Partial support for consensus theory appeared in that the lawyers, who were better educated than the businessmen on average, were more often favourable to the libertarian position. Education, however, did not otherwise affect responses on these issues. Neither did age, sex or religion. The items on which the workers were most favourable to the libertarian view included the extension of civil rights (or the recognition of new rights), holding a critical attitude to government, opposing the proclamation of the War Measures Act (temporarily suspending civil liberties in the country), and a reluctance to view government as being above the law generally. On economic matters they included concern over unemployment and raising social and economic inequalities as problems.

On the issue of equal rights for women, on the other hand, the results were largely supportive of consensus theory. The lawyers and businessmen were the most favourable to rights for women, after the civil liberties members, with the teachers usually next and the workers last. (There were some reversals between the teachers and workers.) Moreover, the differences between the groups were strong, among the strongest found throughout the survey. Education had the predicted effect, although it was not as strong as that of occupation. Women were considerably more supportive of rights for themselves than were men, and these other differences held controlling for sex.

The particular views studied on rights for women included very basic orientations to sex roles, the sharing of household tasks and child care responsibilities, and women holding supervisory positions. There were also questions on perceptions of the capacities of women and the nature and extent of discrimination against women in Canada. The responses indicated a high degree of misinformation about the status of women. Despite the fact that women full-time employees in Canada earn on average only 60 per cent of their male counterparts, and are almost totally excluded from top positions in government, industry, commerce, judiciary, churches, unions and universities[1], less than half the respondents regarded discrimination as serious enough to fit the 'substantial' level in the coding. The proportions claiming that discrimination was non-existent were small, but clearly large numbers saw discrimination as basically a problem of the past.

On the other hand, the responses showed a much greater acceptance of equal rights than would be expected from current practice. Considerably more people agreed in principle with a flexible division of labour between the sexes than practise such an arrangement. Considerably more people approved of women obtaining supervisory positions on the same basis as men (merit) than have ever seen a woman supervisor. (There are very few in any sector of employment in Canada, even in working units which are exclusively female.)

SHARING THE CONTINENT WITH THE AMERICANS

When the subject matter turned to continental integration, the results shifted again. Two questions were of concern: the distribution of views on continentalism across the sample groups, and the relationship between continentalism and civil liberties. In the case of the first it was possible to conduct tests only of conflict theory, for there was no 'objectively correct' position against which perceptions could be assessed for consensus theory. The conflict theory hypothesis was of greatest support for continentalist policies among the businessmen and lawyers, next among the teachers and least among the workers—in accordance with the interests served by such policies. Businessmen and lawyers do stand to gain, if only in the short run, by continentalist policies, while workers clearly suffer, both immediately and in the long run, being laid off and losing their jobs in response to the ailments of the American economy.

The results partially supported the theory. There were no differences among the occupational groups in considering that American influence in Canada posed problems, but there were differences when the *nature* of the problem was considered. The workers were the most

1. Report of the Royal Commission on the Status of Women.

concerned about *economic* aspects of American domination. They were less concerned about political, social and cultural aspects—television, books, scientific research and so forth. Again, though, they had a lower evaluation of the *benefits* of American involvement. The over-all result was a draw. The proportions of respondents stressing the dangers over the benefits ranged from 70 per cent among the civil liberties members to roughly 50 per cent among the other groups (60 per cent of the textile workers), with no significant differences among the occupational groups.

The relatively high level of concern on the part of the civil liberties members was somewhat surprising given that there were a number of Americans in the organization, and the Canadian independence movement has been attacked as fascist in the extreme, and otherwise illiberal. It confirms, though, the view of continentalism as an issue with civil liberties dimensions. From conflict theory, the hypothesis was of greater *opposition* to continentalism with commitment to civil liberties. The reasons for this lie in the nature of the relationship between a weaker partner and a stronger. Continental integration for Canadians means the loss of capacity to make decisions, progressively as size of markets (labour, capital and product) grow. It means constraints as pressures faced by the stronger power are passed on to the weaker, as with American balance of payments problems leading to plant shut-downs in Canada. At the time of the survey it meant involvement with a power at war in Vietnam, and for many years has meant involvement with a country supporting some of the worst dictatorships in the world.

From the consensus approach the hypothesis was of a *positive* association between support for continentalist policies and civil liberties. This is very much the official position of the country, and the one most espoused in universities, schools and the mass media. It is the economic 'advantages' that are typically stressed as the justification for integration, but it is not admitted that these might be paid for by the loss of other freedoms. Indeed continentalism is often defended with the philosophy of nineteenth-century liberalism. The continental citizen has that much more freedom than the mere Canadian as the continent is greater than Canada. The independence movement would *deny* opportunities to Canadians, restricting freedom of movement, choice of employment, cultural activities and so forth.

Integration with the United States also signifies integration with a society with strong democratic traditions, still in evidence in a number of minority movements, notably on civil rights for blacks and women. So far as formal recognition of rights is concerned, the United States has long been in advance of Canada. There is good reason, then, for hypothesizing an association between continentalist views and civil liberties.

It was the conflict prediction, however, that was supported. The test consisted of examining the relationship between continentalism (four items) and civil liberties (six items), with significant results in the direction predicted by conflict theory in thirteen cases. In only one case did the contrary relationship appear, and not to a statistically significant degree.

Finally the relationship between views on civil liberties, attitudes to women and punitiveness were examined. Since the connection between general liberties and these other two matters must be more obvious than was the case for continentalism, this was not counted as hypothesis testing. Rather the exercise served a more modest goal of ascertaining the extent of consistency in response and, in fact, demonstrated a certain degree of consistency.

Respondents who supported traditional civil liberties were more supportive of equal rights for women, and less punitive, than those who did not. This was the case, at least, for items on the extension of civil rights, freedom of expression and perception of injustices. The items on agreement with economic rights and traditional rights were not related to responses in these other areas.

CONCLUSIONS

The pattern of findings for this part of the project was complicated. The overall result was of greater support for conflict theory than consensus, but now there were more findings supportive of consensus theory than in any other part. This occurred in the comparisons across the occupational groups, notably on attitudes to crime and criminals, and on certain of the rights questions. In the case of comparisons between the content of the criminal law and priorities, both as expressed by respondents and in terms of objective risks, it was clearly conflict theory that did better. Apart from the priority given serious violence, and especially murder, in the law, Canadian criminal legislation very much reflects the particular interests of the holders of economic and political power.

When enforcement practices are considered this is even more the case. The great bulk of the enforcement machinery is devoted to the processing of offences trivial in relation to any reasonable list of problems in Canadian society or to the priorities expressed by respondents. Property offenders often get more severe sentences than violent offenders, and public concern over killings by drunken driving is not remotely reflected in the light sentences typically given these offenders. The use of prison sentences for trivial theft offences and non-criminal matters, such as being drunk in a public place, is quite at odds with the concerns we found, and which have emerged in numerous other studies as well.

Perceptions of the nature of crime—the ever rising crime rate and ever shorter sentences—revealed a high level of misinformation. More to the point, the pattern appearing was one supportive of conflict theory. The belief in rising crime serves to justify more repressive measures, as does the view that the trend in sentencing has been towards leniency. The same holds for ignorance that race affects offenders' chances of receiving a prison sentence.

In the tests dealing with comparisons across samples no consistent conclusions could be drawn. The predictions of conflict theory were somewhat better supported than those of consensus, but a number of findings were made in favour of consensus theory as well. There was high and relatively uniform agreement on basic liberties, consistent with the mainstream, consensus approach. Education had the predicted, liberalizing, effect in several issue areas, again consistent with this approach. The working-class authoritarianism approach did badly. Where the order predicted by consensus theory appeared the differences were weak, and the findings in favour of conflict theory are sharply contradictory of working-class authoritarianism. My findings were clearly at variance with those of earlier, American studies, notably Lipset's, of lesser support for basic civil liberties among working-class people.

SOCIAL SCIENTISTS AND LAW AND ORDER

The fact of a high level of misinformation brings us back to one of the first concerns of the study—the role of social scientists in the law and order enterprise. The inaccuracies cannot easily be explained away. They were not randomly distributed in terms of what sorts of policies they support, but all were such as to be supportive of increased severity. Yet accurate information is available, if hardly freely offered about. The material I used came largely from published sources, and my own publications and others underscoring the necessary points have been available for some years now.

To explain why accurate information has not become better known I am inclined to begin, paradoxically, with *too much* data. Statistics Canada publishes volumes of crime, police and judicial statistics annually, in depressing detail, so much so that the average citizen needs considerable help in making sense of it. Moreover, the statistics are 'improved' virtually every year, which means that year-to-year comparisons can only be made by a select group of the initiated. Technically competent persons indeed exist who could give the necessary guidance but, and this is the crucial point, most of them are committed to only one side of the debate. Very few people who have the relevant expertise are free to criticize the official, consensus, position. Most of the experts are civil servants, and bound by oaths not to comment, or are restricted by conditions of government consulting, contract research, or involvement on government boards and commissions.

This is a particularly acute problem in Canada, for the errors and inadequacies in published sources make inside contacts more important than in other countries, simply to obtain necessary data for one's own research. Governments do consider the public relations impact of research they permit, and researchers who publish unfavourable results have subsequently been denied access to material. Another constraint arises in the desire to bring to completion work one has done. Whether this is a desirable aspect of professionalism or a blatant 'publish or perish' ethic matters little. Governments *do* veto publication of unflattering results, and researchers may well feel it better to drop unacceptable material to insure that something sees the light of day.

I have been careful to refer to governments in general in this discussion, for I do not wish to suggest that one-sided presentation of information is a peculiarity of any particular government. I do not know of *any* government that has a good record in this respect, although some are worse than others. Nor does it make much difference which political party is in office. The NDP, the 'socialist' party in Canada, has been no better than the bourgeois parties, any more than has Labour been better than the Conservatives in Britain.

There is a good example of this in Manitoba, a province with an

NDP government since 1972, and a premier who was himself a professor in the social sciences. Moreover, the NDP in Manitoba has claimed to be a flexible, reformist party. The specific example is the government's project to evaluate its corrections system, a laudable if not courageous objective on the surface. Digging more deeply, it seems that the project will serve to obscure the very problems to be solved. Firstly, there was a complete denial of sanctions. There are no more prisons in Manitoba, but institutions that dispense services to people in need of them, 'correctional service delivery agencies'. With prisons abolished there are no more prisoners, but only 'clients'. Curiously, one of the objectives of the project was to 'identify the clients' of the agencies. The fact that roughly half of them are readily identifiable as Indians or Métis was nowhere alluded to.

The main purpose of the project was evaluation of the 'effectiveness' of the system, and especially of 'rational communication' in it. Effective for what, and rational in view of what goals was never stated. Nor was it admitted that there might be *no* solutions, that the needs of different sectors of the population, notably Indians and whites, might be incompatible. Rather the approach implied that more research, a bigger computer and more experts was all that was needed.[1]

The first NDP government in British Columbia embarked on an even more ambitious law and order campaign.[2] Early in 1975 it predicted a doubling of the crime rate by 1976. Increases in the police force were then called for, on account of the projected increase!

The use of social science in the legitimation of government programmes, or to disguise non-action, itself raises a host of other problems. I expect it is responsible for much of the disenchantment with social science currently in fashion—and the subject of the next chapter. There I shall be arguing *against* the attack on the discipline.

1. A letter to the Premier raising these problems elicited a reply from the Minister of 'Social Development', avoiding the substance of the issue. Rather, there was further description of the project, generously dosed with technical terms.
2. Letters to the Premier and the Attorney-General, pointing out the lack of science in such scientific predictions, elicited a bare acknowledgement from the former, and nothing from the latter. The same government, on the other hand, abolished correctional institutions for children shortly after coming into office.

In the meantime, the problem is one to be taken seriously—whether an innocent seduction, as may have been the case in these last examples or the deliberate unscrupulous use of social science, which also happens.

PART III

The State of the Subject

Chapter 8

THE DEBATE ON METHODOLOGY:
POSITIVISM AND PRAXIS

THE ATTACK ON SOCIAL SCIENCE

In the course of criticizing consensus theory a number of writers have launched an attack on 'positivism' which in some cases turns out to be a much broader attack on the whole exercise of theory construction and testing of social science itself. The attack has included both the activity of doing empirical research and the formulation of propositions in causal form. Universities have been under attack in Europe and North America in recent years over very much the same issues, and the end is nowhere in sight. Younger students, especially, must be troubled by the turn of events. Empirical work is too low-brow for many members of the profession, yet the search for the historical roots of theory is scorned as an obsession with an irrelevant past. The result altogether is a widespread malaise with scholarly work. I propose here to deal with only a few of the issues, focusing on the relationship between consensus theory and empirical work, and between empirical work and humanistic values.

Quinney has lengthy criticisms of causal theory in general in both his major works. The 'positivist' was a narrow-minded individual, blindly supportive of the *status quo*, and unconcerned with basic philosophical issues. The authors of *The New Criminology*, also in the course of attacking consensus theory, attacked the premises of the scientific method—'measurement, objectivity and causation'—from which a consensus view was held to follow necessarily. Gouldner, in *The Coming Crisis of Western Sociology*, took pains to stress his concern for theorizing of certain kinds, an 'historically informed social theory'. As well, he expressed his disappointment with young radicals who rejected theory altogether, nevertheless his attack on 'positivism' was broad enough to cover much theory, and he endorsed the still broader attack of *The New Criminology*.

The discussion has been focused for the most part on the inadequacies, and sometimes immoral, qualities of 'positivism'. Whose positivism is seldom made clear, and often the targets of attack have been ill-defined notions like 'ultra positivism', 'determinism', and 'hard determinism'. Effectively I will be arguing that the critics have set up a straw man. The nasty qualities they attack may pertain to something someone may wish to call 'positivism', but not to the work of the major, known nineteenth-century positivists—Comte, Mill, Quetelet and Durkheim[1]. Moreover, certain theorists these critics treat as anti-positivistic, notably Weber, Marx and Engels, committed precisely the same 'errors' they attribute to the positivists.

THE CONSENSUS POINT OF VIEW AND POSITIVISM

A common reason given for the attack on positivism has been its association with conservative, consensus theorizing, in the extreme case the connection being held to be necessary. This is the position taken in *The New Criminology*:

> The positivist attempts the scientific explanation of crime by social action as having the qualities (no more and no less) of things—or objects in the natural world. With this in mind he denudes action of meaning, or moral choice and of creativity. For human behaviour to be studied scientifically it must be akin to the non-human world, it must be deterministically dominated by law-like regulations, it must be reified—have the quality of 'things'. This, then, is at the centre of the positivist hopes for a science of crime and it is in this respect that its theoretical approach stands or falls.
>
> Thus, from the initial three *premises* of the scientific method—measurement (quantification), objectivity (neutrality), and causality (determinism)—are derived a number of *postulates*: a consensus view of the world, a focus on the criminal actor rather than the criminal act, a reification of the social world, a doctrine of non-responsibility for actions, the inapplicability of punishment, and a faith in the superior cognitive ability of the scientific expert (p. 23).

1. Even less do they pertain to twentieth-century 'logical positivism', or the Vienna Circle, but that is not at issue.

Quinney was considerably less explicit about the relationship in *The Social Reality of Crime*, but appears even there to identify the consensus approach with causal analysis. In his later work, *Critique of Legal Order*, the attack is explicit and thorough:

The overriding emphasis of positivistic thought is on the *explanation* of events. And in following a mechanistic conception of the relation of social facts, the positivist usually couches his explanations in terms of causality. What is ignored in this approach to explanation is an *examination* (or even an awareness) of the philosophical assumptions by which the observer operates (p. 3).

The logic of the necessary connection between consensus propositions and the objective of describing general, causal explanations has never been demonstrated. Rather, in each of the cases cited, the authors have simply asserted the relationship to exist, citing examples of theorists who have indeed been consensus-oriented causal theorists. They discuss no authors representing alternative combinations of positivism and theory type, and the reader might well be forgiven for concluding that none such exist. In fact, there have been conflict theorists writing in causal terms as long as there have been consensus. Their numbers have not been as great, but there have been too many of them to be ignored, nor can they properly be treated as inconsequential exceptions. Some of these conflict proponents did empirical work themselves, and those that did not made considerable use of existing published data, critically discussing the material, and often arguing for alternative interpretations.

Numerous examples appeared in the review of the literature— Ducpétiaux, Engels, Bonger, Kropotkin, Colajanni, to note the more important, and Hall, Carpenter, Denis, Pecquer, to include the minor cases. Most of these writers have simply been ignored in the discussions of the critics. Ducpétiaux, Kropotkin, Colajanni and Hall do not appear at all in the discussions of Quinney, Matza, Gouldner and *The New Criminology*. Bonger's *Criminality and Economic Conditions* and Engels's *Condition of the Working Class* are omitted in Quinney. Marx, Engels, and Bonger were discussed in *The New Criminology*, but in such a fashion as to suggest that they really did not contradict the case the authors wished to make.[1]

1. Bonger was attacked viciously. His theory did not meet the full requirements of a Marxist theory of deviance, and his methods were such that his 'theory' probably should not be endowed with 'the status of a theory,

Quinney also announced himself a Marxist in the *Critique of Legal Order*, committed to socialist revolution in the United States through a critical, Marxist sociology. Yet he similarly failed to recognize, in Marx and Engels, prime contradictory cases to his own argument. Positivist thought began with 'realist assumptions', a criticism which must qualify the work of Marx and Engels, if anyone's. Yet these were said to be the assumptions of 'anyone who has not reflected about the problems of perception and experience', a charge totally inconsistent with Quinney's deferential treatment of Marx and Engels. 'At best, the positivist has only a naïve acquaintance with epistemological and ontological concerns' (p. 2).

AN UNDIGNIFIED VIEW OF THE INDIVIDUAL

In some respects a more damning criticism of positivism, and one perhaps even more widely held at the present time, is that it involves an undignified view of the human being. Positivists were said to treat their fellow human beings as 'things', or 'objects' in order to study them empirically. Human behaviour, according to *The New Criminology*, thereby became denuded of 'meaning, moral choice and creativity'. In the case of deviance this meant that criminals never chose to commit their acts, and crime, therefore, could never imply political protest, a very good point if it were true.

Quinney's remonstrations on this point were characteristically milder in his earlier work, but even there he protested that causal explanations were often (although not necessarily) 'mechanistic' (p. 6). By contrast, his own theory accorded individuals the ability to act meaningfully, make decisions and construct social realities. In his later work he portrayed 'the positivist' as a singularly self-seeking and immoral creature. 'There is no questioning of the established order' in positivist thought, (p. 3) no 'asking what could be' and no 'seeking to transcend the established order' (p. 4). Rather, 'social scientists have formed an easy alliance with the ruling class that profits from the preservation of the status quo' (p. 5). Positivistic thought cannot provide a liberating conception of human existence.

(p. 235). Yet his discussion of the empirical literature was at fault as well— a 'crudely statistical technique of verification' (p. 238). To cap it all, it was suggested that Bonger's socialism would not be hard to equate with that of the 'leadership of the Soviet bloc, which are currently engaged in their own "war" against crime, utilizing the characteristically empiricist methodology of positivistic social science'.

Matza, whose *Delinquency and Drift* in 1964 opened the current attack, was perhaps the most insistent on this point.

> Positive criminology rejected the view that man exercised freedom, was possessed of reason, and was thus capable of choice. . . . Determinism . . . was not merely a heuristic principle; it was a vision that likened man to physical and chemical particles. Every event is caused. Human freedom is illusory. (p. 5)

All these criticisms reflect a serious misrepresentation of the major positivists. Not even the Italian school went as far as the charges would have us believe, and the charges are even more off base when sociological work is considered. Lombroso explicitly excluded political criminals from the born-criminal explanation, admitting that some amount of crime was caused for any number of social reasons, including deliberate political protest. Political crimes were committed mainly by the young, who were 'endowed with genius and a singular altruism.'[1] Further, crimes of passion, of which political crime was one type, indicated 'excessive development of noble qualities, sensibility, altruism, integrity, affection.' (p. 118). The abuse of power, predominance of one class, and neglect of public welfare were among the causes of political crime. 'Persecutions,' Lombroso argued, 'make for great changes in men's ideas and feelings' (p. 229).

Matza's examples were all drawn from the Italian school, especially Lombroso and the early Ferri, while the work of the sociologists was totally ignored. It is easy to lampoon the Italian school, and Matza does as good a job of it as anyone. The faults he found, however, were then generalized to all social science. 'Multi-causal theories, bio-psycho-socioeconomic theories' were just as bad as 'arrogant psychiatric' (p. 13). No particular sociologists, psychologists or economists were cited, but rather the principal subject of his attack was Schopenhauer, who seems never to have paid dues to any professional sociology association. According to Matza, the positive school of criminology concurred in Schopenhauer's dictum:

> Every man, being what he is and placed in the circumstances which for the moment obtain, but which on their part also arise by strict necessity, can absolutely never do anything else than just

1. Lombroso, *Crime and Its Causes*, p. 434. In *Crime Politique*, Lombroso described Marx as a man with a 'beautiful physiognomy', which revolutionaries generally had; anarchists were generally of the criminal type (p. 43).

what at that moment he does do. Accordingly, the whole course of man's life, in all its incidents great and small, is as necessarily predetermined as the course of a clock. (p. 5)

Ironically, one of Matza's main criticisms of positivism was the excessive differentiation of the criminal from the non-criminal, a point one would have to make of his own differentiation between the positivist and the non-positivist. Matza exempted the classical theorists, such as Beccaria and Bentham, from the differentiation criticism, and that of an undignified view of the human being (p. 11). Yet Beccaria argued economic conditions as causes of crime, which makes him a determinist. And Bentham's portrayal of rational self-interested calculation was hardly flattering.

The logical connection between determinism and lack of responsibility assumed by the critics also fails to stand up to scrutiny: Italian school theorists, who come the closest to determinism were careful to insist that their theories did not absolve offenders of responsibility for their actions. Most of these writers, including Lombroso and Ferri, advocated more lenient punishments, however still believed life imprisonment to be justifiable for some cases, and capital punishment for others. They argued that determinism held as much for law-abiding members of society as for criminals, in that there were forces that motivated people to enforce the law as well as others to break it. Garofalo, a prominent Italian school writer, advocated more severe penalties, as did others of the school. Further, certain governments with particularly repressive regimes supported Italian school theory officially, sponsoring international congresses in their own countries, and sending delegates to others.

The early arguments for determinism were arguments for leniency or, more precisely, they were arguments against the cruel punishments of the day. The great French psychiatrists used their theories to oppose the death penalty for the sick, the mentally feeble and children. Conflict theorists, arguing economic causes, advanced similar arguments. Deterministic arguments, in short, have been used to support a variety of positions, and probably more often humane objectives than otherwise. The most contemptible views of human beings I found came from the *popularizers* of social Darwinism, and not from actual theorists or empirical researchers themselves. Francis Galton and Havelock Ellis are prime examples. They were determinists, and held views of human nature as despicable as any intimated by the critics, but this hardly makes the case of a logical or necessary connection. Kropotkin, too, was a determinist, but his humanity sings out on every page he wrote.

COMTE: THE CONSERVATIVE EXTREME

Comte is an excellent test case for the contention that the criticisms of 'positivism' do not apply to the major nineteenth-century positivists. For conservatism, commitment to general theory, and deference to natural scientific models, the 'founder of positivism' could hardly be excelled. To show that even he is exempt from the brunt of the charges against it, is to show how seriously misguided the criticism has been. Comte's three-stage theory of evolution applied to all societies at all times, and to all kinds of social and intellectual phenomena. Comte was trained in the natural sciences and, while he never followed a career as a researcher, he drew on this background in much of his scholarly writing. His *Cours de Philosophie Positive* was devoted essentially to the argument that, common to all the sciences, including sociology, were certain underlying philosophical assumptions. Scientists, in the course of doing their work, could be seen to have acted on the basis of these assumptions, and Comte took it as his task to make these explicit. Sociology was the last of the sciences to emerge, after mathematics, astronomy, physics, chemistry and biology, but no different from the others in this fundamental respect.

Comte's credentials as a conservative in theory are no less impressive. 'Order and progress' was the motto of his religion of humanity, and he believed not only that both were possible, but that they were inevitable. Though he lived in a period of war and revolution he never lost confidence that a basic unity in society could be achieved— that conflicting interests could be reconciled.

Nevertheless, for all that can be criticized in Comte's evolutionary propositions and his metaphysics, I can find nothing to object to in his philosophy of science. It does not take us very far, is badly expressed, and is inconveniently interspersed with much other writing, but the ideas themselves are quite reasonable. This should be clear in Mill's summary statement of the position in *Auguste Comte and Positivism:*

We have no absolute knowledge of anything, but phenomena; and our knowledge of phenomena is relative, not absolute. We know not the essence, nor the real mode of production of any fact, but only its relations to other facts in the way of succession or of similitude. These relations are constant; that is, always the same in the same circumstances. The constant resemblances which link phenomena together, and the constant sequences which unite them as antecedent and consequent are termed their laws. The laws of phenomena are all we know respecting them. Their essential nature, and their ultimate causes, either efficient or final are unknown and inscrutable to us. (p. 6)

One is inclined to wonder at this point what all the fuss was about. Laws were descriptive devices in Comte's conceptualization, in much the same way as in later positivism and phenomenology. His notion of causality was not of 'hard determinism', but the making of inferences when certain conditions were met. His objectivist position, too, takes on a new light when the continued hold of the 'essentialist' position is considered. He argued that phenomena were to be explained in terms of objective, material conditions, as opposed to 'essences' inherent in them, which was the conceptualization of Plato and Aristotle and still widely held.

To infer from this that his view of human beings was degrading is quite unwarranted,[1] and completely inconsistent with the rest of his life and work. Comte's human beings were very much moral individuals, capable of making choices. They were limited by biological make-up and external, physical constraints, but a wide area for decision was still left. The laws regulating human conduct were more flexible than those regulating natural, Comte explained, on account of the capacities of human beings to grow and change. His concern for education, and his whole religion of humanity even more so, are manifestations of this essentially optimistic view. Knowledge was a means to an end, to be put to use in the enterprise of bettering humanity.

QUETELET

Quetelet was as committed a positivist as Comte, and guilty to boot of actually having done research in the physical sciences and mathematics. He was probably more influential than Comte in the nine-

1. He regarded women as intellectually inferior beings, but none of the critics of positivism seem to have had this in mind.

teenth century, for several reasons. The analysis in *Physique Sociale* was aimed at a much lower level of theory than Comte's all-inclusive historicism. The work served as a practical example for many nineteenth-century studies, researchers in other countries imitating his methods, and comparing the results. In addition, there was Quetelet's philosophy of science, plainly and constructively outlined.

Quetelet really believed in an objective world, physical and social, which could be described, with varying degrees of accuracy, by general laws. He was a total determinist in the sense of treating complete explanation as a goal to be approached, and chance as representing not yet understood forces. As was evident in the discussion in Chapter 3, he by no means treated explanation in a mechanistic fashion, nor believed that complete explanation would ever be achieved. The laws he sought were not totally invariant, but changed, gradually, within limits.

Accordingly, it was necessary to distinguish *social* forces from the ordinary forces of mechanics—for these social forces, 'under the influence of human will, were modified, and progressively changed their direction and intensity' (p. 113).

The laws that were the task of science to discover at no time implied a determinism at the individual level. General patterns could be discovered only when large numbers of observations were made, and this required both considerable simplification and the achievement of some distance from the objects of study. What were only a large number of rain drops would become a rainbow with the proper distance and perspective. From the sentiments and irrational motivations involved in the decision to marry, at the individual level, tables of marriage rates could be constructed at the aggregate. But marriage rates could not predict which particular individuals would marry in any year, any more than mortality statistics which particular individuals would die. 'Man's free will made impossible any kind of prediction at the individual level' (p. 319). But

> *free will, effaced itself and stayed without sensible effect when the observations were extended on a large number of individuals* (p. 320).
> The moral causes which leave their trace on social phenomena then are inherent in the nation and not in the individuals (p. 321).

Quetelet conceived of individuals as being capable of choice, but there were obvious limitations as to what options they had from which to choose, and they were influenced by their surroundings in making choices. In the case of criminals, the regularity of the patterns occurring convinced him that the causes lay in social organisation; 'unhappy condition of the human species', the lament began:

> We can enumerate in advance how many individuals will soil their hands in the blood of their fellows, how many will be frauds, how many poisoners; almost as one can enumerate in advance the births and deaths that will take place. Society holds in itself the germs of all the crimes that are to be committed. It is (society), in a way, that prepares them, and the guilty one is but the instrument that executes them. Each social state supposes then a certain number and a certain order of crimes that result, as a necessary consequence of its organization (p. 97).

This, however, was not the whole story and the situation was not as discouraging as it might seem at first glance.

> On the contrary when one examines it closely it shows the possibility of improving men, of modifying their institutions, their habits, the state of their instruction and, in general, all that acts on their manner of being (p. 97). I am far from concluding . . . that man can do nothing for his improvement. I believe . . . that he possesses a moral force capable of modifying the laws which concern him; but this force acts only in the slowest manner, in that the causes which influence the social system are not susceptible to any brusk alteration. (p. 316)

The fact that change took so long to be effected, far from suggesting the weakness of human beings, showed one of their 'noblest attributes'. What was accomplished would then be durable, and even the most concerted efforts to destroy it often did not succeed. Very few people, though, had the capacity to exert such a profound impression on their society (p. 98). Quetelet conceded that progress in science had the effect of increasingly removing power from the individual, external causes now explaining what had previously been credited to the individual. But these same laws demonstrated even more the *intellectual* powers of individuals (p. 97).

MILL: LIBERTY, DETERMINISM AND FREE WILL

John Stuart Mill was one of the most eminent writers on positivism in the nineteenth century, producing a comprehensive text on the subject, the *System of Logic*, and a useful book on Comte and positivism. Mill was a complete determinist in deeming complete explanation to be the objective of science. Partial explanations of the type 'if A the majority B', were desirably only a step along the way to 'if A all B'. If accurate knowledge were possible at every stage it would be 'abstractly possible' to foretell all effects.[1]

Mill was one of the strongest advocates of natural science models for sociology, going so far as to assert that the 'backward state of the moral sciences could only be remedied by applying the methods of the physical sciences, duly extended and generalized' (p. 405). Mill's reasons were not crassly opportunistic—the success of the physical sciences—but were based rather on the lack of alternative models. Literature was not much help as a model and historians typically disdained theorizing. Economists were more precise and could be counted on to be theory-oriented, but their models were too abstract. Far from attempting to explain the real world, they stripped it of its most crucial conditions. The use of natural science models, however, at no time implied a simple identification of social phenomena with physical. The differences between them were carefully discussed in *System of Logic*, so much so that Durkheim complained Mill exaggerated them. Altogether it is difficult to reconcile the charge that positivists never reflected on ontological questions with Mill's careful, serious *System of Logic*.

Mill's position on the free will-determinism debate was again not simple. He had to be on the determinist side, in view of his positivistic convictions, but admitted that the doctrine of determinism could be degrading in terms of moral, human values. The free will doctrine might be closer to the truth 'by keeping in view the power of the mind to co-operate in the formation of its own character' (p. 412). Determinism did not signify only the external forces acting on individuals, but those at the command of the individual as well.

> They made us what they did make us, by willing not the end, but the requisite means: and we, when our habits are not too inveterate, can, by similarly willing the requisite means, make ourselves different. . . . We are exactly as capable of making our own character, *if we will*, as others are of making it for us. (p. 410)

All this is perhaps even more obvious when it is remembered that the same Mill who wrote *System of Logic* wrote also the essay *On*

1. *System of Logic*, p. 51.

Liberty. Mill quite outdid even the most progressive of the critics of positivism in according the capacity for moral choice to ordinary human beings—including women as competent in this respect as well as men.

DURKHEIM: A RELUCTANT POSITIVIST

Durkheim described as the principal objective of his work 'the extension of scientific rationalism to human conduct', and the explanation of the origin of social phenomena, their functioning and their evolution or change.[1] Durkheim did not like the term 'positivist' but accepted it as a description of his work; positivism was a logical consequence of his rationalist position. The bulk of his work was clearly in the positivist tradition—the formulation of general laws and their verification.[2] The later functionalism of his *Elementary Forms of the Religious Life* marks a departure in many respects, as does his last work on morality, 'Introduction à la Morale'. He never, however, repudiated his early explicit stand, and it seems perfectly proper to treat him as a positivist, without undue qualification.

The Rules of Sociological Method is one of the classic texts of positivism, and the main source here for his views on methodology. It was in this work that Durkheim elaborated his method of comparative analysis, or indirect experimentation, and established criteria for making decisions on verification of propositions. Inferences could not properly be based on isolated examples, but on systematic observation of series, or different combinations of circumstances. The coincidence of cause and effect in sufficiently large numbers of observations, across sufficiently varied circumstances, could be interpreted as substantiation of a causal proposition.

Durkheim's positivism was no more a simple determinism than that of Comte, Quetelet, or Mill. Causality was something the scientist imputed to certain relationships on the basis of empirical investigation. He was well aware of the complexity of social phenomena and, as a result, the immensity of the difficulties in correctly tracing causal relationships. Much of his criticism of other sociologists in fact dealt with disputes over the appropriate inferences to be drawn from particular data.

Durkheim's view of the state of knowledge in sociology was

1. *Règles de la Méthode Sociologique*, p. ix.
2. *Division of Labour, Suicide*, and 'Deux Lois'.

pessimistic. In the *Rules* he claimed that sociologists were almost completely ignorant about principal social institutions, such as the state and the family—the causes on which they depended, the functions they fulfilled, and the laws of their evolution. Rather, we were only beginning to see through certain false conceptions. Yet, Durkheim lamented, one had only to glance through the works of sociology to see how rare was this sense of ignorance.

Social phenomena were admittedly much more difficult to study than any other, and the sociologist was considerably more constrained methodologically. Most important, the sociologist was seldom free to experiment, although the differences between sociology and the other sciences in this respect were a matter of degree rather than kind. There was, however, one great compensation for the sociologist, in the richness of variation in social data. In no other realm of nature were the structural transformations so great over time or the diversity of particular sub-types (pp. 126–34).

Durkheim, perhaps as much as any of the positivists, made 'objects' of social phenomena, in fact arguing that social facts had to be treated as 'things' to be studied. What he meant by this is perhaps deceptively simple. Social facts had to be approached as being external to the individual researcher, and not readily 'penetrable' by introspection. Earlier generations, for example, had influenced current social conditions in many important ways, but in so complex a fashion that we could not know precisely how (p. xiv). The sociologist could claim more intuitive insight into social phenomena than a geologist into a rock, but the differences across the sciences were again matters of degree rather than kind.

Durkheim's purpose in arguing the objectivist position was to insure that researchers took a suitably humble stance in approaching their data. Researchers had to face the social world as a world of the unknown, and one which would often present them with quite unexpected, and sometimes disturbing results (p. xiv). Objectification, far from justifying mechanistic or simplistic approaches to social study, was intended to do just the opposite.

WEBER: UNDERSTANDING, HISTORY AND CAUSALITY

Weber is typically exempted in attacks on positivism, his 'method' of *Verstehen* being interpreted as a rejection of positivism. Weber's work on methodology was lengthy and difficult, and the fact that not all of it has been translated into English has meant further misunderstanding. My concern here is to show that the implications of the attack on 'positivism' are much greater than has been commonly supposed. I dispute that there are easily definable 'good guys', and 'bad guys', and suggest that the criticisms made of the supposed 'bad guys' apply also to any number of the theorists supposedly on the other side. Neither Weber, nor Marx, can properly be exempted, which makes the 'attack on positivism' an attack on most of social science.

Firstly, Weber never rejected the notion of causality. He believed the formulation of causal laws to be an essential part of the social sciences, or the 'cultural sciences' as he called them. Causal laws were, however, a means to an end, and not the end itself, not such a different position as that taken by the classical positivists. They, too, saw explanation as a means to an end, but toward something along the lines of the betterment of humanity. The end, for Weber, was the understanding of significant events.

> The understanding of *laws* of causality is not the *end*, but only the *means* of research. It facilitates and makes possible the causal imputation of elements of phenomena important for the culture by their singularity.[1]

Weber's position on the generality of laws to be sought reflects this same concern. Generality and usefulness were mutually exclusive objectives. The more general or abstract the law, the less it would enrich understanding of particular events. While there was something to be gained by seeking generality—application to more events—there was a trade-off—less to be said about any of them. To Weber, there was no incompatibility between the search for causal laws and historical study. The proper subject matter of the cultural scientist was the great events of history, but these were to be studied causally. 'Causal importance' was the major criterion the scientist used in selecting from the 'infinity' of particular elements of study available (p. 78). The great events of history were more difficult to study than common recurring matters, but they were, nevertheless, what the scientist ought to be concerned with. Once these objectives were settled

1. 'Objectivité de la connaissance dans les sciences et la politique sociale', in *Essais sur la Théorie de la Science* p. 163.

on, causal importance became relevant, in the selection of what about them should be studied.

'Value neutrality' was never a matter of fact to Weber, or a goal easily achieved. Certainly he held that one should seek conscientiously to be objective in scientific work. On the moral level, teachers owed it to their students to keep their political views out of the classroom. It was irresponsible to exploit one's position as a teacher for political purposes. On the intellectual level, Weber was equally categoric: one's values were an impediment to scientific work. 'Whenever a man of science introduces his personal value judgement, a full understanding of the facts *ceases*.'[1] Values were a legitimate, indeed necessary, concern in selecting problems for study. The importance of the question was to be the prime consideration in selecting problems, and importance was something established relative to values.

Weber's position on the differences between the natural and cultural sciences involves many complications. Suffice it to say that, while he drew a number of distinctions between the two types of sciences, they were never a simple black and white nature. Further, while he did not use natural science examples in his work, unlike both the classical positivists and the Marxists, neither did he reject the natural sciences' concern for general laws. The 'idiographic-nomothetic' distinction was not a matter of absolute difference in his conceptualization. Rather both types of scientists were involved in both descriptive work and the formulation of universal laws.[2] The purpose of his methodology was the reconciliation of the study of important, singular events with the scientific precision normally associated with simpler, repetitive occurrences. The cultural science he sought to advance was one which would avoid the loose speculation of the former, and the triviality of the latter. Weber was properly concerned with the triviality of much of what passed for positivistic work, but his solution was not to abandon scientific principles altogether. It was over the issue of *level of analysis* that he departed most fundamentally from classical positivism. Human individuals were what was most real to Weber and he was concerned with Durkheim's reification of the collective, or at least his inordinate attention to conceptualizations at that level.

Finally, Weber's methodology was always a methodology of

1. 'Science as a Vocation', in *From Max Weber*, p. 146.
2. *Essais*, p. 30.

the real world, to the disappointment of phenomenologists ever since.

> The type of social science in which we are interested is an *empirical science* of concrete *reality*. Our aim is the understanding of the characteristic uniqueness of the reality in which we move.[1]

MARX AND ENGELS: 'VULGAR' MATERIALISM AND CLASSICAL POSITIVISM

Marx and Engels shared with Weber and the classical positivists the same real world assumptions, respect for the scientific method, concern for the search for general laws, and strictures of objectivity in method. With the classical positivists, the Marxists shared also a love of natural science models and a belief in objectification as part of the process of study. There are differences between the dialectical materialism/*praxis* model and classical positivism, but our enthusiasm in finding differences should not make us ignore the similarities. Rather, there are reasons to treat the dialectical materialism model as having evolved, in a sense, from classical positivism. Insofar as dialectical materialism was a revision of Feuerbach's simpler, 'vulgar' materialism, it was a revision of the basic notions of classical positivism as well.[2]

Feuerbach's materialism is the link between the two. As the source of Marx's materialism, it is the source of the similarities with classical positivism. Where Marx and Engels departed from it—for dialectical materialism and *praxis*—they departed also from classical positivism. Marx had made the step to materialism from Hegelian idealism by 1844. It is quite evident in the *Philosophical Manuscripts*, although the *depth* of the break is still disputed. The move to dialectical materialism, from 'vulgar' materialism, occurred very soon after, in 1845. It appears in *The German Ideology* and the 'Theses on Feuerbach'.

---

1. *Methodology of the Social Sciences*, p. 72.
2. *Praxis* signifies the capacity of human beings to make their history, as opposed to their being merely acted-on objects. 'Dialectical materialism' signifies the interplay between individuals as actors, acting on an external world, and as objects acted on by external events. The two concepts, then, are intimately related, so that the use of either term implies the other. Both can be contrasted with 'historical materialism', which signifies the action of material conditions on human history.

There is further discussion in Engels's *Anti-Dühring* and scattered remarks in both Marx's and Engels's later work.[1]

The basic materialist position espoused by Marx and Engels is identical with that of classical positivism. There was, fundamentally, a belief in a real, objective world, acting on conscious human beings. The world was a knowable one, if not known, and the scientist's task was to seek out the laws which explained it. Human beings could be studied as much as material objects, for they too were objects, in the sense of being acted on by others.[2] Externalization and objectification were not necessarily undesirable undertakings, for they implied the ability of humans to stand back and reflect on themselves, which could be an enriching experience.

Both Marx and Engels used natural science examples in their work, and both were impressed with the success of those sciences in their day. Nor was this a question of a peculiar, esoteric taste they shared, or undue susceptibility to the good public image of natural science. Rather, the success of the natural sciences had an important, substantive role to play in the development of dialectical materialism as a methodology. It was necessary to study *things* first, before an understanding of *processes* could be achieved. Sufficient knowledge of the natural world was a necessary first step for the study of the social world in which it was situated.

In Feuerbach's time, knowledge had been arrested at the stage of things; materialism at this level was static or 'vulgar' and this made Feuerbach's own repugnance for it understandable. Three important scientific discoveries changed this situation: the discovery of the cell, the theory of the transformation of energy and the theory of evolution.[3] Each had the essential quality of crossing the boundaries between mechanics, chemistry and biology, to interrelate phenomena previously dealt with in an isolated fashion. Natural science was thereby transformed from an 'empirical science' to a 'theoretical science'. This stage achieved, the development of a human science could be broached. Natural science constituted the base of the 'edifice of human knowledge', but was not the edifice itself, for we live not only in nature, but in human society. The differences between human society and the natural world were profound, and were

1. A much more thorough discussion of these points is planned for another work.
2. *Philosophical Manuscripts of 1844*, p. 362.
3. Engels, 'Fragment non publié' in *Etudes Philosophiques*, 1886.

not adequately taken account of in 'vulgar' materialism. This is plain in several of the 'Theses on Feuerbach':

I. The chief defect in all hitherto existing materialism (that of Feuerbach included) is that the thing, the reality, the sensuousness, is conceived only in the form of *object* or contemplation, but not as sensuous *human activity*, *praxis* not subjectively.

II. The materialist doctrine concerning the changing of circumstances and upbringing forgets that circumstances are changed by men and that it is essential to educate the educator himself. . . . The coincidence of the changing of circumstances and of human activity or self-changing can be conceived and rationally understood only as *revolutionary praxis*.

VIII. All social life is essentially *praxis*. All mysteries which lead theory to mysticism find their rational solution in human *praxis* and in the comprehension of this *praxis*.

Social life could not be understood in the same way as the natural world, for human beings were themselves conscious, feeling beings, as well as objects, reflecting on their experiences in the natural world, and acting in turn on it. Why Feuerbach and others had not moved past early materialism was itself explained by the social conditions of the time. The older materialism, as Feuerbach himself, was a product of bourgeois society, and its conceptualization of the human being as an isolated, abstract person, corresponded to that. The point of view of the new materialism—dialectical materialism—reflected a 'human society, or socialized humanity'.[1]

THE NOTION OF PRAXIS IN CLASSICAL POSITIVISM

The differences between dialectical materialism and classical positivism are still a matter of degree, not kind, even on this crucial point. Quetelet believed that 'man possesses a moral force capable of modifying the laws which concern him.'[2] Similarly, John Stuart Mill asserted, 'We are exactly as capable of making our own character, *if we will*, as others are of making it for us.[3] Science, according to Durkheim, on revealing for us the causes of phenomena furnishes us the means to realize the ends that our will seeks for supra-scientific reasons.[4] Even in Comte the rudiments of *praxis* appear. Laws regulating human conduct were more flexible than those in the

1. 'Theses on Feuerbach', number 10.   2. *Physique Sociale*, p. 316.
3. *System of Logic*, p. 410.   4. *Règles*, p. 48.

natural world, on account of the capacity of human beings to grow and change.[1] Marx and Engels were more optimistic about the scope of the change human beings could make, and the speed, but the germ of the idea is certainly present in the work of the classical positivists.

On the question of the relationship between theory and practice Marx and Engels again went further. The non-Marxist positivists argued for action on the basis of study, while Marx and Engels advocated an *integration*. The difference is a profound one, but again is a matter of a development rather than a total break. Durkheim, among others, stated that knowledge without being directed to the betterment of humanity was of no value. Of course what constituted betterment also differed between them, the classical positivists all being at best reformers. But it is with Weber and his followers that really basic differences appear, Weber insisting on the separation of science from political activity. The Marxist position was much closer to that of the classical positivists than either was to the Weberian.

To what extent Marx intended *praxis* to imply a repudiation of traditional methods of research is not clear and remains a matter of dispute. Some writers claim to find a 'break with positivism' in Marx,[2] while others would prefer that he had gone further.[3] The second thesis on Feuerbach, which I do not interpret as a break, is, however, ambiguous:

> The question whether objective truth can be attributed to human thinking is not a question of theory but is a question of *praxis*. Man must prove the truth, i.e., the reality and the power, the this-sidedness of his thinking in *praxis*. The dispute over the reality or non-reality of thinking that is isolated from *praxis* is a purely *scholastic* question.

At no time, however, did Marx expressly repudiate the methods of ordinary science, and Engels continued to reveal a strong positivism. Marx certainly used ordinary social science methods in his own work. C. Wright Mills maintained that that was *all* he used, that he totally ignored dialectical methodology in his own research.[4] As to Marx's views on the classical positivists of his own day we have almost no information. He was familiar with Quetelet's *Physique Sociale* and

1. *Cours de Philosophie Positive* T. IV, lessons 48 and 51.
2. *New Criminology.*   3. Althusser.   4. *The Marxists*, p. 128.

cited material from it, calling it 'an excellent and learned work'.[1] This occurred in 1853, or well after the formulation of *praxis* and, accordingly, not a position to be attributed to Marx's social democratic phase, vulgar materialism or whatever.

Engels's position was very clear; whatever else *praxis* might mean, it included scientific work, both in the study of nature and society. This was stated unambiguously in 'Idéalisme et Matérialisme', among other places, in a defence of the Marxist faith in the knowability of the world.

> Hume and Kant contest the possibility of the knowledge of the world, or at least of its complete knowledge. The refutation the most striking is *praxis*, notably in experience and activity. We prove the correctness of our conception in producing it. (p. 23)

To illustrate this, Engels cited the discovery of the planet, Neptune, whose existence was first deduced mathematically, and later confirmed by observation (p. 23). The same principle held in the case of social theory. Engels consistently insisted that it was *facts* that had refuted the principal elements of bourgeois economics—the identity of interests between capital and labour and so forth.[2]

Praxis, in Engels's conceptualization, was not incompatible with the search for general, causal explanation. The differences between the natural world and the social world suggested a contradiction, but one that could be resolved. It was, indeed, consideration of these differences that led Marx and Engels to the notion of *praxis* in the first place. In nature, 'blind and unconscious factors' were at work, and it was in their 'alternance' that general laws were manifested.[3] Nothing in the world of nature was produced through a conscious, willed goal.

> By contrast, in the history of society, the active factors have been exclusively men, endowed with reason, and acting with reflection, or passion and following determined goals; nothing was produced without a conscious design, without a willed end. (p. 45)

This difference, however, could not change the fact that the course

1. In a *New York Daily Tribune* article (p. 229 in the reprint). It is interesting that Comte dismissed the same work as 'mere statistics'. Again the line between positivism and *praxis*, as good and evil, proves elusive.
2. *Anti-Dühring*, p. 13.
3. Idéalisme et Matérialisme', p. 44.

of history was determined by general, internal laws. The multiplicity of differing wills had the effect of cancelling each other out.

> Thus, the conflict of innumerable wills and individual actions created in the domain of history a state exactly analogous to that which prevailed in unconscious nature. Goals and actions were willed, but the results which followed them were not, or, if they seemed, at the start, to correspond to a pursued goal, they had, finally, consequences quite other than that which had been willed.

Engels's solution to the problem was precisely the same as Quetelet's—the effects of individual decisions being cancelled out with large numbers. Like Quetelet, again, Engels treated 'what seemed to be chance, on the surface' as laws which had not yet been understood.

LENIN'S ATTACK ON PHENOMENOLOGY

The extent of the common ground between classical positivism and dialectical materialism is again underscored in the attack on both at the turn of the century, and Lenin's counter-attack. Briefly, two opposition movements can be identified. There was a conventional academic group, whose most prominent contributors were Ernst Mach, an Austrian physicist, Karl Pearson, the British statistician, and Pierre Duhem, a French chemist. The second movement involved mainly Russian philosophers, notably Bogdanov and Avenarius, who were Marxists and whose intentions were the development of a new, Marxist philosophy. Lenin interpreted both revisions as attacks on dialectical materialism and, in 1908, responded with a lengthy and vituperative counter-attack, *Materialism and Empirio-criticism*.

Mach's criticism of positivism was perhaps the most fundamental, and it influenced other conventional scientists and back-sliding Marxists, or 'muddle-headed Machists' as Lenin called them. Mach repudiated the central 'real world' conceptualization of classical positivism and dialectical materialism. The physical world was not in any absolute sense different from the psychic; both were formed of the same elements, sensations. The task of the scientist was to describe the relationships among these various phenomena—among physical phenomena (physics), among psychic (psychology) and between physical and psychic (physiology).[1]

Laws should be regarded as nothing more than the descriptions of

1. *Connaissance et l'Erreur.*

these relationships. The notions of cause, effect and necessity were understandable in that they reflected a desire for order in the natural world, and themselves marked a progression in human thought from more casual associations of phenomena. Desirably, they were an intermediate step to careful, descriptive propositions, preferably in functional form. The idea that natural laws *existed* before being recognized by human beings was 'unfortunate' (p. 368).

Pearson's argument for purely descriptive laws was similar, earning him Lenin's scorn as an 'unadulterated idealist'. Like Mach and the others, he had not advanced past the stage of Bishop Berkeley.[1] Pearson stressed that his complaint was with the *mode of expression* of scientific work, and not the substance of any concrete laws; science, indeed, was doing very nicely. But school textbooks should not mislead school children into confusing descriptive concepts, like force, with real things. Force could describe the process of breaking a window, but force did not itself break windows. Pearson's examples, like Mach's, all dealt with natural science, and it is not clear from the *Grammar of Science* to what extent he rejected positivism in social science. From other evidence, it seems that he exempted social science from his critique. Shortly after publishing the *Grammar of Science*, Pearson became the statistical adviser for one of the most ambitious empirical studies in the social control field, Goring's refutation of Italian school theory. In introducing a later edition of the work, Pearson reveals himself as very much at home with the notions of causal theory.[2] The research design was solidly grounded in classical positivist assumptions and Pearson described all this in an approving, and sometimes enthusiastic tone. He even had praise for the criminal anthropological laboratories in the United States (p. xv).

THE DEFENCE OF DIALECTICAL MATERIALISM

Lenin interpreted the assault on the real world as an assault on dialectical materialism and, necessarily, an attack on Marxism itself. This was stated plainly in 'Questions to a Lecturer':

> 3. Does the lecturer acknowledge that recognition of the external world and the reflection of it in the human mind form the basis of the theory of knowledge and dialectical materialism . . . ?

1. *Materialism and Empirio-criticism*, p. 224.
2. *The English Convict*, abr. 1915 edn.

7. Does the lecturer acknowledge that the ideas of causality, necessity, law, etc. are a reflection in the human mind of laws of nature, of the real world? Or was Engels wrong in saying so (*Anti-Dühring*).[1]

The development of dialectical materialism in Marx and Engels was traced in some detail in *Materialism and Empirio-criticism*, with the major elements of law, causality and necessity all defended.

Firstly Engels at the very outset of his argument recognized laws of nature, the necessity of nature—i.e., all that Mach . . . and Co. characterize as 'metaphysics'. . . . Secondly . . . Engels takes the knowledge of the will of man, on the one hand, and the necessity of nature on the other, and . . . simply says that the necessity of nature is primary, and human will and mind secondary. The latter must inevitably adapt to the former. Engels regards this as so obvious that he does not waste words explaining his view (p. 188).

Lenin then defended the 'necessity of nature' doctrine as an essential element in *praxis*. The knowledge of the objective nature of things was necessary for the transformation of 'things-in-themselves' into 'things-for-us', or of 'blind, unknown 'necessity-in-itself' into the known 'necessity for us' (p. 189).

Until we know a law of nature, it, existing and acting independently of and outside our mind, makes us slaves of 'blind necessity'. But once we come to know this law, which acts (as Marx repeated a thousand times) *independently* of our will and our mind, we become the masters of nature. The mastery of nature manifested in human practice is a result of an objectively correct reflection within the human head of the phenomena and processes of nature, and is proof of the fact that this reflection . . . is objective, absolute, eternal truth (p. 190).

Lenin was never a man to mince words but, even so, *Materialism* comes on strong. The aggressiveness of the work perhaps makes sense, when one considers the threats to the Bolshevik movement at the time. Idealist movements in Tsarist Russia were a major form of political protest, and so a form of competition to political revolutionaries.[2] Discontented individuals who were drawn off into radical

1. *Materialism and Empirio-criticism*, p. 15.
2. See Stark's volume on sects in *The Sociology of Religion*.

sects were lost to political action, at least temporarily and, more often, permanently. Idealist intellectual movements had a long history in Russia, and showed no signs of flagging. A heretic epistemology could not safely be ignored as an academic discussion among groups of isolated intellectuals. There were threats from within the Communist movement to be considered as well. The major deviationists claimed to be Bolsheviks, a point used by the Mensheviks in their claim to be the true descendants of Marx. Lenin was evidently embarrassed by this compromising situation, and sought to strengthen the Bolshevik claim to legitimacy with *Materialism*.[1]

THE LEGITIMATE ATTACK

To argue that the 'attack on positivism' has been misguided is not to imply that all is well in the field of sociology, or even that very much is satisfactory in it at all. Rather, I will agree with any critic that many of us get away with a lot of bad sociology. I will agree, also, that most current work is trivial—but must add no more so than in the nineteenth century. I concur with virtually all of the criticisms of contemporary work in Mills's *Sociological Imagination*. But many of these criticisms are the criticisms a classical positivist would level against the field as well. In the social control field especially, a substantial portion of the research published can be shown to be erroneous by the criteria of ordinary positivistic rules, a point argued in Chapter 3. It would seem, as well, that much work in the social control field has been carried out cynically, with the understanding that contribution to knowledge is only a secondary factor in the project, next to public relations. This, too, however, is a criticism that derives from the principles of classical positivism itself.

From outside the positivist perspective, I agree with Marxist-oriented critics that the focus of study has been inordinately on static situations. Researchers have resented change because it disturbs the orderly progress of their research designs, however much the change itself might be more worthy of study. I share the discontent, then, of most of the critics of contemporary sociology, but not the assessment of the problem as lying in the principles of positivism. To understand what went wrong in sociology I suggest exploration along quite different lines: the role of governments in sponsoring and controlling research work, institutional pressures of 'publish or perish' in

1. Vucinich, p. 265.

academe, and the loss of the classical tradition. Governments have long been influential in the shaping of the course of social science theorizing and research, but never so much before as now. The eighteenth-century theorists were largely independent scholars, neither employees of government, nor dependent on government contracts or grants. If they had university connections, these were usually with independent institutions. By the nineteenth century this had changed substantially. The large bulk of the empirical work was done by practitioners working for government agencies. Still, the great theoretical contributions, and a certain amount of the research, were the work of scholars effectively independent of government. By the twentieth century, there were few independents left. Most contributors were professional academics and practitioners, in both cases either employed by governments directly, or closely involved through grants, consulting work and so forth.[1]

Institutional pressures towards the production of large quantities of trivial work have been strong both in academe and government. In the case of government departments, the exigencies of safe findings have meant that difficult, controversial questions have seldom been permitted as research topics. In academe, 'publish or perish' can be blamed for a great deal of trivial work. What is perhaps less obvious is that it has also meant hasty and often equally trivial critiques. The critics of triviality have themselves been subject to the same pressures to get into print quickly and often.

Disdain for the classical tradition is a related problem, again affecting work in both the conflict and consensus orientations. Ignorance of the great theorists, and the great empirical projects, is a sufficient, and possibly a necessary, condition for the formulation of trivial projects. This point has been beautifully argued in Mills's *Sociological Imagination*, in a plea as eloquent as it is ignored. It is my impression that conflict theorists are somewhat less blameworthy in this respect, but the differences are not great, and there is nothing to be gained by blaming consensus theory *per se*.

The decline of the classical tradition, and especially of theory and research on the conflict side, are themselves related to the 'Americanization' of the subject.

American sociology is distinctive for its inattention to classical

1. An American study in the social control field found an association between the use of hard data, support for the *status quo* and government funding. See Galliher and McCartney.

theory,[1] and the conflict tradition was hurt the most by this neglect. Alternatively, the classical tradition would not have suffered so much had not conflict work virtually disappeared. Conflict theory, in turn, was always a European subject, and never a consideration in the formative years of American sociology.

The sequence of events seems fairly clear. Before World War I, sociology was essentially a European subject. Americans contributed to it along the lines established by the European originators. European works were widely reviewed in American journals, and Americans went to Europe to study. After the war, this pattern was never resumed. American writers increasingly cited only American sources, and American journals accorded less and less attention to European works—trends discussed in Chapter 4. A long, declining spiral began. The more European work was ignored, the less important it became to study it—and the less important to study the languages necessary to read it. Without languages, the possibility of retaining contact decreased. This, however, was justified on the grounds that European work was not relevant.[2]

Ironically, the next stage was the export of American sociology, back to Europe, to Canada, and much of the rest of the world. American histories of the subject became *the* histories. The Chicago school became the beginning of recorded time, with Durkheim and Marx playing no greater role than early forbears. Continental European and British sociologists now are often as cut off from the origins of their subject as are American, and show this in issuing the same complaints.

The loss of the classical tradition and ignorance of conflict theory are by no means exclusively American problems and, for this reason, efforts to 'de-Americanize' the subject are likely not to get far. The rejection of quantitative methods as American would seem to be particularly misguided. Rather I would argue for a return to the roots, empirical and theoretical, as the necessary first stage in the restoration of sociology as a serious scientific undertaking.

1. It is not that American sociology is 'atheoretical', as European radicals complain; rather, the level and type of theory has been different.
2. There is a telling indicator of the problem in citation practices, in the predominance of works published in the author's own society in the preceding ten years. A study on the influence of French scholarship in Quebec revealed an even bleaker pattern. The majority of citations in the journals concerned were to the senior members of the authors' own departments! (Le Blanc).

Chapter 9

CONCLUSIONS

This study began with a concern over the law and order issue, and especially the role social scientists have played in lending academic respectability to the demand for ever more and better means of control. It was disconcerting that sociologists act as consultants to programmes which, for all their fancy names, amount to longer sentences for young males of low social and racial status, and increased interference in the lives of ordinary people. I was puzzled by the extent of belief in the 'rising crime rate', a view widely held in industrial societies and Third World societies aspiring to western standards of civilization. Neither it, nor its companion belief in growing leniency in sentencing, seemed ever to have been properly documented. It began to appear that much of the conventional wisdom on crime and punishment was very badly based in fact. There was already reason to suspect much etiological theory, for research standards in that area have been notoriously low. Then a growing awareness of the ideological use of consensus theory gradually undermined what credibility remained. Clearly a rigorous assessment of the theoretical literature, in the light of the best research available, was in order.

Discontented as I was with the field, I was not prepared to accept many of the more recent criticisms of it. I disagreed with the contention that empirical research necessarily meant supporting the *status quo* and that endeavours at general explanations implied an undignified view of human beings. Further, I was not inclined to opt for the phenomenologist's solution to the problem, to shift the level of analysis to how conceptualizations of crime are built up. Fruitful as that approach might be for many questions, it could not be used for the questions I felt to be most important. My objective was to treat consensus theory as a source of propositions to be tested with concrete data, relative to sets of propositions from the competing conflict approach. I had begun to view consensus theory as bad theory, and wished to pursue it on those grounds. Much as one could criticize the law and order approach on moral grounds, it was its factual basis that I wished to pursue.

These concerns led to a lengthy exploration of the literature, reported in Chapters 2–4, and a series of research projects reported in Chapters 5–7. The origin, revision and disappearance of the major theories of crime, law and sanctions was traced, organized around the contrasting approaches of conflict and consensus theory. Conflict theory was defined as any approach in which power was given prominence in the explanation, conflicting interests between those holding power and those not being assumed. Consensus theory meant any other type of explanation, with considerations of power being either secondary or non-existent. What was interesting about this definition was that its use highlighted rather important *structural* differences between the two approaches. In consensus theory, criminal behaviour was crucial; law and sanctions were said to have developed in response to problems posed to a society through the criminality of certain of its members. To understand law and sanctions, one must first understand behaviour, for the nature of the law and the enforcement system depended on the nature of the crime problem. What was said to cause crime in the first place has varied over time and among different theorists, so that different schools can be identified, as between those emphasizing biological factors, psychological, social or various combinations of these. Yet, they all have in common the view of criminal behaviour as the primary factor to the understanding of social control. In conflict theory, by contrast, behaviour was secondary and ultimately explicable in terms of the interests of the holders of power. Law, which was held to reflect rather directly those interests, was important to the explanation of crime, or precisely the opposite relation to that of consensus theory. Sanctions, too, were tied to the power structure, reflecting its interests and, in recent versions, being crucial in the explanation of crime through a process of labelling.

These relations between law, sanctions and behaviour were discussed relatively explicitly by the early theorists. In the twentieth century, however, with increased specialization in the subject, the connections began to be ignored. The sociology of law became a separate subject, taught in the law school, while deviant behaviour became another of the 'white man's burdens' in the sociology department. The great mass of empirical studies in the field were designed so as to exclude consideration of the role of power. The data for such studies pertained almost inevitably to one society, and often only one segment of society, in other words holding constant the effect of power. Conflict and consensus theorists talked past each other. Researchers in the consensus tradition would show any number of problems to be associated with high official crime rates, but without having considered that the interests of the holders of power might explain the same phenomenon better. Conflict theorists would show that changes in the power structure were followed by changes in the nature of the law and enforcement system, but without establishing that it was the change in power that was crucial, rather than some other factor.

My own research projects were designed with these problems in mind. Units were chosen such that factors of *both* conflict theory and consensus varied, so that the effects of each could be tested against the other. For this reason, most of the analysis was based at the level of the nation–state. The tests were directed to the level of *sanctions*, expressed as a rate for the total society. This level, according to consensus theory, is supposed to reflect real crime—for sanctions are a response to the crime problem, and real crime, in turn, is supposed to reflect real social, economic, and psychological problems. According to conflict theory, the level of sanctions depends on the need for formal control measures on the part of the holders of power, and the resources, economic and social, available to them for such purposes. Sharply contrasting predictions, then, follow from the two approaches, and the tests lie in assessing the competing predictions against concrete data.

The data for the tests in Chapter 5 were of police-reported crime of various types, on both adults and children, from Interpol and on juvenile court convictions from the United Nations. A wide range of countries was covered in both data sets, varying in extent of social and economic problems, estimated needs of the power structure, and resources available to them. The tests in Chapter 6 were confined to England and Wales, with variation now over time as problems, needs and resources changed. The indicators included convictions for a number of different offences, adult and children's, police reports, and the rate of use of prisons. There was also a brief analysis of data at the

SLO—K

level of the borough in England and Wales, or again with variation across units differing as to their problems, and the needs and resources available to the holders of power.

Across this diverse set of tests a remarkably similar set of findings emerged. Rates of sanctions were not associated with the ordinary run of social and economic problems. Official crime rates were not higher in societies with widespread poverty, illiteracy, rapid population increase and little formal schooling. Nor were they in societies with heterogeneous populations, unconstitutional regimes, low rates of voting and relatively limited democratic institutions. The only genuine and unambiguous social problem with which high official crime rates were associated was unemployment, a problem historically linked to conflict theory, and entirely consistent with even modern versions of this theory. The only other exception to this pattern held for the rate of murder, which is rather tenuously related to sanctions. Social and economic problems were predictors of the murder rate, although only weakly, but this is hardly what is meant by the 'crime rate' or the 'crime problem'. High rates of sanctions were, rather, associated with prosperity (as indicated by GNP per capita), urbanism, extensive development of the school system, modern, central bureaucracies, widespread mass media, a high proportion of the population voting, and well-developed, representative institutions, in the western sense.

In the case of England and Wales, high official crime and sanction rates were related to economic prosperity, again as measured by GNP per capita, and the development of the welfare state. They were associated with a high rate of enrolment in formal education, and high expenditure on education, rather than to inadequacies in the school system. Again unemployment was a factor, although not as closely related to official crime as the other indicators. Interestingly, official crime rates were higher when the Labour Party was in office, but this seemed to be a result of greater expenditure on the welfare state under Labour, and the relationship disappeared when that was taken into account. Both for the post-war period, and for the whole of the period since 1900, official crime rates were positively associated with expenditure on the police and police force size. This was the finding also in the case of the borough data and, for police force size, for the Interpol set too. Recommendations for increases in police force size and expenditure to reduce crime, would seem to be badly based in view of these facts.

The analysis raised further doubts about 'rising crime'. The claims made of increases in the United Nations' juvenile court data were examined against the actual rates of increase computed from the raw data reported. For most of the countries, the rates were found to be increasing, but not nearly to the extent implied in the discussion. Rather, countries for which the' rates were decreasing or constant were ignored, and trivial increases, very easily due to even the most modest improvements in recording practices, were exaggerated.

For the British data changes in the rates were examined in a number of ways, relative simply to population (as in the above case), but also to police force size and expenditure. Increases were found, both relative to population and police force size, but, in the case of expenditure, there were decreases with some of the official crime indicators. Even in the case of increases moreover, the rises were much more modest than the 'more than doubling' claimed by other authors. Such high increases, it was suggested, depended on the choice of atypical years of comparison, a crime indicator particularly vulnerable to changes in reporting practices and an indicator of policing under-estimating effective police force size. As well, increases were compared across the whole of the 1900–68 period, and nowhere found as great as the claim just discussed.

The test case with Canadian data produced a more complicated pattern of results. The analysis was now expanded to consider a survey on attitudes to criminals and sanctions, and perceptions of crime, criminals, and the workings of the criminal justice system. It was on these questions that some deviant results appeared. The analysis of purely objective statistical data yielded unambiguous findings contrary to the predictions of the conventional wisdom. Apart from traffic, parking offences and other trivial matters official crime rates proved not to be rising in the 1950–66 period. There was no general trend to leniency in sentencing either during this same period, and no trend to reduced disparities in sentencing. Official crime rates were closely related to size of police force, increases in the size of the force accounting for increases in less serious offences, especially traffic and parking violations.

When people's assessments of the seriousness of offences were compared with the seriousness accorded them in the written law and in actual enforcement the results were again in line with the conflict approach. Apart from the seriousness accorded murder relative to property offences, the law was a poor reflection of people's priorities, and the gap was even greater for enforcement *practices*. Trivial property offences and liquor offences not involving harm to others were widely regarded as unimportant, yet are part of the criminal law, and much enforcement time, money and energy is devoted to them. Violent offences, especially involving children, were viewed as much more worthy of punishment than is actually the case. The same holds for motor vehicle deaths, especially when liquor is a factor, and for which punishments are usually mild.

Perceptions of the working of the criminal justice system revealed substantial misinformation, consistently supportive of repressive measures. There was widespread perception of the crime rate as rising and sentences becoming more lenient. Despite the fact that sentences in Canada are among the toughest in the western world, there was considerable belief in their being too lenient. There was much more acceptance of favourable views of psychiatric treatment of criminals than would be justified by an appraisal of the evaluation literature. And there was widespread ignorance of the extent to which Canada's prisons and gaols are custodial institutions for Indians. On all these points respondents were in good company with judges, police chiefs, Ministers of Justice and many social scientists. These are the views of the conventional wisdom, and they are as loosely connected to fact as they are convenient justifications for the use of excessively repressive measures of control.

Predictions from conflict theory as to responses across the various groups in the study, however, were not well borne out. The basic hypothesis was that access to power would affect attitudes and perceptions in crime, civil liberties and other social control issues—the better the access to power the more to gain by repressive measures, and views supportive of them. In the case of specific issues in crime and sanctions this was clearly disconfirmed, as were predictions on certain civil liberties questions (qualifications to freedom of expression) and rights for women. On a number of other, traditional civil liberties, and on views of related political and economic issues, the conflict predictions did appear.

Two approaches from consensus theory were explored, one a mainstream approach emphasizing harmony of interests and perceptions, with differences occurring effectively through differences in education and exposure to information. A working-class authoritarianism approach, developed from Lipset, but adding the notion of positive incentives to illiberal views was also considered. In both, the opposite order was predicted from conflict theory, with education, security of employment and occupational prestige being the crucial factors. The groups were chosen so that those with greater access to power (lawyers and businessmen) were also better educated and held higher status occupations than those with less access to power (teachers, then two groups of workers). Some differences as predicted by consensus theory did appear, but these were too weak to disturb the general negative conclusions on the approach.

CONSENSUS THEORY AS A FRAMEWORK OF ANALYSIS

The findings contrary to consensus theory were sufficiently persistent as to cast doubts on the propriety of using the approach as a *model*, one of the main criticisms of Part I. Throughout the literature there were discussions of competing ideas, and competing research projects, but all *within* the consensus framework. Theorists would debate, for example, *which* particular social problem was the most noxious, without questioning the social problem approach itself. Problems of various sorts may well determine *who* is sanctioned for crimes, and even who commits acts believed to be criminal, but these are quite different matters. The consensus, social problem approach fails as an explanation of levels of official crime and sanctions. There may be justifications for continuing to use it, but it is difficult to think of any that are satisfactory intellectually, let alone morally. The common recommendation for increases in measures of formal control, in view of rising social problems, would seem to be especially invalid. This has been demonstrated in the case of expenditure on policing, but it may not be realized that governments' social welfare budgets often include prisons and other formal control measures. Increases in 'social services', then, may mean more prisons and officials. In the United Nations document used in the study it was pointed out that increases in crime had occurred *in spite of* improvements in education, social welfare, and a generally improved standard of living. The conclusion was that, since these measures did not work, more direct and more stringent means of control were called for. Alternatively, one could conclude that crime was not related to social problems in the first place, but that possibility was not entertained.

A wide range of levels of formal control was revealed. Japan had over 7,000 reported offenders per 100,000 adult population, compared with close to a thousand for England and Wales, 174 for Spain and 117 for India. Even among the Nordic countries, with relatively similar social structures, there was great variation—from over 4,000 in Finland, 1,000 in Sweden to only 340 in Denmark. A high rate of offenders would hardly seem to be a necessity, for many countries manage to make do with less. The message was the same from the British data. The rate of indictable convictions was over three times as great in 1968 as at the turn of the century. Yet, much as one may wish to believe in 'the good old days', can it really be argued that the British population is three times more criminal now than then? With little social security, high unemployment, illegal strikes and violent strike-breaking and all the same problems in Ireland, yet the country survived with its much lower level of formal control. It would seem that authorities have a great deal of leeway with respect to the amount of crime they wish to recognize. The crime rate is not entirely something forced on a society by its deviant members but, to a great extent, represents the level of social control desired, and the means available to attain it.

The last task, and the subject of Chapter 8, was to examine the attack on social science theory and research. This was argued to mean effectively the demolition of a straw man. The 'hard positivism' denounced with so much righteous indignation turned out to bear little resemblance to the beliefs and practices of the major nineteenth-century positivists, specifically Comte, Quetelet, Mill and Durkheim. Further, it was shown in what way certain of the accusations against the positivists applied also to Marxists (notably Marx, Engels and Lenin), and Weber to boot. These included the search for general laws, belief in an external, real world, and objectification of human beings for purposes of study. The claim that ordinary social science methodology is still relevant and useful for a number of serious tasks rests mainly on the work reported in Chapters 5–7. Or, my defence of social science methodology is essentially a *practical* one.

By way of a final comment, perhaps I should make clear that I am not advocating any permanent acceptance of social science methodology in its present form. My contention has been rather that the method is capable of far more than it is given credit for, that it has been found guilty unjustly, by association. It is not that I am content with it, but find it a reasonable place to start.

Technical Notes to Chapters

CHAPTERS 2–4

The objective was to gain as complete an understanding as was possible of the range of theories proposed over the ages. Since I was interested in the interplay between conflict and consensus approaches, and between theoretical and empirical research, it was important to establish precise time sequences of the emergence of an idea, its evolution and re-statement or abandonment. I was concerned, then, to find the 'original authors' of theoretical propositions, authors of major revisions, and contributors of major empirical works and criticism. This means only, of course, giving credit to the earliest source to my knowledge, and there were certain limits to that. One major constraint was that works had to be *published* to come to my attention, or at least be classified as published somewhere in the indexes, catalogues and bibliographies I consulted. Further, the material had to be available through Paris, London or Toronto libraries. I did not conduct any systematic search for unpublished manuscripts, although a few did turn up in the course of the work, and these were used.

The second major contraint was language. I was confined to material published in English or French, or otherwise abstracted or summarized in English or French. One never knows, of course, what has been missed in other works; however, there is reason to believe that the omissions are not too serious. Up until this century large numbers of works were translated in full and many others became available through journal and congress abstracts and bibliographic papers. The major theorists and researchers for most of the period of the study read several European languages, and citation of works in four languages was common. Hence I am fairly confident that important contributors were not missed in the search. Once the names of apparently important sources became known the task then became one of finding some of their work in English or French. For most writers this was possible—if not a full-scale book, at least a paper or two at a congress.

The actual literature search was begun with lists of authors already known or thought to be important contributors. For the very important authors, like Durkheim and Spencer, I examined all their available published works. I did not *read* everything, but scanned the material, checked tables of contents and indexes, and consulted secondary sources on them. I then systematically searched subject indexes of the British Library, the Bibliothèque Nationale, and the British Library of Political and Economic Science in search of works which had not appeared through reading the better known authors. Other bibliographies used were Berriat-Saint-Prix, Culver, Cumming, Fink, Jousse, and Le Blanc.

Authors for whom any original propositions appeared in this search were then made the subject of a further search, at least of all their earlier works, if not their later. (I normally examined these later works, but went to less trouble to obtain them if they were not readily available.) When it seemed that the 'original statement' of an important idea had been located I then examined its sources—the author's citations, footnotes or bibliography. A good proportion of the cited works were then read, or abstracts, summaries or references to them were checked. It was not possible or practicable to read or consult all of these, for some references were in languages I did not read, and many were unpublished or otherwise unavailable in the libraries in which I worked. When one of the cited works appeared to merit credit for an original proposition, it, too, was subjected to the same search, until all references were eventually exhausted.

The early years of the major journals in the field were systematically searched in a similar way: *L'Année Sociologique, Archives d'Anthropologie Criminelle*, the *Journal of Criminal Law and Criminology*, the *Asylum Journal of Mental Science*, and the *American Journal of Sociology*. These journals were the major sources for material published in languages other than English or French and were useful for book reviews, abstracts and summaries of work as well as articles. All of them extensively reviewed foreign publications, especially German, Italian and Russian works. *L'Année Sociologique* was by far the most useful in this respect, but even the *American Journal of Sociology* in the years before World War I gave considerable coverage to European scholarship. The *AJS* leaned rather more to the Italian school than the French, but basically served as a general review. It was also a major source for early American work. The *Archives*, although published in French, was something of a house organ for the Italian school. It was both a good secondary source for Italian publications, and for the many Italian school publications in Russian. *L'Année Sociologique* was also important in its early years as the vehicle of publication of Durkheim's work in deviance. After 1906, it was confined exclusively to a reviewing function.

Errors in the search procedure, that is, failure to search where one would have found an earlier or better exponent of a proposition, or failure to find alternative propositions, could have occurred in several ways. Writers from before the mid-nineteenth century were not very thorough in citing their sources. Some cited no sources, or only a handful of the great philosophers. Sometimes the citations were inadequate for purposes of finding the work later. Further, until very recently, inadequate attention was paid to *dates* of publication. Sometimes, for example, a second edition of a work would be cited without any notation to that effect. A reader seeking early reference to an *idea* would then incorrectly skip over such a reference.

At no time did I rely entirely on secondary sources for acceptance of a theoretical proposition, but I did use secondary sources extensively for dismissal of works from the search. Thus there may have been relevant ideas in works reviewed by scholars who did not share my theoretical interests, or who did, but still managed to overlook the point in question.

CHAPTER 5

The Interpol data were taken from *International Crime Statistics*. Where data for a particular year between 1961 and 1966 were missing, data from 1960 were used instead if they were available. In eleven cases the averages were based on only five years, and in four cases on only four. Population data were obtained from the United Nations *Demographic Yearbook*. Where population by age was not available for any year it was estimated with the proportion of the under twenty age group for the nearest year available, of the total population for the year in question. In cases for which total population was unavailable it was estimated as being midway between the total of the year before and after.

Interpol began publishing official crime statistics in 1950, with only a small number of countries reporting, and numerous gaps in particular offence categories. Since then, the number of countries reporting has increased markedly, and comprehensiveness of reporting improved as well. By confining the study to the years of the 1960s, the worst irregularities in the series are avoided. Averaging of the data also minimizes the effects of errors in reporting. Interpol warns that definitions of crime vary from country to country, as do recording procedures, hence comparisons across countries are not warranted. Insofar as the data are used as measures of criminal behaviour or immorality, I agree, but as indicators of official crime rates and sanctions, comparisons are valid.

The sources for the United Nations data were as follows:

United Nations Secretariat, *New Forms of Delinquency—Origin, Prevention and Treatment*, 1960, A/Conf. 17/7, for Austria, Belgium, Finland, Formosa, France, Democratic Republic of Germany, Federal Republic of Germany, Greece, Italy, Japan, South Africa, Sweden, United Kingdom, United States and Yugoslavia.

United Nations General Assembly, *Progress achieved by the non-self-governing territories in pursuance of Chapter XI of the Charter*, A 14181, for Barbados, Bermuda, British Honduras, Fiji, Guyana, Hong Kong, Madagascar, Mauritius, Singapore, Uganda and Zanzibar.

United Nations Department of Economic and Social Affairs, *Comparative Survey of Juvenile Delinquency—The Middle East*, rev. edn., New York, 1965, for Iraq, Jordan, Turkey and the United Arab Republic.

The sources for data on the explanatory variables were

GNP per capita, from Russett and Alker, pp. 155–7; United Nations *Statistical Yearbook*.
Intersectoral inequality. Lorenz coefficient of intersectoral inequality, from Phillips Cutright, 'Inequality: a cross-national analysis', *American Sociological Review*. vol. 32, 1967, p. 577.
Land inequality, Gini index, from Russet and Alker, pp. 239–40.
Unemployment, percentage working age group unemployed, from Russett and Alker, pp. 189–90.
Labour force participation, proportion of population fifteen and above in the paid labour force, from *Demographic Yearbook*, 1964. (For the juvenile court tests, proportion of males in paid labour force over population 15 and above.)
Radios, per population, from Russett and Alker, pp. 120–2.
Bureaucracy, countries dichotomized between those having a 'generally effective and responsible civil service or equivalent

performing in a functionally specific, non-ascriptive social context', and others, from Banks and Textor, pp. 112, 113.

Higher Education, enrolment in institutions of higher learning, proportional to population aged five to nineteen, from Russett and Alker, pp. 214–16.

Police force, size per population, unpublished data supplied by the International Criminal Police Organization, St. Cloud, France.

Data collection index, scored from the number of items (listed below) on which the country published data: annual estimates of total population 1961–66 (*Demographic Yearbook*, 1967); economically active, by marital status (*Demographic Yearbook*, 1964); Percent population urban by age (*Demographic Yearbook*, 1967); percent population unemployed (*Statistical Yearbook*, 1968); long-term migrants (*Demographic Yearbook*, 1966); students enrolled in schools and public expenditure on schools (*Statistical Yearbook*, 1968); annual estimates of national income and gross domestic production 1961–6 (*Statistical Yearbook*, 1968).

Illiteracy, proportion of population fifteen and above illiterate, from *Demographic Yearbook*, 1963, 1964; Russett and Alker, pp. 222–224; U.N. *Compendium of Social Statistics*, 1963.

School enrolment, school enrolment proportional to population aged five to nineteen, from Russett and Alker, pp. 218–20.

Family size, child–woman ratio, from the *Demographic Yearbook*, 1965.

Urbanism, percentage urban population, from the *Demographic Yearbook*, for 1960 or latest year available in series. (For juvenile court tests data from Russett and Alker.)

Population increase, average annual population increase, from the *Demographic Yearbook*—rates averaged for whatever years were available in the series.

Religious heterogeneity, countries dichotomized between those with 80 per cent or more of its population of the same religion, and others, from Banks and Textor, p. 71 and the *Encyclopaedia Britannica*.

Linguistic heterogeneity, countries dichotomized between those with 85 per cent or more of their population speaking the same language and with no significant minority, and others, from Banks and Textor, pp. 72–5 and the *Encyclopaedia Britannica*.

Racial heterogeneity, countries dichotomized between those with 90 per cent or more of the population of the same race, and others, from Banks and Textor, p. 72.

Constitutional status, countries dichotomized between those conducted with reference to recognized constitutional norms, and others, Banks and Textor, p. 83.

Government stability, countries dichotomized between those with stable governments since World War I or with a constitutional change in the inter-war period and others, from Banks and Textor, p. 84.

Executive stability, the ratio of the number of years the country was independent over the number of chief executives, between 1945 and 1961, from Russett and Alker, pp. 103–4.

Voting proportion, average proportion of voting age population voting, from Russett and Alker, pp. 84–6.

Political representation and franchise index, see Phillips Cutright and James G. Wiles, 'Modernization and political representation: 1927–66', *Studies in Comparative International Development*, vol. 5, 1969, pp. 24–41. The actual scores for countries included in the above-mentioned article were supplied by Phillips Cutright, and the others were computed using the directions in the article, p. 34.

Newspaper circulation, proportional to population, from Russett and Alker, pp. 108–10.

CHAPTER 6

Data Sources, 1948–68

Total population, wherever cited, from United Kingdom, *Annual Abstract of Statistics*, 1969; United Nations, *Demographic Yearbook*, 1967, pp. 130, 142–3.

Population aged five to nineteen from *Annual Abstract of Statistics*, 1969, p. 10; 1966, p. 85; 1963, p. 83; 1952, pp. 9, 10; 1938–50, pp. 9, 10; 1938–49, pp. 9, 10; 1938–48, pp. 8, 9.

Population aged ten to forty from *Annual Abstract of Statistics*, 1969, pp. 19, 383; 1970, p. 10; *Demographic Yearbook*, 1967, pp. 196–7; 1965, p. 250–1; 1964, pp. 150–1; 1963, pp. 220–1; 1961, pp. 156–7; 1960, pp. 244–7; 1959, p. 164; 1958, p. 135; 1957, p. 147; 1956, p. 176; 1955, pp. 259, 273; 1954, p. 132; 1953, p. 126; 1951, p. 141; 1949–50, p. 159.

GNP (in 1963 prices)/total population. GNP from United Kingdom, *National Income and Expenditure*, 1969, pp. 16, 17.

Government Social Security expenditure (in 1963 prices)/total population. *National Income and Expenditure*, 1969, p. 64; 1965, p. 62. (Includes expenditure on education, national health, child care, school meals and Social Security benefits. Comparable data for 1948 and 1949 were not available).

School enrolment/population aged five to nineteen. Enrolment data from *Annual Abstract of Statistics*, 1969, pp. 89, 85.

School expenditure in 1963 prices (total expenditure on education/ school enrolment). *Annual Abstract of Statistics*, 1970, pp. 16, 17.

Police Force (female and male officers and full-time auxiliaries)/ total population. Police data from *Annual Abstract of Statistics*, 1969, p. 68; 1968, p. 64; 1966, p. 64; 1956, p. 64.

Expenditure on police/total population, from the *Statesman's Yearbook*, each year's data published the year following. No data published for 1949. The data were deflated by the retail price index, *London and Cambridge Key Statistics*, 1970.

Unemployment rate (percentage of the total paid labour force unemployed). United Nations *Statistical Yearbook*, 1968, p. 108; 1961, p. 58; 1955, p. 81.

Government consumption expenditure (in 1963 prices)/total population. *National Income and Expenditure*, 1969, pp. 17, 16.

Crime Statistics from *Criminal Statistics (England and Wales)* unless otherwise noted.

Indictable convictions, 1968, p. xxix; 1966, p. xxvii; 1963, p. xxiv; 1962, p. 72; 1956, p. xxix; 1953, p. xxiv; 1950, p, xxii.

Summary convictions, 1968, p. lvi; 1961, p. xiv; 1956, p. xlv.

Indictable police reports, 1968, p. 7; 1964, p. 7; 1962, pp. 4, viii; 1952, pp. 4, viii.

Larceny, 1968, p. lvi; 1962, p. xlv; 1953, p. xxxvi.

Violence against persons, 1968, p. lv; 1962, p. xliv; 1953, p. xxxv.

Breaking and entering, 1968, p. lvi; 1962, p. xlv; 1953, p. xxxvi.

Fraud, receiving and false pretences, 1968, p. lv; 1962, p. xliv; 1953, p. xxxv.

Sex offences, 1968, p. lvi; 1962, p. xlv; 1953, p. xxxvi.

Convicted murderers and murder suspects, 1968, p. xxxix; 1966, p. xxxvii; 1956, p. xxxvi.

Murder victims, 1968, p. xxxix; 1966, p. xxxvii; 1956, p. xxxvi.

Juvenile (under 17) convictions, 1968, pp. 194–5; *Statesman's Yearbook*, 1967, pp. 194, 196; *Criminal Statistics (England and Wales)*, 1966, p. xlviii; 1957, p. xlv; 1949, p. viii; 1948, p. 27.

Juvenile (under 17) summary convictions, 1968, p. 199; *Statesman's*

Yearbook, 1966, p. 199; 1965, p. 199; 1964, p. 199; 1963, pp. 62, 66; 1962, pp. 62, 66; 1961, pp. 62, 66; 1960, pp. 62, 66; 1959, pp. 62, 66; 1958, pp. 62, 66; 1957, pp. 62, 66; 1956, pp. 64, 68; 1955, pp. 64, 68; 1954, pp. 64, 68; 1953, pp. 64, 68; 1952, pp. 64, 68; 1951, pp. 64, 68; 1950, pp. 64, 68; 1949, pp. 64, 68; 1948, pp. 52, 56.
Prison population (average daily population in prisons and borstals), *Annual Abstract of Statistics*, 1969, p. 70; 1968, p. 70; 1966, p. 70; 1956, p. 69.

Data Sources, 1900–68.

Total population. *Annual Abstract of Statistics*, 1915, p. 381; 1936, p. 4; 1922, p. 319; 1948, p. 7; 1959, pp. 142–3; 1967, p. 143; 1969, p. 6.
Police expenditure by local authorities (excl. capital expenditure)/ total population. *Annual Abstract of Statistics*, 1915, p. 56; 1926, p. 50; 1940, p. 236; 1948, p. 224; 1960, p. 263; 1949, p. 233; 1952, p. 264; 1969, p. 315.
Authorized police strength/total population. *Annual Abstract of Statistics*, 1915, p. 384; 1926, p. 248; 1936, p. 105; 1948, p. 46; 1958, p. 66; 1969, p. 68.
Summary convictions/total population. 1900, p. 65; 1901, p. 63; 1902, p. 93; 1904, p. 11; 1905, p. 11; 1907, p. 11; 1908, p. 63; 1909, p. 61; *Annual Abstract of Statistics*, 1926, p. 289; 1930, p. 77; 1936, p. 109; 1948, p. 47; 1951, p. 59; *Criminal Statistics (England and Wales)*, 1950, p. xxii; 1953, p. xxiv; 1956, p. xxix; 1957, p. 72; 1958, p. 72; 1959, p. 72; 1960, p. 72; 1961, p. 72; 1962, p, 72; 1963, p. xxiv; 1966, p. xxvii; 1968, p. xxix.
Indictable convictions/total population. 1901, pp. 11, 64; 1902, pp. 69, 92; 1904, p. 11; 1905, p. 11; 1906, p. 11; 1909, p. 11; *Annual Abstract of Statistics*, 1915, pp. 411–12; 1922, pp. 345–6; 1926, p. 288; 1936, p. 109; 1938, p. 110; 1939, p. 111; 1948, p. 47; 1951, p. 59; *Criminal Statistics (England and Wales)*, 1956, p. xiv; 1961, p. xiv; 1968, p. lvi.

CHAPTER 7

SAMPLE SELECTION
The choice of lawyers and businessmen as representatives of the 'holders of power' of conflict theory should require little explanation. Lawyers are themselves important in big business (as many as 14 per

cent of Porter's economic elite of Canada). They form the largest occupational group in Parliament and the provincial legislatures. Many senior civil servants are lawyers by training. In the criminal justice field lawyers hold virtually all the top positions dealing with legislation, and many of those in probation, parole and prison administration, apart from being the judges and prosecutors. Lawyers in Canada are quite literally the writers of the law, the interpreters, and they have a great deal to do with its application as well. They have high incomes on average and enjoy high prestige in the community.

The holders of great wealth in the country are largely businessmen. They constitute the second largest group in Parliament and the provincial legislatures. They dominate the regulatory boards and commissions, through government appointments, and otherwise exercise considerable influence informally. They are influential, too, in the direction of cultural institutions, notably universities, art museums and orchestras, and such welfare institutions as hospitals and child protection agencies. They tend to be ranked lower than lawyers, especially judges, in social esteem, but still enjoy considerable prestige.

How junior members of these groups, ordinary businessmen and lawyers at the beginning of their careers, can be seen as representing the upper echelons requires some explanation. None of the respondents were themselves the 'holders of power' envisaged in conflict theory. Rather they must be thought of as members of broader segments, to which the powerful belong. The actual holders of power are socialized within this larger group, interact with members of it in their work, social and family life, education and so forth. The larger segment serves as an ongoing reference group to the current holders of power. Members of the broader group, in turn, reflect back the views of the more powerful members, acting as opinion leaders to the rest of the community.

The actual source of businessmen for the study was a businessmen's association, for men only, known for its pro-business views. All the 83 members were asked for an interview, and 60, or 72 per cent, were interviewed. The interviews were held at the respondent's home or place of business, as he preferred. One quarter of those interviewed had university degrees, and a further 42 per cent had some university training. Politically, the men supported parties of the centre-right: 55 per cent Liberal, 42·5 per cent Conservative, and only 2·5 per cent, or one person, supported the socialist, New Democratic Party.

The lawyers' sample was drawn from the Ontario Bar Admission course, which all law graduates in the province must take, after articling, before being called to the Bar. All the 60 women enrolled were asked for an interview, and 35, or 70 per cent, were interviewed. For the men, a one-in-seven sample was drawn, of which 56, or 62 per cent, were interviewed. The interviews were conducted at Osgoode Hall.

The teachers' group was the largest in the study, but the sampling the least adequate. Names were drawn randomly from among the 1,300 teachers attending summer courses at McMaster University, 83 men and 132 women, of whom 65 men and 106 women were interviewed, or 78 and 80 per cent respectively of the samples. The interviews were held in spare offices on campus.

Two groups of workers were chosen, textile workers employed at a carpet factory in Brantford, Ontario, and a mixed group of manual workers living in the industrial, east end of Hamilton, Ontario. The textile workers were all members of a Canadian union, the Canadian Textile and Chemical Union, while half of the Hamilton East group were not union members at all and a quarter each were in Canadian and American unions. The textile workers' sample was drawn from the union's list of employees currently working and living in the city. An equal number of women's and men's names were drawn, with random selection within each sex. Altogether 50 women and 54 men were interviewed, representing response rates of 55 and 57 per cent respectively. The interviews were held in respondents' homes.

Textile workers are relatively badly paid workers and job security is not good. The workers at this particular plant are among the better off in the industry, but do less well than other industrial workers in the area. A department employing highly specialized workers had been closed down in the year preceding the fieldwork and many workers had had to take less skilled jobs at lower rates of pay. The company otherwise has the reputation of being a good employer, and the product is of high quality.

The Hamilton East sample was drawn from a stable, working-class residential district, close to the major steel and manufacturing plants. The area had the advantage of not having suffered urban renewal, and being far enough away from the university to have escaped most surveys. The sample area was comprised of the three census tracts with the highest proportions of persons employed in 'manufacturing and production' in the 1961 Census. Voters' lists corresponding to these tracts were obtained, persons with non-manual or ambiguous occupations listed eliminated, and names randomly drawn. (Since enumerators often neglect to ask women voters their occupations many more women had to be eliminated than men, and the sampling adjusted accordingly.) The great advantage of using the voters' list was that it was up-to-date, having been drawn up for the 1972 federal election, only a month before the fieldwork. The interviewing had to be brought to a close before the full list had been interviewed, with only 34 women and 27 men having been interviewed. The interviews all took place at respondents' homes. The average level of education was higher in the Hamilton East group than among the textile workers, but in both cases con-siderably lower than in the other groups. A quarter of the Hamilton East group had no more than elementary schooling, while as many as 48 per cent of the textile workers had not gone past this level. The workers from both groups were, on average, much older than the members of the middle-class groups. More of the workers, as well, were church members.

The civil liberties group consisted of all the members of the Hamilton Civil Liberties Association willing to be interviewed, 28 women and 39 men (80 per cent in both cases). The members were largely well-educated professional people; 66 per cent had at least one university degree and 61 per cent held professional positions. Of those who gave a federal party identification, 63 per cent were NDP supporters, 31 per cent were Liberal, and only 6 per cent Conservative.

THE QUESTIONNAIRE

The questionnaire was developed at intermittent stages over a period of several years. Questions on attitudes to crime and sanctions had been included in several smaller studies, beginning in 1969, and differ-ent approaches tried out on volunteer subjects (mainly university faculty and students). Exploratory interviewing was done in the summer of 1970 on a broad range of the civil liberties and crime questions. The interview schedule eventually used went through its final pre-testing and revision in the four months preceding the field-work, with householders of Toronto and Hamilton kind enough to be interviewed the respondents. The actual fieldwork was done in the six months July–December, 1972.

The approach settled on was a simple question-and-answer interview, beginning with very open-ended questions, followed by progressively more specific probes. Some questions were covered by a printed agree-disagree type form at the end of the interview, simply to save time. Otherwise the gadgetry approaches tried out at various stages (rating scales and forced-choice questions) were all abandoned. The interviews were conducted by the writer, research assistant, and four professional interviewers, all women. The interviews took roughly 40 to 50 minutes to complete, the interviewer recording the responses on the spot. (There were no tape recordings.) The interviewers did their own coding, the writer the checking. The coded material was punched and computer analysed at the university computer centre.

ANALYSIS

Demographic differences among the groups meant that precautions had to be taken against spurious findings. Studies have shown greater punitiveness and lesser attachment to civil liberties on the part of older persons, the less well-educated, women, and church-goers, all of whom were over-represented in the workers' groups. Findings of greater punitiveness and anti-libertarian attitudes among workers in this study would be favourable to consensus theory, but insofar as due to demographic considerations would require quite different interpretation. The results were accordingly analysed with controls for age, sex and religion. It was not possible to control for education in the same way, as noted in the text, but, wherever possible, comparisons were made between 'more' and 'less' well educated groups. Thus some distinction between the effects of education and occupation could be made. The material reported in the text represents only a small fraction of the data collected and analysed. Space limitations affected most drastically the 'soft' data, the uncoded responses to the open-ended questions, much of which was quite interesting.

Bibliography

CHAPTER 1

Bailey, W. C., 'Correctional outcome: an evaluation of 100 Reports',
1966 *Journal of Criminal Law, Criminology and Police Science*,
vol. 57, pp. 153–60.

Barlow, D. (ed.), *A review of selected criminological research on the*
1971 *effectiveness of punishments and treatments*, University of
Toronto, Centre of Criminology.

Black, Donald J. and Albert J. Reiss, 'Police control of juveniles',
1970 *American Sociological Review*, vol. 35, pp. 63–77.

Canadian Committee on Corrections, *Toward Unity: Criminal*
1969 *Justice and Corrections*, Ottawa: Queen's Printer.

Chiricos, Theodore G. *et al.*, 'Inequality in the Imposition of a
1972 Criminal Label', *Social Problems*, vol. 19, pp. 553–72.

Giffen, P. J., 'Rates of Crime and Delinquency', in W. T. McGrath
1965 (ed.), *Crime and its Treatment in Canada*, Toronto: Macmillan,
pp. 59–90.

Goldman, Nathan, *The differential selection of juvenile offenders for*
1964 *court appearance*, National Council on Crime and Delinquency.

Hogarth, John, *Sentencing as a Human Process*, University of
1972 Toronto Press.

Le Blanc, Marc, *Délinquance Juvénile*, Ph.D. thesis, Université de
1969 Montréal.

McCord, William and Joan, *Origins of Crime*, New York: Columbia
1959 University Press.

McDonald, Lynn, 'Crime and Punishment in Canada: A Statistical
1969 Test of the "Conventional Wisdom" ', *Canadian Review of
Sociology and Anthropology*, vol. 6, pp. 212–36.

1972 (ed.), *A study of certain correctional institutions with particular
reference to their effect on drug offenders*, Ottawa: Commission
of Inquiry into the Non-Medical Use of Drugs (unpublished
report).

Murphy, B. C., *A quantitative test of the effectiveness of an experimen-*
1970 *tal treatment programme for delinquent opiate users*. Ottawa:
Canadian Penitentiary Service (unpublished report).

Piliavin, I. and Scott Briar, 'Police encounters with juveniles',
1970 *American Sociological Review*, vol. 35, pp. 63–77.

Powers, Edwin C. and Helen Witmer, *An Experiment in the Prevention*
1951 *of Delinquency*, New York: Columbia University Press.

Prévost Commission, 'Trends in Quebec Criminality'; vol. 3, tome 1.

Stratton, John R. and Robert M. Terry (eds.), *Prevention of Delin-*
1968 *quency*, New York: Macmillan.

Terry, Robert N., 'Discrimination in the handling of juvenile offenders
1970 by social control agencies', in P. C. Garabedian and Don C.
Gibbons (eds.), *Becoming a Delinquent*, Chicago: Aldine,
pp. 78–92.

Waller, Irving, *Men Released from Prison*, University of Toronto
1974 Press.

Wilkins, L. T., *Evaluation of Penal Measures*, New York: Random
1969 House.

Wolfgang, Marvin E., R. M. Figlio and T. Sellin, *Delinquency in a*
1972 *Birth Cohort*, University of Chicago Press.

CHAPTER 2

PRE-EIGHTEENTH CENTURY

Aristotle, *The Basic Works of Aristotle*, New York: Random House,
1964   (ed. Richard McKeon).
Ethica Nicomachea (trans. W. D. Ross), pp. 928–1112.
Politics (trans. Benjamin Jowett), pp. 1114–1316.

Augustine, St., *The City of God Against the Pagans*, London:
413–426.   Heinemann, 1957 (trans. G. E. McCracken).

Berriat-Saint-Prix, Ch., *Etudes sur les Principaux Criminalistes qui ont*
1855 *écrit en Français ou en Latin depuis le XVIème siècle*, Paris:
Guyot et Scribe.

Hobbes, Thomas, *The Elements of Law; Natural and Politic*, London:
1650 Simpkin, Marshall, 1889.
1651 *Leviathan*, Oxford: Basil Blackwell, 1946.

Machiavelli, Niccolo, *The Prince*, New York: Collier & Son, 1910
1532 (trans. N. H. Thomson).

More, Thomas, *Utopia*, New York: P. J. Collier, 1910 (trans. R.
1516 Robinson).

Plato, *The Republic*, Chicago: Kern, 1918 (trans. A. E. Taylor).
Laws, London: Oxford University Press, 1931 (tran. B.
Howett).

Porta, J. B. della, *Le Physionomiste*, Paris: Tardier, 1808.
1601

Salisbury, John of, *The Statesman's Book*, New York: Russell &
1159   Russell, 1963 (trans. and ed. John Dickinson).

Winstanley, Gerrard, *Selections from his Works*, London: Cresset,
1649   1944, (ed. Leonard Hamilton).

EIGHTEENTH CENTURY

Beccaria, Marquis de, *An Essay on Crimes and Punishment*, London:
1764/6   Symonds, 1804 (abridged). *Traité des Délits et des Peines*,
        Lausanne, 1766 (trans. A. Morellet, from 3rd. Italian edn.).

Bentham, Jeremy, *A Fragment on Government and an Introduction to the*
1780   *Principles of Morals and Legislation*, Oxford: Blackwell, 1948.

1776   *The Limits of Jurisprudence Defined*, Part Two of 'An Intro-
        duction to the Principles of Morals and Legislation', New
        York: Columbia University Press, 1945.

        The Rationale of Punishment, London: Howard, 1830 (ed.
        Dumont from unpub. early papers).

Brissot de Warville, A. M., *Théorie des Lois Criminelles*, 2 vols.,
1781   Paris: Aillaud, rev. edn., 1836.

Colquhoun, P., *A Treatise on the Police of the Metropolis*, London:
1796   Fry, 5th edn., 1797.

Ferguson, Adam, *Institutes of Moral Philosophy*, Basel: James
1772   Decker, 1800.

Fielding, Henry, *An Enquiry into the causes of the late Increase of*
1751   *Robbers, Works*, London, 1806, vol. 10, pp. 333–467.

Godwin, William, *Enquiry Concerning Political Justice and its*
1793   *influence on Morals and Happiness*, 2 vols., Toronto: Uni-
        versity of Toronto Press, 1946.

Holbach, Baron Paul H. D. von, *Système Social ou Principes Naturels*
1773   *de la Morale et de la Politique avec un examen de l'influence du*
        gouvernement sur les moeurs, London.

Hume, David, *An Inquiry into the Principles of Morals*, New York:
1751   Liberal Arts Press, 1957.

Jousse, Daniel, *Traité de la Justice Criminelle de France*, 2 vols.,
1771   Paris: Debure.

Linguet, S. N. H., *Théories des Lois Civiles*, London.
1767

Mably, Gabriel-Bonnot de, *Théories Sociales et Politiques*, Paris:
1784   Gustave Sandré, 1849.

1789 'Principes de Morale', *Oeuvres Complètes*, vol. 10, London.

Montesquieu, Baron, *The Spirit of Laws*, New York: Hafner
1748 (trans. T. Nugent), 1949.

Morelly, fils, *Code de la Nature*.
1755

Smith, Adam, *Essays on Moral Sentiments*, London: Alexander
1744 Murray, 1872.

1776 *An Inquiry into the nature and causes of the Wealth of Nations*,
London: Black & Tait, 1838.

anon. *An Enquiry into the effects of Public Punishments upon Criminals*
1787 *and upon Society*, Philadelphia: James.

CHAPTER 3

Alimena, B., 'Relation entre la predisposition héréditaire et le
1896 milieu domestique pour la provocation du penchant criminel',
Fourth International Congress of Criminal Anthropology,
Geneva, pp. 48–9.

Angeville, Comte A. d', *Essai sur la statistique de la population*
1836 *française*, Paris: de Delloye.

Aubry, Paul, 'Influence de la Presse sur la criminalité', *Fourth*
1896 *International Congress of Criminal Anthropology*, Geneva,
pp. 28–34.

Baldwin, James Mark, *Social and Ethical Interpretations in Mental*
1897 *Development*, New York: Macmillan.

Baudin, L., *Folie et Criminalité. Les criminels sont-ils des fous?*
1888 Besançon: de Dodivers.

Benelli, G. 'L'anthropologie dans les prisons', *First International*
1885 *Congress of Criminal Anthropology*, Rome, pp. 495–500.

Bonneville, A., *De la Récidive*, Paris: Cotillon.
1844

Booth, Charles (ed.), *Life and Labour of the People of London*,
1896 London: Macmillan, vol. 8.

Bournet, Albert, *De la Criminalité en France et en Italie*, Paris:
1884 Baillière.

Buckham, Thomas R., *Insanity considered in its Medico-Legal*
1883 *Relations*, Philadelphia: Lippincott.

Candolle, Alph. de, 'Considérations sur la statistique des délits',
1830 *Bibliothèque Universelle de Genève*, pp. 159–86.

Cargill, Wm., 'Educational, Criminal, and Social Statistics of
1838 Newcastle-upon-Tyne', *Journal of the Statistical Society*,
vol. 1, pp. 355–61.

Carpenter, Mary, *Juvenile Delinquents, their condition and treatment*,
1853 London: Cash.

Cavaglieri et Florian, 'Criminalité et vagabondage', *Fourth Interna-*
1896 *tional Congress of Criminal Anthropology*, Geneva.

Clay, John, 'Annual Report to the Visiting Justices: Criminal
1839 Statistics of Preston', *Journal of the Statistical Society*, vol. 2,
pp. 84–103.

Colajanni, Napoleone, 'La Question Contemporaine de la Crimina-
1888 lité', *Revue Socialiste*, vol. 7, Paris; pp. 59–68.

1901 'Le Socialisme et sa propagande en rapport avec la criminalité',
Fifth International Congress of Criminal Anthropology,
Amsterdam, pp. 231–3.

Corre, A., *Les Criminels*, Paris: Octave Doin.
1889

1894 *L'Ethnographie Criminelle*, Paris: Reinwald.

Dallemagne, J., *Les Théories de la Criminalité*, Paris: Masson.
1896

Darwin, Charles, *The Origin of Species*, London: John Murray, 6th
1859 edn., 1902.

David, Louis, *L'Identification Anthropométrique des Recidivistes*,
1895 Bordeaux: Gounouilhs.

Denis, Hector, 'L'Influence de la crise économique sur la criminalité
1885–6 et le penchant au crime du Quetelet', *Bulletin de la Société
d'Anthropologie de Bruxelles*, vol. 4, pp. 220–8.

Despine, Prosper, *De la Contagion Morale*, Marseille: E. Camoin.
1870

Dicey, A. V., *Lectures on the Relation between Law and Public
1898 Opinion in England during the Nineteenth Century*. London:
Macmillan, 1930.

Down, J. Langdon, *Mental Affections of Childhood and Youth*,
1887 London: Churchill.

Drahms, August, *The Criminal: his personnel and environment*, New
1900 York: Macmillan.

Drill, D., 'Des principes fondamentaux de l'école d'anthropologie
1892 criminelle', *Third International Congress of Criminal Anthropology*, Brussels, pp. 37–40.

1896   'Les fondements et le but de la responsabilité pénale', *Fourth International Congress of Criminal Anthropology*, Geneva.

Ducpétiaux, Édouard, *De la Justice de Prévoyance*, Brussels:
1827   Cautaerts.
1827   *De la Mission de la justice humaine et de l'injustice de la peine de mort*, Brussels: Cautaerts.
1835   *Statistique compareé de la criminalité en France, en Belgique, en Angleterre et en Allemagne*, Brussels: L. Hauman.

Durkheim, Emile, *De la Division du Travail Social*, Paris: Félix
1893   Alcan, 4th edn., 1922.
       The Division of Labor in Society, New York: Free Press, 1966 (trans. George Simpson).
1890–1900   *Leçons de Sociologie, Physique des Moeurs et du Droit*, Paris: Presses Universitaires de France, 1950.
1897   *Le Suicide*. Paris: Félix Alcan.
1917   'Introduction à la morale', *Revue Philosophique*, pp. 79–97.
1899–1900   'Deux Lois de l'Evolution Pénale', *L'Année Sociologique*, vol. 4, pp. 1–65.

The Economist, 'Relations between Crime and Material Welfare',
1856   15 March, pp. 280–1.

Eaton, J., *On Crime and Education*, U.S. Commissioner of Education.
1879

Ellis, Havelock, *The Criminal*, London: Walter Scott, 4th rev. edn.,
1890   1910.

Engels, Friedrich, *The Condition of the Working Class in England*.
1845   Oxford: Basil Blackwell, 1971. (trans. and ed. W. O. Henderson and W. H. Chaloner).
       Socialisme Utopique et Socialisme Scientifique, Paris: Derveau, 1880, (trans. P. Lafargue).

Esquirol, Dr., *Note sur la Monomanie-Homocide*, Paris: Baillière.
1827

Féré, C. H., *Dégénérescence et Criminalité*, Paris: Félix Alcan.
1888

Ferri, Enrico, *Sociologie Criminelle*. Paris: Rousseau, 1893, (tran. by
1881   author from 3rd Italian edn.). 1917, *Criminal Sociology* Boston: Little, Brown (trans. J. I. Kelly).
1898   *La Justice Pénale*, Brussels: Veuve Larcier, 1898.
1925   *Congrès Pénitentiaire de Londres*, Paris: Godde, 1926.

1894   *Socialism and Positive Science*. London: Independent Labour Party, 1905 (trans. Edith C. Harvey from the French edn. of 1896/9).

Fink, Arthur E., *Causes of Crime: Biological Theories in the United*
1938   *States 1800–1915*, New York: Barnes.

Fletcher, Joseph, 'Progress of Crime in the United Kingdom',
1843   *Journal of the Statistical Society*, vol. 6, pp. 218–40.

Francotte, Xavier, *L'Anthropologie Criminelle*. Paris: Baillière.
1891

Fregier, H. A., *Des classes dangereuses de la population dans les*
1840   *grandes villes et des moyens de les rendre meilleures*, Paris: Hachette, 1971, microfiche.

Frigerio et Ottolenghi, 'Organes et fonctions des sens chez les
1885   criminels'. *First International Congress of Criminal Anthropology*, Rome, pp. 35–8.

Gall, F. J., *Sur les fonctions du cerveau*, 6 vols., Paris: Baillière.
1822

Galton, Francis, *Inquiries into Human Faculty and its Development*,
1883   London: Macmillan.

Garofalo, Baron R., *Criminology*, Boston: Little, Brown, 1914
1885   (trans. R. W. Millar).

1895   *La Superstition Socialiste*, Paris, Félix Alcan.

Georget, Dr., *Nouvelle Discussion Médico-Légale sur la Folie ou*
1828   *Aliénation Morale*, Paris: Migneret.

Giddings, Franklin Henry, *Principles of Sociology*, New York:
1899   Macmillan.

1901   *Democracy and Empire*, New York: Macmillan.

de Greef, Guillaume, *Introduction à la Sociologie*, 2 vols., Brussels:
1886   Mayolez.

Gross, Hans, *Criminal Psychology*, Boston: Little, Brown, 1918.
1897

Guégo, Henry, *Étude Statistique sur la Criminalité en France de 1826*
1902   *à 1900*, Paris: Michalon.

Guénoud, 'La criminalité en Suisse', *Fourth International Congress*
1896   *of Criminal Anthropology*, Geneva.

Guerry, A. M., *Essai sur la statistique morale de la France*, Paris:
1833   Crochard (microfiche).

1864   *Statistique Morale de l'Angleterre Comparée avec la Statistique Morale de la France*, Paris: Baillière.

Guillot, Ellen E., Social Factors in Crime, University of Penn-
1943   sylvania Ph.D thesis.

Hall, Charles, *The Effects of Civilisation on the People in European*
1850   *States*, London: Gilpin, 1905.

Hill, Frederic, *Crime: Its Amount, Causes and Remedies*, London:
1853   John Murray.

Hoffbauer, J. C., *Médecine Légale relative aux aliénés et aux sourds-*
1827   *muets ou les lois appliquées aux désordres de l'intelligence*,
        Paris: Baillière.

Jackson, Randle, *Considerations on the Increase of Crime*, London:
1828   Hatchard.

Jelgersman, G., 'Les caractères physiques, intellectuels et moraux
1892   reconnus chez le criminel—ne sont d'origine pathologique',
        Third International Congress of Criminal Anthropology,
        Brussels, pp. 32, 36.

Johnstone, John, *Medical Jurisprudence*, Birmingham: Belcher.
1800

Joseph, H. S., *Memoires of Convicted Prisoners*, London: Chester.
1853

Kellor, Frances, 'Criminal Anthropology and its Relation to Crimi-
1898–99   nal Jurisprudence', *American Journal of Sociology*, vol. 4,
           p. 515.
1899–1900   'Psychological and Environmental Study of Women
             Criminals', *American Journal of Sociology*, vol. 5,
             pp. 527–43.

Lacassagne, A., *De la Criminalité chez les Animaux*, Lyon: Bourgeon.
1882
1882   *L'Homme Criminal comparé à l'homme primitif*, Lyon: Giraud.

Laschi, Rodolphe, *Le Crime Financier*, Paris: Masson (*Bibliothèque*
1901   *de Criminalité*, xxiv).

Laurent, Emile, *L'Anthropologie Criminelle de les Nouvelles Théories*
1893   *du Crime*, Paris: Société d'Éditions Scientifiques, 2nd edn.

Lauvergne, H., *Les Forçats*. Paris: Baillière.
1841

Letourneau, Ch., *L'Évolution de la Morale*. Paris: Delahaye et
1887   Lecrosnier.

Lodhi, A. Q. and Charles Tilly, 'Urbanization, Crime, and Collective
        Violence in 19th Century France', *American Journal of
        Sociology*, vol. 79, pp. 296–318.

Lombroso, Cesare, *L'Homme Criminel*. Paris: Félix Alcan, 1887.
1871   (2nd French edn.).

Lombroso, Cesare, *Crime: Its Causes and Remedies*, Boston: Little,
   Brown, 1918 (trans. H. P. Horton).

Lombroso-Ferrero, Gina, *Criminal Man according to the classification
   of Cesare Lombroso*, Montclair, N.J.: Patterson Smith, 1972.

Lucas, Prosper, *Traité philosophique et physiologique de l'Hérédité
1847–50   Naturelle*, 2 vols., Paris: Baillière.

MacDonald, Arthur, *Abnormal Man*, Washington: Government
1893   Printing Office, Bureau of Education Circular no. 4.

1893   *Le Criminel Type*, Paris: Masson.

1902   *A Plan for the Study of Man*, Washington: Government
   Printing Office.

Macedo, Francisco Ferraz de, *L'Encephale Humain*, Geneva: C.
1889   Schuchardt.

Maine, Henry Sumner, *Ancient Law*, London: John Murray, 15th
1861   edn.

Maliarewsky, Jean, 'Les modes de prévenir l'évolution de la crimi-
1896   nalité', *Fourth International Congress of Criminal Anthropology*,
   Geneva.

Mannheim, H., ed., *Pioneers in Criminology*, London: Stevens, 1960

Marro, Antonio, 'Influence of the Puberal Development upon the
1899–1900   moral character of children of both sexes', *American
   Journal of Sociology*, vol. 5, pp. 193–219.

Marx, Karl and Frederick Engels, *The German Ideology*, Moscow:
(1845)   Progress Publisher, 1964 (trans. C. Dutt).

Marx, Karl, *Contribution à la critique de l'économie politique*, Paris:
1859   Giard et Briere, 1909 (trans. Laura Lafargue from 2nd
   German edn.). *Contribution to the Critique of Political Economy*,
   New York: International Library (tran. N. I. Stone from 2nd.
   German edn.), 1904.

   'The State and Law', in T. B. Bottomore and M. Rubel (eds.),
   *Karl Marx: Selected Writings in Sociology and Social Philo-
   sophy*, Harmondsworth: Penguin.

Maudsley, H., *Le Crime et la Folie*, Paris: Baillière, 3rd edn., 1877.
1874

1870   *Body and Mind*, London: Macmillan.

1867   *The Pathology of Mind*, London: Macmillan, 3rd edn.
   (rewritten), 1879.

Mauss, Marcel, *La Réligion et les Origines du Droit Pénal*, Paris:
1897 Leroux, extrait de *La Revue des Religions*, vol. 35, no. 1.

Mayhew, Henry, *London Labour and the London Poor*, London:
1861 Mark Cass, 1967, vol. 4.

Mayhew, Henry and John Binny, *The Criminal Prisons of London and*
1862 *Scenes of Prison Life*, London: Griffin.

Mayo, Thomas, *Elements of the Pathology of the Human Mind*,
1838 London: John Murray.

Meyer, Ernest, *Criminels et Malades*, Paris: Thorin.
1886

Minovici, 'Rémarques statistiques relatives à l'anthropologie du
1896 criminel', *Fourth International Congress of Criminal Anthropology*, Geneva.

Mirehouse, John, *Crime and its Causes: with observations on Sir*
1840 *Eardley Wilmot's Bill*, London: Cleaver.

Moreau-Christophe, L. M., *Du Problème de la Misère et de sa solution*
1851 *chez les peuples anciens et modernes*, 2 vols., Paris: Guillaumin.

Morel, B. A., *Traité des Dégénérescences physiques, intellectuelles et*
1857 *morales de l'espèce humain*, Paris: Baillière.

Morgan, John, *Religion and Crime: or, the condition of the people*,
1840 London: Hooper.

Morrison, William Douglas, *Crime and its Causes*. London: Iwan
1891 Sonnenschein.

Naecke, P., 'Considérations générales sur la psychiatrie criminelle',
1896 *Fourth International Congress of Criminal Anthropology*,
Geneva, pp. 1–11.

Nicholson, David, 'The Morbid Psychology of Criminals', *Journal of*
1873–4 *Mental Science*, vol. 19, pp. 222–32, 398–409.

Ottolenghi and Rossi, 'Deux cents criminels et prostituées', *Année*
1897–8 *Sociologique*, vol. 1, pp. 428–30.

Owen, Robert, *A New View of Society: or, Essays on the Principle of*
1813 *the Foundation of the Human Character*, London: Cadell &
Davies.

1836 *Book of the New Moral World*, London: Wilson.

Pecqueur, C., *Des Améliorations Matérielles*, Paris: Gosselin.
1840

1842 *Théorie Nouvelle d'économie sociale et politique*, Paris: Capelle.

Piepers, M. C., 'La Notion du crime au point de vue évolutioniste',
1901 *Fifth International Congress of Criminal Anthropology*,
Amsterdam.

Pinel, Philippe, *Traité Médico-Philosophique sur l'aliénation mentale*,
1799 *ou la Manie*, Paris: Richard, Caille et Ravier.

Plint, Thomas, *Crime in England; Its Relation, Character and Extent*,
1851 London: Gilpin.

Prichard, James Cowles, *On the different Forms of Insanity in Relation*
1842 *to Jurisprudence*, London; Baillière.

Prins, Adolphe, *Criminalité et Répression*, Brussels: Librairie
1886 Européene, C. Muquardt.

Proal, Louis, *La Criminalité Politique*, Paris: Félix Alcan.
1895

Proudhon, P. J., *Manuel de Speculateur à la Bourse*, Paris: Garnier,
1854 3rd edn., 1857.

1858 *De la Justice dans la Révolution et dans L'Église*, Paris:
Garnier.

Quetelet, Alphonse, 'Du Nombre des Crimes et des Délits dans les
1829 provinces ... 1826–28', *Correspondance Mathématique et
Physique*, vol. 5, pp. 177–87.

1830 'Sur la constance qu'on observe dans le nombre des crimes qui
se commettent', *Correspondance Mathématique et Physique*,
vol. 6, pp. 214–17.

1831 *Recherches sur le Penchant au Crime aux Différens Ages*,
Brussels: Académie Royale.

1835 *Sur l'homme et le développement de ses facultés ou Essai de
Physique Sociale*, Paris.
A Treatise on Man and the Development of his Faculties,
Edinburgh: Chambers, 1842, (trans. R. Knox).
*Physique Sociale, ou Essai sur le développement des facultés de
l'homme*, 2 vols., Brussels: Muquardt, 1869.

Rawson, W., 'An Inquiry into the statistics of crime in England
1839 and Wales', *Journal of the Statistical Society*, vol. 2, pp. 316–
344.

1840 'An Enquiry into the Condition of Criminal Offenders in
England and Wales, with Respect to Education', *Journal of
the Statistical Society*, vol. 3, pp. 331–52.

Ray, Isaac, *Medical Jurisprudence of Insanity*, Boston.
1838

Richard, Gaston, 'Les Crises Sociales et la Criminalité', *L'Année*
1898–99 *Sociologique*, vol. 3, pp. 15–42.

Ross, E. A., *Social Control*, Citizen's Library of Economics, 1901.
1898–99

Rostand, Eugène, *Criminalité et Socialisme*, Paris: Comité de Defense
1898   et de Progrès Social.

1897   *Pourquoi la criminalité monte en France et baisse en Angleterre*,
        Paris: Bureaux de la Reforme Sociale.

Roukavichnikoff, 'Commentaires au 5 ème séance', *Third Interna-*
1892   *tional Congress of Criminal Anthropology*, Brussels, pp. 209–
        210.

Saint-Aubin, M., *Le Criminel*, Grenoble: Bratier et Dardelet.
1889

Sampson, M. B., *Criminal Jurisprudence Considered in relation to*
1843   *cerebral organization*, London: Highley.

Soury, Jules, 'Le Crime et les Criminels', *La Nouvelle Revue*, Paris,
1882   vol. 4, pp. 510–20.

Spencer, Herbert, *The Man Versus the State*, London: Williams &
1860   Norgate, 1884.

1874–1877   *The Principles of Sociology*, 3 vols., London: Williams &
            Norgate, 3rd edn. rev., 1893.

1850   *Social Statistics*. Osnabrück: Otto Zeller, abr. and rev., 1966.

1873   *The Study of Sociology*, Ann Arbor: University of Michigan,
        1966.

Star, Frederick, 'Study of the Criminal in Mexico', *American*
1898   *Journal of Sociology*, vol. 3, pp. 13–17.

Sumner, William Graham, *Folkways*, Boston: Ginn.
1906

Sutherland, Alexander, *The Origin and Growth of the Moral Instinct*,
1898   2 vols., London: Longman.

Taladriz, Alvarez, 'La Criminalité dans ses rapports avec l'ethno-
1885   graphie', *First International Congress of Criminal Anthropology*,
        Rome.

Talbot, Eugene, *Degeneracy*, London: Walter Scott.
1898

Tamburimi, 'Contribution de l'identité de la délinquance congénitale
1885   et de la folie morale', *First International Congress of Criminal
        Anthropology*, Rome, p. 431.

Tarde, Jean Gabriel de, *La Criminalité Comparée*, Paris: Félix Alcan,
1886   5th edn., 1902.

1890   *Penal Philosophy*, London: Heinemann, 1912 (trans. Rapelje
        Howell).

1890   *Les Lois de L'Imitation*, Paris: Félix Alcan, 2nd edn., 1907.

1901 'La criminalité économique et les phenomènes économiques', *Fifth International Congress of Criminal Anthropology*, Amsterdam, pp. 197–204.

Tarnowsky, Pauline, *Étude Anthropométrique*, Paris: Lecrosnier et
1889 Babé.
1908 *Les Femmes Homicides*, Paris: Félix Alcan.

Taverni, Romeo, and Dr. Magnan, 'De l'enfance des criminels dans
1885 ses rapports avec la prédisposition naturelle au crime', *First International Congress of Criminal Anthropology*, Rome, pp. 20–32.

Thiry, Fernand, 'Applications administratives de l'anthropologie
1896 criminelle', *Fourth International Congress of Criminal Anthropology*, Geneva, pp. 20–7.

Thomas, Dorothy S., *Social Aspects of the Business Cycle*, London:
1925 Routledge and Kegan Paul.

Thompson, William, *An Inquiry into the principles of the Distribution*
1824 *of Wealth most conducive to Human Happiness*, London: Longman.

Thomson, J. Bruce, 'The Psychology of Criminals', *Journal of Mental*
1870 *Science*, vol. 16, pp. 321–50.

Tristan, Flora, *Promenades dans Londres*, Paris: Delloye.
1840

Tschisch, Wladimir, 'L'affaiblissement psycho-physique de la
1901 personalité, une des principales causes du crime', *Fifth International Congress of Criminal Anthropology*, Amsterdam.
1901 'Les types criminels d'après Dostowesky', *Fifth International Congress of Criminal Anthropology*, Amsterdam.

van Hamel, G. A., 'L'anarchisme et le combat contre l'anarchisme au
1896 point de vue de l'anthropologie criminelle', *Fourth International Congress of Criminal Anthropology*, Geneva, pp. 111–19.

Villiers, Le comte H. G. C. de, 'L'Abolition de la Peine de Mort',
1899 *La Revue Socialiste*, Paris: Cerf.

Voisin, Félix, *Du Traitement Intelligent de la Folie*, Paris: Baillière.
1847

von Liszt, Franz, 'Aperçu des applications de l'anthropologie
1892 criminelle', *Third International Congress of Criminal Anthropology*, Brussels.

Vuacheux, M. F., *Étude sur les causes de la progression constatée dans*
1898 *la criminalité précoce*, Paris: Imprimerie Nationale.

Ward, Lester, F., *Dynamic Sociology*, 2 vols., New York: Appleton.
1883
1903   *Pure Sociology*, New York: Macmillan.
Waugh, Benjamin, *The Gaol Cradle*, London: Isbister, 4th edn., 1880.
1875
Wines, F. H., *Punishment and Reformation*, New York: Thomas
1895   Crowell.

CHAPTER 4

Addams, Jane, *Democracy and Social Ethics*, New York, Macmillan.
1902
1910   *The Spirit of Youth and the City Streets*, New York: Mac-
        millan.
Aichhorn, August, *Wayward Youth*, New York: Viking, 2nd edn.,
1925   1935.
Alexander, Franz and Hugo Staub, *The Criminal, the Judge, and the*
1929   *Public*, London: Allen & Unwin, 1931 (trans. Gregory
        Zilboorg).
Alexander, Franz and Sheldon Selsnick, *The History of Psychiatry*,
1966   New York: Harper & Row.
Andry, Robert G., *Delinquency and Parental Pathology*, London:
1960   Methuen.
Aschaffenburg, Gustav, *Crime and its Repression*, Boston: Little,
1903   Brown, 1913.
Bandura, Albert and R. H. Walters, *Adolescent Aggression*, New
1959   York: Ronald Press.
Barnes, Harry E. and Negley K. Teeters, *New Horizons in Crimi-*
1943   *nology*. Englewood Cliffs, N.J: Prentice-Hall.
Becker, Howard S., *Outsiders*, New York: Free Press.
1963
Belby, José, 'La Délinquance des Schizophrènes', *Actes du IIe*
1950   *Congrès International de Criminologie*, Paris, pp. 75–96.
Berman, Harold, J., *Soviet Criminal Law and Procedure*. Cambridge,
1966   Mass: Harvard University Press.
Bonger, William Adriaan, *Criminality and Economic Conditions*,
1905   London: Heinemann, 1916 (trans. H. P. Horton).
1933   *An Introduction to Criminology*, London: Methuen, 1936.
1943   *Race and Crime*, New York: Columbia University Press.

Bouhdiba, Abdelwahab, *Criminalité et Changements Sociaux en Tuni-*
1965   *sie*, Tunis.
Bowlby, E. J. M., *Maternal Care and Mental Health*, Geneva: World
1952   Health Organization.
1948   *Crime and the Mind*, Philadelphia: Lippincott.
Bronner, Augusta F., 'A research on the proportion of mental
1914–15   defectives among delinquents', *Journal of Criminal Law
        and Criminology*, vol. 5, pp. 561–8.
Burt, Cyril, *The Young Delinquent*, London: University of London
1925   Press, 4th rev. edn., 1944.
Carrara, 'L'Importance des anomalies physiques des criminels
1911   dans la théorie et dans la pratique médico-légale', *Seventh
        International Congress of Criminal Anthropology*, Cologne,
        pp. 147–51.
Chassell, Clara Frances, *The Relation between Morality and Intellect*,
1935   New York: Columbia University Bureau of Publications.
Clinard, M. B., *Anomie and Deviant Behaviour*, New York: Free
1964   Press.
Cloward, Richard A. and Lloyd E. Ohlin, *Delinquency and Oppor-*
1960   *tunity: A Theory of Delinquent Gangs*, Glencoe, Illinois:
        Free Press.
Cohen, Albert K., *Delinquent Boys: the Culture of a Gang*, New York:
1955   Free Press.
Cohen, Jerome, *The Criminal Process in the People's Republic of
1968   China, 1949-1963*, Cambridge: Harvard University Press.
Comfort, Alexander, *Authority and Delinquency in the Modern State:
1950   a criminological approach to the problem of power*, London:
        Routledge & Kegan Paul.
Connor, Walter D., *Deviance in Soviet Society*, New York: Columbia
1972   University Press.
Cook, Shirley J., 'Canadian narcotics legislation, 1908–1923: a
1969   conflict model interpretation', *Canadian Review of Sociology
        and Anthropology*, vol. 6, pp. 36–46.
Culver, Dorothy C., *Bibliography of Crime and Criminal Justice
1939   1932-1937*, Montclair, N.J: Patterson Smith.
Cumming, Sir John, *A Contribution towards a Bibliography dealing
1935   with Crime and Cognate Subjects*, London: Metropolitan
        Police District (3rd edn.).
Current Digest of the Soviet Press, 'A Selection of Law and Order
1972   Stories', vol. 24, no. 6, pp. 8–10, 14.

Dahrendorf, Ralf, *Class and Class Conflict in Industrial Society*,
1959 London: Routledge & Kegan Paul, 1963.
1961 'On the Origin of Inequality', in *Essays in the Theory of
       Society*, London: Routledge & Kegan Paul; 1968.
Darrow, Clarence, *Crime: its cause and treatment*, London: Harrap.
1922
Debuyst, Christian, *Criminels et Valeurs Vécues*, Louvain: Publica-
1959 tions Universitaires.
Downes, David M., *The Delinquent Solution*, London: Routledge &
1966 Kegan Paul.
Djekebaev, U.S., 'Crime in Socialist Society and its Principal
1975 Features', *Soviet Sociology*, vol. 14, pp. 62–85.
East, Norwood, *Society and the Criminal*, London: HMSO.
1949
Elkin, W. A., 'Criminal Statistics, 1933', *Howard Journal*, vol. 4,
1934 pp. 154–8.
Ellwood, Charles A., 'Lombroso's Theory of Crime', *Journal of
1911–12 Criminal Law and Criminology*, vol. 2, pp. 716–23.
Ehrlich, Eugen, *Fundamental Principles of the Sociology of Law*,
1913 New York: Russell & Russell.
Eysenck, Hans, *Crime and Personality*, London: Paladin, rev. edn.,
1964 1970.
Ferguson, T., *The Young Delinquent in his Social Setting*, London:
1952 Oxford University Press.
Fernand, Mabel Ruth, *et al.*, *A Study of Women Delinquents in New
1920 York State*, Montclair, N.J: Patterson Smith, 1968.
Freud, Sigmund, *The Ego and the Id*, London: Hogarth vol. XIX of
1923 the Standard Edition of *The Complete Psychological Works of
       Sigmund Freud*.
Friedlander, Kate, *The Psychoanalytical Approach to Juvenile Delin-
1947 quency*, London: Kegan Paul.
Fyvel, T. R., *The Insecure Offenders: rebellious youth in the welfare
1961 state*, London: Chatto & Windus.
Garfinkel, Harold, 'Conditions of Successful Degradation Ceremon-
1956 ies', *American Journal of Sociology*, vol. 61, pp. 420–4.
Gatrell, V. A. C. and T. B. Hadden, 'Criminal Statistics and their
1972 interpretations', E. A. Wrigley (ed.), *Nineteenth-century
       Society*, Cambridge University Press, pp. 336–96.
Ginsberg, Morris, *On Justice in Society*, Harmondsworth: Penguin.
1965

Glaser, Daniel, *The Effect of a Prison and Parole System*, Indianapolis:
1964   Bobbs-Merrill.

Glover, Edward, *The Roots of Crime: Selected Papers on Psychoana-*
1960   *lysis*, London: Imago, vol. 2.

Glueck, Sheldon and Eleanor, *Physique and Delinquency*, New York:
1956   Harper.

1950   *Unravelling Juvenile Delinquency*, Cambridge: Harvard
        University Press.

Goddard, Henry, H., *The Kalikak Family*, New York: Macmillan.
1913

Goffman, Erving, *Asylums*, Garden City, N.Y: Anchor.
1961

Goring, Charles, *The English Convict: A Statistical Study*, London:
1913   HMSO.

Grapin, Pierre, 'Possibilités d'une contribution de l'anthropologie
1950   évolutive à la criminologie', *Actes du XIème Congrès Interna-*
        tional de Criminologie, Paris, pp. 75–96.

1973   *L'Anthropologie Criminelle*, Paris: Presses Universitaires de
        France.

Greef, Etienne de, *Introduction à la Criminologie*, Brussels: Vanden-
1937   plas, 2nd edn., 1946.

Grimberg, L., *Emotion and Delinquency*, London: Kegan Paul.
1928

Gurvitch, Georges, *Sociology of Law*, New York: Philosophical
1940   Library, 1942.

Haikerwal, B. S., *Economic and Social Aspects of Crime in India*,
1934   London: Allen & Unwin.

Hall, Arthur, *Crime in its Relations to Social Progress*, New York:
1902   Columbia University Press.

Hall, Jerome, *Studies in Jurisprudence and Criminal Theory*, New
1958   York: Oceana.

1935   *Theft, Law and Society*, Indianapolis: Bobbs-Merrill, 2nd
        edn., 1952.

Healy, William, *Mental Conflicts and Misconducts*, Boston: Little,
1928   Brown.

Healy, William and Julia Lathrop, *The Individual Delinquent*, Boston:
1915   Little, Brown.

Henderson, Charles Richmond, *The Cause and Cure of Crime*,
1914   London: Cazenove.

Hesnard, A., *Psychologie du Crime*, Paris: Payot.
1963

Hirschi, Travis, *Causes of Delinquency*, Berkeley: University of
1969   California Press.

Hoag, Ernest B., and E. H. Williams, *Crime, Abnormal Minds and the*
1923   *Law*, Indianapolis: Bobbs-Merrill.

Hobhouse, L. T., G. C. Wheeler and M. Ginsberg, *The Material*
1915   *Culture and Social Institutions of the Simpler Peoples*, London:
        Routledge & Kegan Paul.

1922   *The Elements of Social Justice*, London: Allen & Unwin.

Hobsbawm, E. J., *Bandits*, Harmondsworth: Penguin.
1969

1959   *Primitive Rebels*, Manchester: Manchester University Press.

Hollander, Bernard, *The Psychology of Misconduct, Vice and Crime*,
1922   London: Allen & Unwin.

Holmes, Thomas, *Psychology and Crime*, London: Dent.
1912

Hooton, E. A., *The American Criminal*, Boston: Harvard University
1939   Press.

Horney, Karen, *Our Inner Conflicts*, London: Kegan Paul.
1946

Hourwich, I. A., 'Immigration and Crime', *American Journal of*
1911–12   *Sociology*, vol. 17, pp. 478–90.

International Social Science Council, *Social Sciences in the U.S.S.R.*,
1965   Paris: Mouton.

Jefferey, C. Ray, 'The development of crime in early English society',
1957   *Journal of Criminal Law, Criminology and Police Science*,
        vol. 47, pp. 647–66.

Karpman, Ben, 'A Survey of contributions of American psychoanaly-
1950   sis to criminology,' *Actes du IIe Congrès International de*
        Criminologie, Paris.

Kinberg, Olof, *Les Problèmes Fondamentaux de la Criminologie*, Paris:
1930   Cujas, 1957.

Kolaly, Mohamed El, *Essai sur les causes de la criminalité actuelle*
1929   *en Egypte*, Paris: Librairie Generale du Droit.

Kropotkin, Pierre, *Les Prisons*, Paris: Bureau de la Révolte,
1890   2nd edn.

1892   *La Loi et L'Autorité*, Paris: Publications de la Révolte.

1889   *La Morale Anarchiste*, Paris: Temps Nouveaux.

1902 Kropotkin, P., *Mutual Aid*, London: Heinemann, popular
edn., 1915.

1924 *Ethics, Origin and Development*, New York: Dial Press.

Laignel-Lavastine, Pr. M. and V. V. Stanciu, *Précis de Criminologie*,
1950 Paris: Payot.

Lander, Bernard, *Toward an Understanding of Juvenile Delinquency*,
1954 New York: Columbia University Press.

Lange, Johannes, *Crime as Destiny: a study of criminal twins*, London:
1929 Allen & Unwin, 1931.

Laski, Harold J., 'The Criminal Statistics', *Howard Journal*, vol. 4,
1936 pp. 257–62.

LeBlanc, Marc, 'Inventaire de la Recherche criminologique au Que-
1970 bec: 1949–1969', *Acta Criminologica*, vol. 3, pp. 171–207.

Lemert, Edwin C., *Social Pathology*, New York: McGraw-Hill.
1951

Lévy-Bruhl, Lucien, *La Morale et la Science des Moeurs*, Paris:
1903 Félix Alcan.

Lofland, John, *Deviance and Identity*, Englewood Cliffs, N.J.:
1969 Prentice-Hall.

Lydston, G. Frank, *The Diseases of Society, the vice and crime prob-
1904 lem*, Philadelphia: Lippincott.

McCord, Wm. and Joan, *Psychopathy and Delinquency*, New York:
1956 Grune & Stratton.

McDonald, Lynn, *Causes of Drug Use and Dependence*, Ottawa:
1971 Commission of Inquiry into the Non-Medical Use of Drugs
(unpublished report).

Macnaughton-Smith, Peter, 'The second code: toward (or away
1968 from) an empiric theory of crime and delinquency', *Journal of
Research in Crime and Delinquency*, vol. 5, pp. 189–97.

Martin, J. P. and D. Webster, *The Social Consequences of Conviction*,
1971 London: Heinemann.

Maxwell, J., *Le Crime et la Société*, Paris: Flammarion.
1909

Mead, George H., 'The Psychology of Punitive Justice', *American
1918 Journal of Sociology*, vol. 23, pp. 577–602.

Mensbrugghe, André von den, *L'Élimination Darwinienne dans la
1907 Répression*, Brussels: Polleunis.

Merton, Robert K., *Social Theory and Social Structure*, New York:
1957 Free Press.

Michon, Emile, *Un Peu de l'ame des Bandits*, Paris: Dorbon Ainé.
1917

Miner, James B., *Deficiency and Delinquency*, Baltimore: Warwick &
1918   York.

Morris, Terence, *The Criminal Area*, London; Routledge & Kegan
1957   Paul.

Mosby, Thomas S., *Causes and Cures of Crime*, St. Louis: Mosby.
1913

Murchison, Carl, *Criminal Intelligence*, London: Oxford University
1926   Press.

Murphy, B. C., *A quantitative test of the effectiveness of an experimen-*
1970   *tal treatment program for delinquent opiate addicts*, Canadian
        Penitentiary Service, Abbotsford, B.C. (mimeo).

Otterström, Edith, *Delinquency and Children from Bad Homes*, Lund:
1946   Carl Bloms.

Pailthorpe, Grace W., *Studies in the Psychology of Delinquency and*
1932   *Crime*, New York: Macmillan.

Parsons, Philip, *Crime and the Criminal*, New York: Knopf.
1926

Parsons, Talcott, *The Social System*, Glencoe, Illinois: The Free
1951   Press.

    1962   'The Law and Social Control', in William M. Evan (ed.), *Law
            and Sociology*, New York: Free Press of Glencoe, pp. 56–72.

    1961   *et al.* (eds.), *Theories of Society*, New York: Free Press of
            Glencoe.

Pinatel, Jean, *La Criminologie*, Paris: Spes.
1960

Pound, Roscoe, 'Scope and purpose of sociological jurisprudence',
1911   *Harvard Law Review*, vol. 24, pp. 591–619.

    1942   *Social Control through Law*, New Haven: Yale University
            Press.

    1943   'A survey of social interests', *Harvard Law Review*, vol. 57,
            pp. 1–39.

Quinney, Richard, *Social Reality of Crime*, Boston: Little, Brown.
1969

Quiros, C. Bernaldo de, *Modern Theories of Criminality*, Boston:
1908   Little, Brown, 1911 (trans. A. de Salvio).

Radzinowicz, Leon. 'Economic pressures', in Radzinowicz, Leon
1968   and M. E. Wolfgang, (eds.), *Crime and Justice*, vol. 1, New
        York: Basic Books, 1971, pp. 420–42.

Rao, S. Venugopala, *Facets of Crime in India*, New Delhi: Allied.
1962

Renda A. and F. Squillace, 'Folie criminelle en Calabre', *Fifth Inter-*
1901 *national Congress of Criminal Anthropology*, Amsterdam.

Rhodes, Henry T. F., *Genius and Criminal; a study in rebellion*,
1932 London: John Murray.

Rocher, Guy, *Introduction à la Sociologie Générale*, 3 vols., Paris:
1968 HMH.

Rosenblum, Victor G., *Law as a Political Instrument*, New York:
1962 Random House.

Rozengart, Gecel, *Le Crime comme produit social et économique*,
1929 Paris: Jouve.

Rubenfeld, Seymour, *Family of Outcasts*, New York: Free Press.
1965

Samuel, Viscount, *Is the Criminal to Blame or Society?* Clarke Hall
1938 Lecture 4.

Saxena, Srî P. N., 'The Criminal Tribes of India', *Actes du XIème*
1950 *Congrès International de Criminologie*, Paris.

Schlapp, Max G., and Edward H. Smith, *The New Criminology: a*
1928 *consideration of the chemical causation of abnormal behaviour*,
New York: Boni & Liveright.

Schoff, Hannah Kent, *The Wayward Child*, Indianapolis: Bobbs-
1915 Merrill.

Schur, Edwin M., *Our Criminal Society*, Engelwood Cliffs: Prentice-
1969 Hall.

Schwartz, Richard D. and Jerome H. Skolnick, 'Two Studies of
1964 Legal Stigma', in Howard S. Becker (ed.), *The Other Side*,
New York: Free Press, pp. 103–17.

Seelig, Ernest, *Traité de Criminologie*. Paris: Presses Universitaires
1951 de France, 1956 (trans. I. Petit and M. Pariser).

Sellin, Thorsten, *Culture Conflict and Crime*, New York: Social
1938 Science Research Council.

Sethna, M. J., *Society and the Criminal*, Bombay: Leaders' Press.
1952

Shargorodski, M. D., 'The causes and prevention of crime', in
1964 Alex Simirenko (ed.), *Soviet Sociology*, London: Routledge
& Kegan Paul, 1967, p. 24.

Shaw, Clifford, *Delinquency Areas*, Chicago: University of Chicago
1929 Press.

1931   *Natural History of a Delinquent Career*, Chicago: University of Chicago Press.

Shaw, Clifford and Henry D. McKay, *Juvenile Delinquency in Urban*
1942   *Areas*, Chicago: University of Chicago Press.

Sheldon, William H., *Varieties of Delinquent Youth*, New York:
1949   Harper.

Slawson, J., *The Delinquent Boy*, Boston: Badger.
1926

Smart, Frances, *Neurosis and Crime*, London: Duckworth.
1970

Smith, M. Hamblin, *Psychology of the Criminal*, London: Methuen.
1922

Solomon, Peter H., *Soviet Criminology: the effects of post-Stalin*
1970   *politics on a social science*, Columbia University M.A. Thesis, Faculty of Political Science.

Sorokin, Pitirim, *Contemporary Sociological Theories*, New York:
1928   Harper.
1937   *Social and Cultural Dynamics*, New York: American Book, vol. 2.

Spaulding, Edith R. and William Healy, 'Inheritance as a Factor in
1913–14 Criminality', *Journal of Criminal Law and Criminology*, vol. 4, pp. 837–58.

Stone, Julius, *Social Dimensions of Law and Justice*, Stanford: Stan-
1966   ford University Press.

Sutherland, 'Resultats de la deportation en Australie', *Année*
1901–02 *Sociologique*, vol. 6, pp. 443–4.

Sutherland, Edwin H. and Donald R. Cressey, *Principles of Crimino-*
1966   *logy*, Philadelphia: Lippincott, 7th edn.

Szabo, Denis, *Criminologie*, Presses de l'Université de Montréal.
1965

Tannenbaum, Frank, *Crime and the Community*, New York: Colum-
1951   bia University Press.

Thomas, William I., *The Unadjusted Girl*, London: Routledge &
1924   Kegan Paul.

Thrasher, Frederic M., *The Gang*, Chicago: University of Chicago
1927   Press.

Timasheff, N. S., *An Introduction to the Sociology of Law*, Cam-
1939   bridge, Mass.: Harvard University Committee on Research in the Social Sciences.

Tobias, John J., *Crime and Industrial Society in the Nineteenth*
1967 *Century*, London: Penguin, 1972.

Toby, Jackson and Marcia L., 'Low School Status as a Predisposing
Factor in Subcultural Delinquency', Rutgers University
mimeo, U.S. Office of Education.

Topping, C. W., *Crime and You*, Toronto: Ryerson.
1960

Trasler, Gordon, *The Explanation of Criminality*, London: Routledge
1962 & Kegan Paul.

Turk, Austin T., *Criminality and Legal Order*, Chicago: Rand
1969 McNally.

Van Kan, Joseph, *Les Causes Economiques de la Criminalité*, Paris:
1903 Storck.

Van Waters, Miriam, *Youth in Conflict*, London: Methuen.
1926

Varma, Sri Paripurnanand, 'The anthropological aspect of crimin-
1950 ology', *Actes du IIe Congrès International de Criminologie*,
Paris, pp. 245–55.

Vold, George B., *Theoretical Criminology*, New York: Oxford
1958 University Press.

Walker, Nigel, *Crime and Punishment in Britain*, Edinburgh: Edin-
1965 burgh University Press.

Westermarck, Edward, *The Origin and Development of the Moral*
1906–8 *Ideas*, 2 vols., London: Macmillan.

Wilson, Albert, *Education, Personality and Crime*, London:
1908 Greening.

1910 *Unfinished Man.* London: Greening.

Wilson, Harriet, *Delinquency and Child Neglect*, London: Allen &
1962 Unwin.

Work, Monroe N., 'Crime Among the Negroes of Chicago', *Ameri-*
1900–01 *can Journal of Sociology*, vol. 6, pp. 204–23.

Yen, Ching-Yueh, 'Crime in Relation to Social Change in China',
1934–5 *American Journal of Sociology*, vol. 40, pp. 298–308.

Young, Pauline, V., 'Defective Social Intelligence as a Factor in
1938 Crime', *American Sociological Review*, vol. 3. pp. 213–17.

CHAPTER 5

Banks, Arthur S. and Robert B. Textor, *A Cross-Polity Survey*,
1963 Cambridge, Mass.: MIT Press.

Bell, Daniel, *The End of Ideology*. New York: Free Press.
1960
Biderman, Albert D., 'A Case Example: Crime Rates', in Raymond
1966   A. Bauer (ed.), *Social Indicators*, Cambridge, Mass.: MIT
        Press, pp. 111–29.
Edwards, Allen, *Statistical Methods for the Behavioral Sciences*,
1954   New York: Holt, Rinehart, 3rd edn., 1973.
Ferdinand, Theodore N., 'The Criminal Patterns of Boston since
1967–68   1849', *American Journal of Sociology*, vol. 73, pp. 84–99.
Powell, Elwin H., 'Crime as a Function of Anomie', *Journal of*
1966   *Criminal Law, Criminology and Police Science*, vol. 57, pp.
        161–71.
Russett, Bruce M. and Hayward R. Alker, *World Handbook of*
1964   *Political and Social Indicators*, New Haven: Yale University
        Press.
Warner, Sam Bass, *Crime and Criminal Statistics in Boston*, Cam-
1934   bridge, Mass.: Harvard University Press.
Willbach, Harry, 'The Trend of Crime in New York City', *Journal of*
1938–9   *Criminal Law and Criminology*, vol. 29, pp. 62–75.
1940–1   'The Trend of Crime in Chicago', *Journal of Criminal*
        Law and Criminology, vol. 31, pp. 720–7.

CHAPTER 6

Carr-Hill, R. A. and N. H. Stern, 'An Econometric Model of the
1973   Supply and Control of Recorded Offences in England and
        Wales', *Journal of Public Economics*, pp. 289–318.
Cooper, Beryl P. and Garth Nicholas, *Crime in the Sixties*, Conserva-
1963   tive Party Political Centre, Bow Group.
Durant, Mary, Margaret Thomas and H. D. Willcock, *Crime*,
1972   *Criminals and the Law: A Study of Public Attitudes*, London:
        HMSO.
Jones, H., *Crime in a Changing Society*, Harmondsworth: Penguin.
1965
Labour Party Study Group, *Crime—a challenge to us all*, London.
1964
Lodge, T. S., 'Criminal Statistics', *Journal of the Royal Statistical*
1952   *Society*, vol. 115, pp. 489–500.
McClintock, F. H., *Crimes of Violence*, London: Macmillan.
1963

McClintock, F. H. and N. Howard Avison, *Crime in England and*
1968   *Wales*, London: Heinemann.

Mays, J. B., *Crime and the Social Structure*, London: Faber & Faber.
1963

Sullerot, Evelyne, *Woman, Society and Change*, London: Weidenfeld
1971   & Nicolson (World University Library).

Walker, Nigel, *Crime, Courts and Figures*, Harmondsworth: Penguin.
1971

Wilkins, Leslie T., *Social Deviance*, London: Tavistock.
1964

1969   *Evaluation of Penal Measures*, New York: Random House.

CHAPTER 7

Adorno, Theodore *et al.; The Authoritarian Personality*, New York:
1950   Harcourt, Brace.

Akman, D. D., A. Normandeau, S. Turner; 'The Measurement of
1967   Delinquency in Canada', *Journal of Criminal Law, Criminology
       and Police Science*, vol. 58, pp. 330–7.

Archambault Report, Royal Commission to investigate the Penal
1938   System of Canada.

Bax, Belfort, 'La Nouvelle Éthique', *Revue Socialiste*, pp. 641–58.
1891

Bernstein, Basil; *Class, Codes and Control*, London: Routledge &
1971   Kegan, Paul.

Boydell, Craig L., Carl F. Grindstaff; 'Public Opinion and the Crimi-
1972   nal Law: an Empirical Test of Public Attitudes Toward Legal
       Sanctions', in Craig L. Boydell, *et al.* (eds.), *Deviant Behaviour
       and Societal Reaction*, Toronto: Holt, Rinehart, pp. 165–80.

Bronfenbrenner, Urie; 'Socialization and Social class through time
1958   and space', in E. C. Maccoby, *et al.* (eds.), *Readings in Social
       Psychology*, New York: Holt, Rinehart.

Erlander, Howard G., 'Social Class and Corporal Punishment in
1974   Childhood: A Reassessment', *American Sociological Review*,
       vol. 39, 1974, pp. 68–85.

Gibbons, Don C., 'Crime and Punishment: a study in Social Atti-
1961   tudes', *Social Forces*, vol. 47, pp. 391–7.

Heumann, Hans W. B., John K. Manning and Douglas A. Schmei-
1973   ser, *The Native Offender in Canada* (report prepared for the Law
       Reform Commission of Canada), Ottawa, mimeo.

Hoggart, Richard, *The Uses of Literacy*, London: Chatto & Windus.
1957

Law Reform Commission of Canada, *The Principles of Sentencing and*
1974   *Dispositions* (Working Paper No. 3), Ottawa: Information
          Canada.

Léauté, Jacques, *et al.*, 'Sondage sur l'Estimation de la Gravité
(1970)   Comparée des Principales Infractions', *L'Année Sociologique*,
          vol. 21, pp. 111–150.

Lipset, Seymour Martin, *Political Man: Essays on the Sociology o,*
1959   *Democracy*, New York: Doubleday.

Macnaughton-Smith, Peter, 'Permission to be slightly free: a study
1972   of the granting, refusing and withdrawing of parole in
          Canadian Penitentiaries' (unpublished manuscript).

Mäkelä, Klaus, 'Public Sense of Justice and Judicial Practice', *Acta*
1960   *Sociologica*, pp. 42–67.

McDonald, Lynn, 'Crime and Punishment in Canada: a statistical
1969   Test of the "Conventional Wisdom" ', *Canadian Review of*
          Sociology and Anthropology, vol. 6, pp. 212–36.

Miller, S. M. and Frank Riessman, 'Working-class authoritarianism:
1961   a critique of Lipset', *British Journal of Sociology*, vol. 12,
          pp. 263–276.

Normandeau, André, 'Les "déviations en affaire" et les "crimes en
1970   col bleu" ', in Denis Szabo (ed.), *Déviance et Criminalité*
          Paris: Armand Colin, pp. 332–41.

Podgorecki, Adam, *et al.*, *Knowledge and Opinion about Law*, London:
1973   Martin Robertson.

Prévost Commission, *La Société Face au Crime*, Annexe 4.
1969

Rose, Arnold M. and Arthur E. Prell, 'Does the Punishment fit the
1955   Crime?' *American Journal of Sociology*, vol. 61, pp. 247–59.

Rossi, Peter H., *et al.;* 'The Seriousness of Crimes: Normative
1974   structure and Individual Differences', *American Sociological*
          Review, vol. 39, pp. 224–37.

Segerstedt, Torgny T., Georg Karlsson and Bengt G. Rundblad
1949   'Research into the General Sense of Justice', *Theoria*, vol. 15,
          Parts I–III, pp. 323–38.

Sellin, Thorsten and M. W. Wolfgang, *The Measurement of Delin-*
1964   *quency*. New York: John Wiley.

Spinley, B. M., *The Deprived and the Privileged*. London: Routledge
1953   & Kegan Paul.

Waller, I. and Chan, J. 'Prison Use: a Canadian and International
1974 Comparison', *Criminal Law Quarterly*, vol. 17, pp. 47–71.
Young, Michael and Peter Willmott, *Family and Kinship in East*
1957 *London*, London: Routledge & Kegan Paul.

CHAPTER 8

Althusser, Louis, *Pour Marx*, Paris: Maspero.
1965
Comte, Auguste, *Cours de Philosophie Positive*, 6 vols., Paris:
1830–42 Bachelier.
> *The Positive Philosophy.* (trans. and abridged version of the
> *Cours*, by Harriet Martineau).
Durkheim, Emile, *Les Règles de la Méthode Sociologique*, Paris:
1895 Presses Universitaires de France, 1947.
> *The Rules of Sociological Method*, Chicago: University of
> Chicago Press, 1938 (trans. Sarah A. Solovay and John H.
> Mueller).
Engels, Friedrich, 'Idéalisme et Matérialisme' in Marx and Engels,
Études Philosophiques. Paris: Editions Sociales, 1947.
> 'Ludwig Feuerbach and the End of Classical German
> Philosophy', in Marx and Engels, *Selected Works*, Moscow:
> Foreign Languages Publishing House, 1958, pp. 361–402.
Galliher, John F. and James L. McCartney, 'The Influence of
1973 Funding Agencies on Juvenile Delinquency Research', *Social
Problems*, vol. 21, pp. 77–90.
Gouldner, Alvin W., *The Coming Crisis of Western Sociology*, New
1970 York: Avon.
LeBlanc, Marc, 'Inventaire de la Recherche criminologique au
1970 Quebec', *Acta Criminologica*, vol. 3, pp. 171–207.
Lenin, V. I., *Materialism and Empirio-criticism*. London: Lawrence
1908 & Wishart (Vol. 14 of *Collected Works*).
Lombroso, C. and R. Laschi, *Le Crime Politique et les Revolutions*,
2 vols., Paris: Félix Alcan, 1892, (trans. A. Bouchard).
Lombroso, Gina Ferrero, *Criminal Man According to the Classification
of Cesare Lombroso*, Montclair, N.J.: Patterson Smith, 1952.
Mach, Ernest, *La Connaissance et l'Erreur*, Paris: Flammarion, 1908
1905 (trans. Marcel Dufour).
Marx, Karl, 'Theses on Feuerbach' in Marx and Engels, *Selected
1845 Works*, Moscow: Foreign Languages Publishing House, 1958.

1844   'Critique of the Hegelian Dialectic and Philosophy as a
       Whole', in *Philosophical Manuscripts of 1844*, Moscow:
       Foreign Languages Publishing House, 1959.

1853   'Capital Punishment', *New York Daily Tribune*, reprinted in
       T. B. Bottomore and M. Rubel, *Karl Marx; Selected Writings
       in Sociology and Social Philosophy*, Harmondsworth: Penguin.

Marx, Karl, and Friedrich Engels, *The German Ideology*, Moscow:
1845   Progress Publisher, 1964 (trans. C. Dutt).

Matza, David, *Delinquency and Drift*. New York: John Wiley.
1964

Mill, John Stuart, *System of Logic*, 2 vols., London: Parker, 3rd.
1851   edn.

1866   *Auguste Comte and Positivism*, London: Trubner, 2nd. edn.

Mills, C. Wright, *The Sociological Imagination*, New York: Oxford
1959   University Press.

1962   *The Marxists*, Harmondsworth: Penguin, 2nd. edn., 1973.

Pearson, Karl, 'Introduction' to Charles Goring, *The English Convict*,
1915   London: HMSO (abridged edn.).

Quetelet, Alphonse, *Physique Sociale*, Brussels: Muquardt, 1869,
1835   2nd edn.

Quinney, Richard, *The Social Reality of Crime*, Boston: Little, Brown.
1970

1973   *Critique of the Legal Order*, Boston: Little, Brown.

Stark, Werner, *Sociology of Religion*, New York: Fordham Univer-
1967   sity Press vol. 2.

Taylor, Ian, Paul Walton and Jock Young, *The New Criminology*,
1973   London: Routledge & Kegan Paul.

Vucinich, Alexander, *Science in Russian Culture 1861–1917*, Stanford:
1970   Stanford University Press.

Weber, Max, *Essais sur la Théorie de la Science*, Paris: Plon, 1951
1903–17   (trans. Julien Freund).

       The Methodology of the Social Sciences, New York: Free
       Press, 1949 (trans. and ed. E. A. Shils and H. N. Finch).

       From Max Weber: Essays in Sociology, London: Kegan Paul,
       1947 (trans. and ed. H. H. Gerth and C. Wright Mills).

NAME INDEX

SUBJECT INDEX

alcohol, 38, 93, 116, 128
American sociology, 85–6, 111, 115, 119, 121, 251, 281–2
anomie, 48, 74, 76, 100–3, 120, 130, 150
atavism, 83–5, 94, 131, 133

biological theories, 48–9, 53, 65, 77, 89, 92–5, 114, 127–8, 131
born criminals, 49, 81–5, 87

capitalism, 22, 55, 116, 127–9
capital punishment, 31, 89, 181
  and consensus theory, 49, 262
  and conflict theory, 40, 48, 54
  views on in Canada, 244–6
Chicago school, 93, 100–2, 120, 282
civil liberties, 238–49, 288
class interests, 40, 42–3, 115, 123, 228–32, 241–2, 248
climate, 34, 93, 117, 131, 134
communism, 116, 117
conflict theory
  definition of, 19–24
  tests of
    in Canada, 242–50
    U.K., 183–7
    cross-nationally, 155–64
    summary results on: 154–5, 175–176, 187, 211–12, 250–1
  acceptance of, 58

consensus theory
  definition of, 19–24
  tests in Canada, 226, 242–50
  U.K., 183–7
  cross-nationally, 155–68
  summary results on, 154–5, 175–176, 211–12, 250–1
Conservative Party, 69
  views on crime, 180–2
  effect on crime rates, 193–7, 203–205
continentalism, 248–50
crime prevention, 15, 103
crime rates/official crime, 54, 61, 64–5, 252, 286
  choice of indicators
    U.K., 297–8
    Canada, 15
    cross-national study, 145, 293–4
    Australia, 94
criminal anthropology, 75–6, 83–6, 92–4, 278
criminal behaviour, 23, 69, 72, 115–116, 284
  definition of, 19, 23
criminal law, 23, 129–30, 284
  definition of, 18, 23
  theories of, 27–37, 39–44, 53–4, 66–73, 77, 86, 108–11, 115, 130
  bad law as cause of crime, 41–2, 49–50, 128
  views on in Canada, 226–29
culture conflict, 102–3